Triumph of Will
SONIA GANDHI

Yusuf Ansari

Tara-India Research Press, New Delhi

India Research Press
B-4/22, Safdarjung Enclave, New Delhi — 110 029.
Ph.: 24694610; Fax : 24618637
www.indiaresearchpress.com
e-mail : contact@indiaresearchpress.com ; bahrisons@vsnl.com

2006

Yusuf Ansari 2005/2006 ©® India Research Press, New Delhi.

ISBN : 81-87943-93-9

Cataloguing in Publication Data
Yusuf Ansari
Triumph of Will : SONIA GANDHI
by   Yusuf Ansari

Includes bibliographical references and index.
1. India.   2. Politics — India.   3. South Asia/Subcontinent - Politics. 4. Biography.
I. Title. II. Author

Printed in India at Focus Impressions, New Delhi — 110 003.

'Oh, weep no more! For once again Life's Spring
Shall throne her in the meadows green, and o'er
Her head the minstrel of the night shall fling
A canopy of rose leaves, score on score.'

Divan-e-Hafiz

In Memory of
My great grandfather
S. Dr. Mukhtar Ahmad Ansari Al-Khazrej
(1880-1936)
Soldier, Stalwart and Staunch Secularist

Contents

Introduction   1

PART I – Ripe for Dissolution   5

ONE
Whither Nehru?   9

1.   Election Fever
2.   Murder at Twilight
3.   The Scholar Prime Minister
4.   A New Congress Government
5.   The Emergence of Dr. Manmohan Singh
      and the New Economic Policy
6.   Congress and the Myths of Muslim Appeasement

TWO
A Period of No Confidence   55

7.   The Costs of Appeasement and the Babri Crisis
8.   Assemblies in the South
9.   Factions and Friction
10.   A Letter of Resignation

THREE
Down and Out in Uttar Pradesh   67

11.   The Deficit Vote-Bank
12.   Fireworks in Amethi
13.   'My Kingdom for an Elephant'

FOUR
An Unhappy Ship   85

14.   Sleaze and Scandal and the Hawala Windfall

15. The Eleventh General Election Staying Afloat,
    But Losing It

16. Narasimha Rao Comes to Grief

PART II – The Rise and Stumble of Sonia Gandhi   **105**

FIVE
A Sterile Interlude and a Change of Leadership   **109**

17. In Bed with the United Front
18. The Avuncular Mr. Kesri
19. 'Only Madam Can Keep the Party Together'
20. The Panchmari Conclave
21. Uttar Pradesh Changes Tracks
22. The Emergence of Digvijay Singh
23. A Winter of Content

SIX
A Crisis of Leadership   **145**

24. For Want of a Vote the Government is Lost
25. The Case of Mr. Pawar
26. Engineering a Coup
27. Resignation
28. The Rebels are Tarred
29. Restoration

SEVEN
The Thirteenth General Election   **173**

30. The Kargil Crises and the Brink of War
31. Malice in Wonderland
32. The Varied Roles of Sushma Swaraj
33. The Middle Class Jumps Ship
34. The Management of Defeat

PART III – 'In the Crucible of Leadership'   193

EIGHT
Of Coteries, Committees and Courtiers   197

35. Winning Small Change
36. Breeding Discontent
37. The Quiet Death of the Bengal 'Mahajot'
38. UP Fear and Loathing in Lucknow
49. Death of an Airman
40. The Leadership Election

NINE
'Blood, Sweat, Toil and Tears'   229

41. Reaching Out
42. The Lost Generation and the Generation that Lost
43. Gujarat Torched, India Enflamed
44. Himalayan Respites

TEN
'Say Not the Struggle Nought Availeth...'   257

45. Debacle in the Heartland
46. In Shining Armour
47. Making Cosmos Out of Chaos

Epilogue : The Second Renunciation or Nehru Found   275

Appendices   283
Acknowledgements   313
Index   315

Introduction

Writing to his daughter Indira Gandhi from prison, in 1934, Pandit Jawaharlal Nehru wondered:

> What, indeed, am I? I find it difficult to answer that question. I have been a dabbler in many things; I began with science at college, and then took to the law, and, after developing various other interests in life, finally adopted the popular and widely practised profession of gaol-going in India!

While he was already a national leader and an international figure at the time, it would be a full thirteen years before Pandit Nehru became the first Prime Minister of an independent India, in 1947. More than 70 years after the above-quoted excerpt was penned, Sonia Gandhi, the present-day head of the house of Jawaharlal Nehru, declined the office of Prime Minister. The parallels between the two figures are close enough to justify further study, for the question has persisted, 'What, indeed, is Sonia Gandhi?'

Born in post-war Italy in 1946, educated in Europe and Britain, married to Rajiv Gandhi in India, witness to the assassination of her mother-in-law Indira in 1984, widowed in mid-life, mother to her children, a riddle to her contemporaries, the leader of the Congress Party in 1998, the uncrowned saviour of Indian secularism and finally and most recently, the hope of millions of her countrymen who renounced the hard won seat of power. The question still remains, 'what, indeed, is Sonia Gandhi?'

No politician in Indian history, with the possible exception of the 16th century Mughal Emperor Babur, has aroused so much vitriol and distrust today, without any significant cause, as has Sonia Gandhi. No politician in modern India has had to defend issues and values whose creation they were not responsible for but which had to be defended because they were an ideological inheritance, as has Sonia Gandhi. No public figure has been attacked more vociferously and personally by their own contemporaries for simply being who they were, as has Sonia Gandhi. And yet, no public figure in the present national political scenario has emerged as unscathed and as deeply popular, despite this sustained onslaught, as has Sonia Gandhi.

Naturally, this is not a comprehensive biography of Sonia Gandhi but an interim study of her as the leader of the Indian National Congress Party and as a central figure in contemporary Indian politics. Her life is still in need of future achievements and therefore of future assessments. The age-old argument of whether an individual persona guides events or whether events are the reproduction of circumstances becomes a raging debate when one surveys the Indian political scene, and Sonia Gandhi's place in it. More time is needed, more challenges have yet to be received and despatched and more milestones need to be crossed before we can confirm this argument in favour of her personality.

Nonetheless, any study of this figure necessitates an understanding of the politics and events which projected her into our national consciousness. While this book is a biographical account of her political career, readers will find little about Sonia Gandhi the individual in the first part of this book. The narrative is linear, and therefore begins with a study of the early 1990s; the Rajiv Gandhi assassination, the New Economic Policy (NEP), the politics of the Ramjanmabhoomi agitation and those other events and personages which defined the 90s. Sonia Gandhi, in this book, as indeed in real life, arrives when events demand her intercession, once there, she stays on. For a historian, particularly one studying contemporary politics in India it is more important to discover what Sonia Gandhi did, rather than condemn her for doing it. Therefore, positioning her much publicised 'we have the numbers' declaration in 1999, after the fall of the second NDA government, against her decision not to participate in government formation in 1998 is more important than merely criticising her political moralities in 1999. Similarly the time has not yet come to fully ascertain her opinion about religion in politics, though she certainly knocked the romance out of 'Hindutva' politics in 2004.

The only thing worse than bad politics is cynicism about bad politics, and unfortunately that cynicism is dripping through every pore of my own generation of Indians, the 'post-Indira generation', that is, those of us in their thirties or less. It is that generation of Indians which this book seeks to interest. The political traditions of the Independence movement ceased to exercise any real influence on the Indian polity by the time I came of age. The political movements of the late 1980s and 1990s disinherited me and those of my generation of the legacy of Nehruvian thought and Gandhian restraint and their respective political moralities.

I began research on this book in 1998, during my second year at the LSE and my first in the Congress Party. At the time, I had not deliberated writing a book on the subject of Indian politics, it was more a collection to help me stay 'on message' with the pace of events in India. It was only in 2000, during my tenure at the newly created Department of Policy Planning and Coordination (or DEPCO as the late Madhavrao Scindia christened it) that I first had the idea of marshalling my research into a narrative. Subsequently, I was present at meetings and deliberations by senior members of the Congress establishment, often having been elevated there over and above what my years and experience would normally have permitted. However, this provided me, over the years, sometimes even as a participant, with invaluable experience and the opportunity to witness the culture and workings of the party leadership, first hand.

In essence then, this is the story of a public figure, narrated through her public actions and it is about the consequences of her political actions on public life and thinking in present-day India.

ONE

Ripe for Dissolution

In 1991 the people of India were offered a choice to elect a new government. This was the second time in just three years that circumstances necessitated a General Election. The immediate cause for this was Chandra Shekhar's resignation as Prime Minister. This book begins at that juncture of political disarray.

The background to the immediate political crisis covered here was the implementation of the Mandal Commission Report by the V.P. Singh government in 1990. While the controversy generated by this engulfed political exchanges, the right-wing reacted by mobilising political opinion along sectarian grounds to carve out their own piece of the political pie. Thus was laid the division of the political sphere – some would say permanent – along the dual divides of caste and creed.

The Congress Party became the first victim of a general national crisis, generated by the politics of Mandal and communalisation. This part traces the beginnings of that development. The political decline and social irrelevance of the Congress Party coincided with a growing dislocation between political representatives and a democratic consensus. Worse was to come, in the midst of the election campaign, former Prime Minister and leader of the Congress Rajiv Gandhi was assassinated. The full context and circumstances of that gory and tragic event are yet to be unravelled. This book can only accord an interim account of what happened. For the Congress Party Rajiv Gandhi's assassination was an unbearable and incongruous alteration in its practice of politics. Following the assassination, Sonia Gandhi became the entity around whose silence the Congress Party and its politics revolved.

Thus, the book begins on a note of detachment; 'Ripe for Dissolution' and 'Whither Nehru?' are the beginning because they describe the start of a new, more right-wing Congress Party that had little in common with Nehru's Congress or his 'National Consensus', they are the beginnings of a new Congress, a recollection of a phase. Without this phase, this break from the Congress of the past, there would have been no vacuum or requirement for Sonia Gandhi to enter politics. 'Murder at Twilight' symbolises this break in a more physical sense, it portrays Rajiv Gandhi's assassination and the double blow it dealt, first at a personal level for his family and then at a political level for his party and Indian politics.

This part of the book ('Ripe for Dissolution') is not really about Sonia Gandhi the person, it covers the factors and conditions which necessitated her plunge into politics, conditions without which her need for political participation would have been hollow and irrelevant. Therefore chapters such as; 'A Period of No Confidence', 'Down and Out in Uttar Pradesh', and 'An Unhappy Ship' , which do not describe Sonia Gandhi the participant are important because they underline the need for her intervention, both in the affairs within the Congress and the larger polity.

These chapters also describe, in great detail, the state of the nation and the social and economic mileu of India, within which its politics functioned throughout the 1990s. Factors that played a role are all mentioned and argued about in this part of the book, including; 'The New Economic Policy' (NEP), the Babri crisis and its social and political consequences, the pulls and pressures of inner-party politics, issues such as corruption, rise of regional politics and electoral fortunes are covered here. There is considerable attention paid to the individuals and personalities who directed and participated in the events of the time, both within the Congress and outside it. The rise of Narasimha Rao by accident and his fall through ineptitude, after a controversial but complete term in office is vividly recounted.

This attention to individuals, through these collective vignettes, is crucial, because in subsequent chapters they establish their position with regard to the persona of Sonia Gandhi, as their leader, their colleague, their opponent and in all those other various avatars that she personifies for different eyes.

The following chapters conclude with the defeat of the Congress Party in the 1996 general election and the consequent confusion which that defeat ensured within the ranks of the party leadership.

Whither Nehru?

Election Fever – Murder at Twilight – The Scholar Prime Minister – A New Congress Government – The Emergence of Dr. Manmohan Singh and the New Economic Policy – Congress and the Myths of Muslim Appeasement

Election Fever

The brain-fever bird had begun singing her song all over India, but it wasn't her pleasant warnings or the torment of the approaching summer that held the attention of the country in March 1991.

The magic lamp of Indian politics and its odious incense of chaos has lured to its scent innumerable personalities. It has intoxicated their tempers, sometimes consumed them. The attraction to possess and rub this life source never ceases, for the inducement of its slowly scorching flame is the acquisition of power itself. The power to decide the fate of one-sixth of humanity and chart the course of the world's largest democracy. The power to bring change to one of the oldest civilisations in human history. Ultimately, the power to assert an individuality upon a national consciousness.

The Mahatma had tempered its temptations with the touch of his austere spiritualism which appeared to flow unhindered from his ascetic and mystical figure. Pandit Jawaharlal Nehru in turn had effortlessly balanced its allures with a constitution of charm and confinement and thus imposed his own standards of political thought on the process of Indian politics. His daughter Indira Gandhi reincarnated this power in its most veracious form; she personified it first as the mother of her people and then as the Hindu Goddess of strength Durga. These forms of feminine shakti[1] aside, she gave power back its essence.

---

1. Strength and potency.

In March 1991 no one possessed this power any more. Barely four months after being sworn in as Prime Minister, Chandra Shekhar and his government had resigned amidst strange circumstances. The events leading up to his resignation perhaps made the transitory provenance of his government inevitable. Therefore they do require examination. In the intervening period between Rajiv Gandhi's departure from the office of Prime Minister in 1989, to Chandra Shekhar's ascent to power in 1990, India itself had been altered by forces of social change. Their ineluctable contribution was violence, turmoil and confusion. Necessary attributes to any pressing and perilous policy which is brought into circulation without the benefit of an exhaustive debate and adequate discussion. As leader of the opposition, Rajiv Gandhi had observed this change in the instincts of the government. He now sought to work against it. The option of cobbling together an alternative front and forming a new government was available to Gandhi[2]. Instead, he opted to go to the country for a fresh mandate. Parliament was dissolved. The Election Commission hastily prepared its schedule for May.

The hundred and six-year-old Congress Party led by yet another member of its "democratic dynasty" had seen worse days. The memories of the late 1980s, so resonant of defeat and abdication had given way to a sense of positive anticipation for an election campaign in which a host of Congress candidates sought to redeem the stigma of failure and corruption that had refused to ebb in the last general election. The brief interregnum of opposition politics had surprisingly proved to be a blessing for a party so used to sitting on treasury benches and in high office. The wear and tear of government and the prolonged accumulation of public disenchantment and indifference had required considerable repair. While the National Front government tried hard to make the transition from politics to administration the Congress Party had between 1989 and 1991 managed to recover in some measure that margin of goodwill and support

---

2.   The Congress Party, with 193 seats was the largest single party in Parliament.

which had deserted it in the 1989 election. The cutting edge of the Bofors[3] controversy, that *raison d'etre* of the National Front's (NF) climatic rise had been effectively blunted, not so much due to effective damage control by the Congress but because of a failure by the NF to live up to its own rhetoric which had served it so well in opposition. Since 1989, three governments had fallen but investigations into the Bofors scandal had revealed little. Certainly none of the personal allegations made by V.P. Singh against Rajiv Gandhi had yet come to light. The Raja of Manda had delighted in personalised vitriol and afterwards reaped its benefits as his coalition government displaced the ruling Congress for only the second time in Indian parliamentary history. In office the proclamations of the election campaign proved far too excessive to materialise.

Alternatively, Singh's experiments, for all their acclaimed sincerity, with Mandal[4] politics, and his government's policy and outlook on the issue of reservations in general, more than anything else divided the country and created an entirely new generation of ostensible social reformers and "class warriors". Mandal was in intent a policy of empowerment. No case can be made for perpetuating the bondage of quashed sections of society, in this regard it was crucial. That is the reason why the policy needed to be explained, its justifications amplified for those who did not understand them. Instead it fuelled new dynamics of social relationships into the state. The details of this complex and controversial period are discussed at length in subsequent chapters. The newly emerging fissures and the residual violence which they necessarily incorporated highlighted the vagaries of the caste system to an entire generation of Indians unaware and unaffected by them. These children born in an Independent India may have been grounded in the basic

---

3. The Bofors scandal erupted when allegations were made against the Rajiv Gandhi government for having received kickbacks in commissions on the purchase of the Swedish howitzers.

4. The Mandal Commission had recommended the reservation of almost 52 per cent of all government jobs for the Scheduled Castes, Backward Classes and Scheduled Tribes. The report, first written in the late 1970s was re-circulated and passed into law in August 1990 by the V.P. Singh-led National Front government.

foundations of the caste system, many of them abhorrent and difficult to escape in a society where caste is seen as not only the essence of a man's identity but also the arbiter of his potential. It was the violence which its reform provoked that was a new experience for this "generation next". In colleges and universities study circles gave way to struggle committees and students marched on the streets, only to be repulsed by the overwhelming force of the state whom they were marching against. Many in their frustration immolated themselves. Simultaneously this attempt at social engineering pushed one of the coalition constituents of the NF, the right-wing communalist Bharatiya Janata Party (BJP) to begin work in earnest on its most ambitious project yet, of "Hindu" revivalism, the Ram-Janamabhoomi, Babri Masjid movement[5]. This was the great leap rightwards that finally tore apart V.P. Singh's fragile coalition government. George Fernandes[6] recalls L.K. Advani telling him, "You have left us with no choice but Hindutva[7] ". The politics of Mandal and the subsequent reaction which brought the caste splits in Hindu society out in the open forced the BJP to react with a more vociferous Ayodhya campaign, until then a largely local issue. The issue had not even surfaced in their agenda till as late as 1984. However, it now became necessary to awaken this politics of Hindutva to combat the policies of Mandal. Until now the Ayodhya dispute was in the safe hands of the Hindu clerics, the swamis, sants and sadhus who felt a justifiable unease with the slow pace at which it was progressing. The BJP came into the picture to maximise its political viability for their own political cause.

Singh was aware that he must protect the secular foundations of his government but he remained wary of upsetting the right-wing. Confrontation with his partners in government became unavoidable when

---

5. See Chapter 7, "The Costs of Appeasement and the Babri Crisis."
6. Former trade unionist and opposition leader. Defence Minister in the Vajpayee-led NDA government.
7. Hindutva essentially signifies the way of Hindu lifestyle and thinking. It is an amalgam of centuries of tradition and experience. The right-wing in India however have interpreted it in a more combative and militant vein and link it to Hindu reassertion, through militant means, if need be.

L.K. Advani, the BJP President began his Rath Yatra or chariot ride from Somnath[8] to Ayodhya[9]. This Toyota truck, itself a contradiction for the proponents of an indigenous economy ploughed the vast tracts of India for votes, leaving in its wake the furrows of human suffering, the sum total of which is difficult to calculate. The Rath Yatra was more than a mere journey of Hindu symbolism. It was a pilgrimage of provocation using political means designed to intoxicate the Hindu mind with religious imagery and speeches and thus effect total polarisation for votes. The party symbol of the BJP was painted pointedly and pronouncedly on the ostensible rath thus dismissing claims that it was a religious or cultural drive designed to awaken religious thoughts. Whatever it may not have been it succeeded as a political objective. India was simultaneously engulfed in two fires. While the flames of caste feelings, long suppressed erupted into violence, the plague of sectarian distrust, draggedly festering was encouraged to spread into communal frenzy. India's destiny as a nation was threatened not just substantially, but in full measure. Neither movement questioned its right to burn its own children on the pyre of political chauvinism. The pain, India was told, had to be borne by the present, to atone for the past and to enliven the future.

In time V.P. Singh instructed the Chief Minister of Bihar, Laloo Prasad Yadav to arrest L.K. Advani when he entered that state and dismantle his chariot of chaos, which Yadav willingly and incredibly did in Samastipur, without causing bloodshed. In the Indian cycle of karma, every occurrence must invite repercussions and the end of the yatra could only result in the fall of V.P. Singh. Atal Behari Vajpayee, at the time a member of the BJP's National Executive revealed to the press, "We had an understanding with the government and the understanding was that Advaniji would be allowed to complete his Rath Yatra." The BJP with its 82 MPs promptly withdrew support to V.P. Singh's National Front government.

---

8. A temple town in Gujarat, in western India. The Somnath Temple was sacked by the Afghan invader, Mahmud Ghazni in medieval times. Since it has come to symbolise, particularly for a section of Hindu society, a monument of renewal and revival.

9. A temple town in Uttar Pradesh. The epicentre of the Janamabhoomi crisis. Hindus revere it as the birthplace of Ram. See subsequent chapters.

Already facing dissent from within through the Jat leader Devi Lal[10] his Deputy Prime Minister, and defeat from without from the BJP, Singh none the less decided to test a vote on the floor of Parliament and for the first time in India's parliamentary history a government lost a vote of confidence. Swift machinations and manoeuvres both by the Congress and by the now split Janata Dal, led to the formation of a minority government under Chandra Shekhar, who with 45 MPs and outside support extended to him by the Congress was sworn in as India's eighth Prime Minister in November 1990. Like his *bete noire* V.P. Singh, Chandra Shekhar too was originally a Congressman, and had once been a member of the CWC[11] to boot, though unlike V.P. Singh he had never held any ministerial office. This lack of experience with governance however, did not hamper his resolve to lead a government now. A mixture of dissatisfaction and resentment with the Congress leadership of the time and a latent disregard for the establishment had effected his estrangement with Indira Gandhi in the 1970s[12]. Henceforth, for the next fifteen years he became that example of a political exile who is never welcome to the boiler-room of politics where its policies, decisions and stratagems are grounded and produced. Previously, the fall of Rajiv Gandhi from power in 1989 created the possibility of an entry for him. Among the half a dozen faces for the candidature of Prime Minister it was Chandra Shekhar's that gained acceptance for most of the election in 1989. At the same time V.P. Singh's famous aside that, "I shall be a disaster as Prime Minister" could only mean, as it did for Chandra Shekhar, that he was the preferred candidate of the Janata Dal centre and the Left. The disadvantages which isolation, especially self-imposed isolation, in politics entails became all too evident when, unknown to him, and perhaps to many others, the

---

10. Jat leader from Haryana was Deputy Prime Minister in the V.P. Singh government and the most senior member in the cabinet. He had by then resigned from the cabinet.
11. CWC, the Congress Working Committee. It is the highest executive body of the Indian National Congress.
12. As a "Young Turk", Chandra Shekhar believed that the Congress government was not doing enough to implement its socialist programmes in government.

power jockeys of the newly formed Janata Dal, all old hands like Arun Nehru[13] and Devi Lal, decided to install V.P. Singh as Prime Minister without due consultations with Chandra Shekhar. Meanwhile, he was led to believe, as had been decided earlier that Devi Lal was the Front's Prime Ministerial candidate. This strategy had met with Chandra Shekhar's approval, Devi Lal being the most senior among the National Front's leaders. To his shock, he became aware of the change in candidate, from Devi Lal to V.P. Singh only minutes before the dramatic "coronation" actually occurred in the Rashtrapati Bhavan. Although managing to keep a straight face through the ceremony, Chandra Shekhar was seen walking out of the hall, full of rancour at what he took as a personal betrayal of his trust. He would not remain disappointed for long. Chandra Shekhar's chance came in 1990 when in order to avoid an early election and to visit retribution upon V.P. Singh, Rajiv Gandhi decided to render him support to form a government, provided he could wean away the required one-third of his party the Janata Dal (JD). Consequently, the National Front faced its first ever split in a series of many. It would be reborn as the United Front in 1996 and then as the People's Front in 2001, and at each juncture it would seek the backing of the Congress in some measure. This consistent dependence on Congress support since 1991 demolishes the precept that a Third Front can occupy a centrist position of power in national politics in India, on its own. The single factor for opposition unity until 1991 was its anti-Congressism, after 1991 this was mitigated and the regional parties gathered around the twin poles of either the BJP or, to a lesser extent the Congress.

Whether Chandra Shekhar's second honeymoon with the Congress would have lasted is difficult to ascertain even with hindsight. The Congress, however, was certainly not prepared to play guardian to his wishes, perceived or apparent, of continuing on as Prime Minister for longer than was necessary. His mandate for office was not, after all, the

---

13.   Arun Nehru, cousin of Rajiv Gandhi. Began his career in the Congress but later joined V.P. Singh. Served in government as well. He is now in the BJP.

legitimate mandate of the people. He was Prime Minister by leave of the Congress, not the electorate. The appearance of two Home Guards outside the residence of Rajiv Gandhi whose motive was never and probably will never be known, raised apprehensions about government surveillance and spying, leading to a boycott of Parliament by the Congress Party. Consequently, Chandra Shekhar, uncertain and flustered gave in his papers to the President of India, R. Venkataraman on March 6, 1991.

In a reply to why the Congress had brought down the Chandra Shekhar government, Rajiv Gandhi stated:

> There seems to be a feeling that we are the ones who precipitated the resignation of the government. At no time did we withdraw support.[14]

The people of India accepted this view. Two years of instability and violence necessitated a change of government. The electorate was divided as never before but India's grand old party looked set to benefit most from this variance in political preferences.

Murder at Twilight

"A Great Hope fell, You heard no noise, The ruin was within."[15]

It was against this background that India's tenth general elections were staged. The battle-lines were set in a triangular contest. The stridently nationalist, as it then was, BJP stood against a more refreshed Indian National Congress led by Rajiv Gandhi. The spoilers were represented by a multitude of smaller regional parties, caste and class formations and breakaway groups, loosely organised under the aegis of the now crumbling National Front.

If one observes the history of the post-Independence Congress Party, it is easy to sight regular periods of elation and disillusionment for the

---

14.   Interview. March 6, 1991.
15.   Emily Dickinson.

party consistently following each other like the music of a carefully arranged opera. The grand illumination of Independence and Pandit Nehru's statesmanship, which painted a vision of a resurgent Asian conglomerate led by India and China itself was paradoxically dissolved by the disillusionment following the Indo-China war of 1962. Similarly the hype that followed 1967, of Indira Gandhi's *Gharibi Hatao* (Eradicate Poverty) slogan and socialist programmes in 1971 which sought to empower the disadvantaged classes of India was irrevocably damaged by the trauma of the Emergency years. This dark period in turn was forgotten and replaced by the broader euphoria of Rajiv Gandhi's arrival on the scene in 1985. The Congress swept the polls in an overwhelming landslide symbolising change and resurgence[16]. That too did not last and with seemingly regular alacrity, Rajiv Gandhi's administration and the Congress Party as a political organisation fell victim to crisis after crisis both of their own making and external. The election of 1991 left no one in any doubt that Rajiv Gandhi and the Congress Party were on their return to power, from whence the recovery of that all important political prestige too was not far distant. The party prepared itself for office once more and the mood of the country, and the views cf its opinion makers and outside observers supported this buoyancy. Rajiv Gandhi it was felt among the circles of power and influence, had redeemed himself and had matured as a leader both at home and abroad. The party had stayed together after its defeat in 1989, despite immense pressure upon it, which in the normal course of events may have led to a split. Moreover his decision, even as he remained the Leader of the Opposition, to fly to Moscow and Tehran during the Gulf conflict of 1991 in order to influence diplomatic opinion against the Gulf War had shown initiative, while no such diplomacy was pursued by the government itself. Instead, Chandra Shekhar's administration compromised the policy of Non-alignment by refuelling American aircraft on their way to the theatre of war.

So while public perception gathered in his favour and in turn was favourably converted into mass support by his party, Rajiv Gandhi

---

16. The Indian National Congress won 405 of the 542 seats contested.

travelled widely and extensively, covering almost every parliamentary constituency in the country. His own constituency of Amethi he left in the experienced hands of his wife Sonia who was recognised well in the region and knew the area and its people. She was assisted by their daughter Priyanka and travelled whenever possible with Rajiv Gandhi to other parts of the country. The election campaign was an intensive one. The Congress was playing for high stakes, the other parties were defending them. Opinion polling at the time was a crude science still in development in India and it is difficult to sight the presence of a "wave" in anyone's favour, however psephologists and analysts claimed that the Congress was the frontrunner. A cover of *India Today* showed Rajiv Gandhi "Taking the Lead" ahead of his rivals. Indeed even he broke from inhibitions and protocols, many of them previously attached to him in his office as Prime Minister. His security cover had been reduced and required serious review. Gandhi was accessible even innovative, often plunging, quite literally, into the swelling crowds at the meetings he addressed. His own morale was high, as some of his friends later recalled, "the magic was working with the people." Everywhere, Congress candidates requested his presence. His residence 10 Janpath, was inundated with ceaseless calls and letters asking for dates for his meetings. In the rush of elections many demands, were readily given, scrutiny being minimal.

On April 21, Rajiv Gandhi arrived in Madras for the Marina Beach rally with his AIADMK ally, Dr. J. Jayalalitha.[17] The meeting went off well but the size of the crowds, the content of the speeches and the general reception are of no concern or consequence. It would emerge much later, that present among the crowds at the Marina Beach rally were the people at whose hands Rajiv Gandhi would meet his death. It is chilling , even in retrospect, to visualise that perhaps Rajiv Gandhi saw the figure of his assassin stalking him among the crowd, analysing his security detail, studying him closely without any realisation of the motivations behind the killer's mind.

---

17.   Former swimming champion and film actress, Dr. Jayalalitha has been a prominent figure in Tamil politics. She is currently Chief Minister of Tamil Nadu.

The decision to assassinate the former Prime Minister had been taken in the jungles of Jaffna in northern Sri Lanka almost six months ago. Safely encapsulated by thick jungles with only the Elephant Pass, the scene of many bloody battles, connecting them to the rest of Sri Lanka and the Palk Straits separating them from India, the LTTE, or Liberation Tigers of Tamil Eelam deliberated upon the consequences of Rajiv Gandhi's return as Prime Minister of India. In his last government, Gandhi had forged the Indian Peace Keeping Force (IPKF) to aid the beleaguered Sri Lankan government in it's war against the LTTE and its leader Prabhakaran. Many reserved their judgement on the move, however that is a subject of argument beyond the purview of this book. The IPKF damaged the military capacity of the LTTE in a big way. Together with the Sri Lankan armed forces the Indian "army of occupation" as the LTTE called them was able to establish military superiority over significant territories previously held by the LTTE. For the Congress government and its Prime Minister, the operations in Sri Lanka reflected a necessary and successful geo-political statesmanship. For Prabhakaran, the Indian action devastated the accumulated experience and resources of many years. More importantly, for his support base among the native Tamil population, who, like him viewed the Indian presence as an occupying force, the IPKF was the real enemy. Excesses were reported, accidents of mistaken identity occurred. In time indifference among the locals gave way to hostility. This episode of the IPKF in Sri Lanka formed the basis of the decision to assassinate Rajiv Gandhi and thus scuttle any revocation of that strategy through deterrence. Who, among his successors would send the troops back in? The fear among the LTTE leadership of his return prompted them to order his execution.

Meanwhile, the election campaign continued relentlessly towards its end. After covering almost 35,000 kilometres and addressing innumerable meetings and rallies throughout the country, Rajiv Gandhi returned to New Delhi on May 19 to cast his own vote in that round of polling the following day. The third and final round of the election was due to end on May 24. The gruelling close to the campaign was drawing near and on the morning of May 20, Rajiv Gandhi flew off once more. Sonia Gandhi gives an account of their last meeting:

> In the evening he was to touch Delhi again, but only to change from the helicopter to a plane that would take him to Orissa. That afternoon we received a message at about 4:15 that he was on his way home. He walked in beaming. We were delighted at the unexpected chance to spend a few more minutes together. He had a quick wash and a snack. He spoke briefly on the phone to Rahul, to wish him well for his coming test and to give him his love. He said goodbye to Priyanka. Once again, it was time for him to go. I would now see him, as he himself announced cheerfully, "in just two more days". We bade each other a tender goodbye...and he was off. I watched him, peeping from behind the curtain, till he disappeared from view...This time forever.[18]

The day was spent canvassing in Andhra Pradesh and Tamil Nadu. That night he arrived at the small town of Sriperumbedur, which lies between Madras and Kanchipuram. As always the crowd had been waiting since the evening. His assassin Dhanu, the human bomb and her accomplices waited for him among them. As he alighted from his vehicle, she edged closer towards him, her presence provoked neither alarm nor suspicion among the large crowd, few could have guessed the enormity of the consequences that would follow. The assassin garlanded a beaming Rajiv Gandhi and pretended to bend down to touch his feet in reverence, as he in turn reached down to lift her. Dhanu activated the detonator of the bomb she had tied along a belt around her waist. The belt held six grenades, each of those made up of 80gm of the highly explosive C4-RDX enclosed within a casting of TNT. Death came instantly to all those within 10 metres of the epicentre of the explosion. The pursuit of politics and power had extracted a heavy price from the Nehru-Gandhi family and from the Congress Party. It appeared to an emotional and deeply shocked Congress that no amount of sacrifice would appease the household gods of India's oldest political tradition. Many questioned the utility of this

---

18. *Rajiv.* Sonia Gandhi. Viking, by Penguin Books. 1992.

sacrifice. Such an occurrence challenges the premise of justice in politics, while it is often unfailing in its fairness to level and even personalities and their actions, few could have seen in Rajiv Gandhi's death any fair play of that hidden hand of providence. What his second term as Prime Minister could have done both for the Congress and the country is debatable and subject to speculation. However, his absence at this crucial juncture revealed that both the Congress and the polity needed him to guide them, politics and governance and administration and ideology would all have benefited with his able and dynamic hand at the helm of affairs. The sequence of events following his death would prove this assertion to be true. As Parel observes in *The Political Calculus:*

> Failure, when it is due to the premature termination of excellence, only reveals the tragic predicament of men and the ruthless omnipotence of fortune. It does not diminish the stature of a great man, one who knows how to act politically.

That night a severe storm lashed vast parts of India. The winds and gales were indicative of misfortune, murmured the holy men.

As news of the tragedy filtered back, first to Madras and then to New Delhi and finally to the rest of the country, politicians, many of them riding the crescendo of their election campaigns gave up their activities and began pouring into Delhi. Sonia Gandhi and her daughter flew to Madras to bring the body home in an aircraft of the Indian Air Force. The aura of tragedy around the widow and daughter of the former leader was absolute. They were able to summon fortitude from an invisible but inexhaustible reservoir of courage and stoicism.

Rajiv Gandhi lay in state in Delhi's Teen Murti Bhavan[19], where his grandfather and mother had lain before him. In the scorching heat they came, thousands and thousands more, the living, breathing masses of the

---

19. At first built by Lutyens as the residence of the Commander-in-Chief of the British forces in India. Teen Murti was converted into the official residence of the Indian Prime Minister after Independence. Nehru was the only PM to ever use it. It was subsequently turned into a museum.

country whose circumstances he had worked so hard to change. They had heard he was dead, they did not want to believe it, the multitudes whose lot he had tried to better. Across India thousands of school children stood in two minutes silence for the young leader, uncontrollable tears rolling down their faces. To the young he personified pledges given by age to youth, once more doomed to be unfulfilled. In her villages, India's poor wailed for compassion. As they had wept for the orphaned son they cried now for the widowed wife and her two fatherless children. Amidst the Vedic chants and shlokas rose the slowly deafening roar of "Rajiv Gandhi Amar Rahe" "Rajiv Gandhi remains immortal". They all came together not merely to pay a symbolic homage but to unite in protest and to cry, "enough"! For with Rajiv Gandhi passed away a promise; which had spoken of passage; from the old to the new. With his death a progression ceased.

Often, in such tragic circumstances, thinking and planning is pulverised. Seemingly indestructible personalities crumble before such an unexpected onslaught of fate and fortune. So it was within the corridors of the Congress too. Many of its leading lights were too stunned with disbelief to even begin thinking of the consequences. Nevertheless, it is also true that the arrival of emergency and despair gives rise, in a few minds to the power of initiative too. While many nervous minds were too preoccupied to think of the succession, others had begun plotting already. Behind the sepulchral visages, and solemn silences some Congressmen had already begun to formulate their options. Most indeed were keen to establish what was uppermost in the minds of colleagues in order to buffer and strengthen their own private opinions before they went public.

The mental trend was growing towards installing Sonia Gandhi as the heir. Certainly the party faithful would accept it, the people might given the strong undercurrent of shock and sympathy prevalent in the country. No one considered that Sonia Gandhi, the grieving widow, facing up to the sum of all her previous fears which had come alive, might not agree to their suggestions and their vibes. So when a group of Congressmen, led by R.K. Dhawan[20] resolutely met her in Delhi a few days later asking her to "take over" as their new leader they may have been forgiven their surprise at her refusal. No one had considered her point of view, none had observed her silence of mourning, some hadn't even respected it. Sonia Gandhi had never envisaged a career in politics. Her association with politics was tempered with trauma and tension. In the early days life for the couple was serene enough. Rajiv Gandhi served as a pilot in the national airline and Sonia was content to remain a home-maker. They tolerated political life because it was the centre of gravity of their household. However, as a member of Indira Gandhi's family, Sonia Gandhi's own sense and sensitivity towards politics and politicians alike cannot be disregarded. In the immediate aftermath of the Emergency, life within Indira Gandhi's household was in a phase of tumult and uncertainty. Sonia Gandhi provides a personal glimpse of how life changed dramatically after the Emergency:

> Through all her difficulties she (Indira Gandhi) had turned to the family for moral support, and we had shared her concerns and the ups and downs of her political life...In early 1977, Rajiv's mother lifted the Emergency and soon after declared elections. Her government fell, and the Janata government took over. We moved from the PM's residence to 12 Willingdon Crescent. The change was not merely of location. Politics entered our lives directly and palpably as my mother-in-law's political associates, supporters and workers moved freely in and out of the house. The new government launched a political vendetta against the family, embroiling Rajiv as well. Lies and rumours were planted in the newspapers to suggest that we had amassed wealth by illicit means and were preparing to flee the country to avoid arrest...Like everyone else in the family, Rajiv and I were followed by the CBI wherever we went.[21]

Subsequently, when Sanjay Gandhi died in an air-crash it was Rajiv to whom Indira Gandhi turned for political sustenance and support. Rajiv's

---

20.   R.K. Dhawan, a member of the CWC.
21.   *Rajiv.* Sonia Gandhi. Viking, by Penguin Books. 1992.

decision to enter politics met with protestations and a vehement reluctance from Sonia Gandhi:

> My mother-in-law for all her courage and composure was broken in spirit. There was only one person in her world to whom she could turn for help. For the first time in the fifteen years that we had known each other, there was tension between Rajiv and me. I fought like a tigress – for him, for us and our children, for the life we had made together, his flying which he loved, our uncomplicated, easy friendships, and, above all, for our freedom: that simple human right that we had so carefully and consistently preserved.[22]

The severity of her feelings were slowly but sharply suppressed as she accepted and ingratiated herself with the inevitability of circumstance. Politics and his party had chosen Rajiv Gandhi to lead them. And while his legacy could be a rewarding condition it demanded his responsibility as well. Sonia Gandhi gave in, another sacrifice was made, this one of a tranquil and contented family life together:

> Finally, I realised that I could no longer bear to watch Rajiv being torn apart. He was my Rajiv, we loved each other, and if he felt that he ought to offer his help to his mother, then I would bow to those forces which were now beyond me to fight, and I would go with him wherever they took him.[23]

Time did not serve her well for scarcely had the impact of this tragedy subsided than Indira Gandhi was assassinated in 1984.

Rajiv Gandhi once confessed that Sonia never really got over the death of her mother-in-law. Alone and dazed it was after all Sonia who carried Indira Gandhi's body, limp, riddled and bleeding profusely to the hospital, it was in her arms that India's matriarch died. Rajiv's assassination was a final hard blow. Indira Gandhi had the comfort of Nehru to pacify her loss when Feroze Gandhi died. Even with Sanjay's death, Rajiv Gandhi stepped in to provide a relief that could not appear from elsewhere. In turn Rajiv Gandhi was comforted by Sonia's presence when his mother

---

22.   Ibid.
23.   Ibid.

died, thus forming an umbilical family chain who stood firmly alongside the successive burning funeral pyres as pillars of comfort. The urns of ashes passed from one generation to the next.

For Sonia Gandhi and her two children there was no such figure available. Rahul and Priyanka Gandhi barely in their twenties were suddenly without their father. She was a widow alone and vulnerable. For Sonia Gandhi politics had become a scourge that consumed the lives of her family members with an insatiable ferocity.

When they met her the leaders of the Congress Party led Sonia Gandhi into a high plain and showed her the legacy to which she was the heir. It would all be hers if only she would accept their offerings. They showed her vistas and scenes which would give her control over the party and thus the country. They proffered her the crown saying it was hers by right. They offered to pass on the lamp of total power to her. She turned away from these temptations. She would not relent. Her refusal was the result of a will which banished all indecision. There was no distraction in her rejection of these riches, no questions, no lingering confusion. It was a clear and simple renunciation.

It was as Rajiv's wife and companion that she came to know the country she had chosen as her own. While Indira Gandhi had guided her and eased her transformation into Indian womanhood, Rajiv Gandhi had symbolised her relationship with modern India itself. That symbol had now been severed leaving her without a guide to negotiate her existence. The scars of sacrifice, too brutal and too many required time to heal themselves. Time was also needed to rationalise the future which appeared dark, blackened by the loss of her husband. Shattered, alone, borne by sentiment and mindful of her duties to her impressionable children, Sonia Gandhi spurned all offers and all audiences. She shut herself behind an impenetrable purdah through which no feelings of either injury or ambition were radiated. Instantly she became a figure of multiple speculations. A symbol of sacrifice for many, a sphinx to be suspected by some, to a few others, particularly in the Congress Party she represented a force over whose silence they would scheme and suspend their own political ambitions. For the press her "mystique" became an obsession of intrigue in those uncertain years.

The leaders who had gone to her thought they were doing the right thing, a non Nehru-Gandhi hadn't led the party since Lal Bahadur Shastri[24] in 1964. Most Congressmen and women had begun and sustained their political careers under the leadership of Pandit Nehru, Indira Gandhi, Sanjay Gandhi, Rajiv Gandhi or a combination of those leaders. An alternative wasn't visible, and even if he was who but a member of the family could control the factionalism and "bloodbath" that was bound to break out sooner rather than later. The enormity and scale of the party's loss only now began to sink in. The party appeared leaderless, naturally Rajiv Gandhi, young himself in political years had not groomed anyone to succeed him. In the last few years of his life, when he was out of power, Rajiv Gandhi did not even have any particular favourites who might have succeeded him.

The cremation took place in Delhi on May 24th. On May 27th, incidentally the 27th death anniversary of his grandfather Pandit Jawaharlal Nehru, a special train carried Rajiv Gandhi's remains to his ancestral home in Allahabad[25]. The next day these ashes were immersed in the sacred confluence of the Ganga and the Jamuna, the Triveni, his years joining those of his ancestors. As Sonia Gandhi sat on the eroding edges of these holy waters, behind her the abandoned creation of her family, the modern day Congress Party suddenly came to life.

Their thoughts began to turn to the installation of a "compromise candidate", who could unify both the right and the left of the party, a consensus man who could be cajoled or coerced as the circumstances required. Thoughts began to turn towards the rural heartlands of Andhra Pradesh. The party had found its man.

---

24. Lal Bahadur Shastri succeeded Nehru as Prime Minister and remained Prime Minster between 1964-1967. Died during peace negotiations with Pakistan in Tashkent in 1967.
25. Anand Bhavan. The Nehru Family home, bequeathed to the nation by Indira Gandhi.

The Scholar Prime Minister

"...He felt transformed from a solitary individual into a very different entity. His own life mattered no more. His joy and sorrow, his family and friends, his likes and dislikes – all were subsumed in a much greater whole. It was the universal and all inclusive existence of mankind, in the infinite continuum of time, space and human emotions. The phenomenon struck him as the spiritual interpretation of democracy...As he pondered over these matters, he was struck by the truth about himself, for the umpteenth time: he was unaffected by, and therefore irrelevant to, the context of political power."[26]

The Insider – P.V. Nərasimha Rao

Pamulaparti Venkata Narasimha Rao was born in 1921 in the district of Karimnagar, situated in present-day Andhra Pradesh. The excerpt above is from a semi-autobiographical work by Narasimha Rao in which he describes the thoughts of the protagonist Anand (himself) when he is sworn in as a Minister. No doubt Rao has drawn on his own extensive experience of oaths and offices. In 1991 when he became first the President of the Congress Party and then the Prime Minister, Rao must have felt much more than a convergence of ordinary human emotions. A lifetime in politics had conveyed him eventually to the doorstep of absolute power. The accumulation of all his experience and skill would now be needed to prolong his hold on that power, both individually and for his party.

His selection as leader was by no means a foregone conclusion as some commentators have suggested. The CWC which had chosen Sonia Gandhi at first had within its ranks equally experienced the persuasive party grandees. Arjun Singh, the aristocratic Congress MP from Madhya Pradesh could claim the crown if the selection was being made on experience and seniority alone. The factionalism in his home state and the lack of adequate support among the parliamentary party counted

---

26. *The Insider.* Narasimha Rao.

against him. However, in time this could be transformed. Arjun Singh was familiar with the transitory nature of his chosen vocation. Permanence is after all merely an illusion in politics. His eyes ever wistful, he would wait.

The case was equally strong, but of different denominations for Sharad Pawar, the "Maratha strongman" who delivered votes and other political accessories whenever required. However, his past record of changing loyalties and the absence of a national following demolished his chances. Pranab Mukherjee, a savant of the Nehruvian mould and a die-hard loyalist of Indira Gandhi possessed the erudition but did not consider the need to engage in electoral contests. His influence and practice of politics were limited to the red benches of the upper house the Rajya Sabha. However, no one combined experience of power with political finesse in a greater degree than N.D. Tiwari, the former Chief Minister of UP[27]. A Brahmin leader who enjoyed stature even outside his own community, "NDT" was a man reputed to have held more ministerial portfolios than any living leader. He wielded his many arms of political talent, like the God Nataraj, with balance and equipoise. His temper was flushed with the patience and symmetry which comes from the prolonged contemplation of power and its administration. N.D. Tiwari had first started out under Pandit Nehru himself. Nevertheless the complete destruction of the Congress Party in his home state of Uttar Pradesh mitigated the extension of parsimonious willingness to support him. In 1991, only five Congress MPs were returned from Uttar Pradesh. Tiwariji, was among the losers, as a result he lost out on considerably more than just his parliamentary seat. Finally, and the inclusion at the end does not moderate the measure of his chances of success, came Madhavrao Scindia. In him the party could count on youth, he was 48, as well as experience, he had been returned to parliament in successive elections since 1971. The Maharaja of Gwalior was perhaps the most successful example in Indian politics of the patrician-turned-parliamentarian. Newly elected Congress MPs, particularly the

27.   Narain Dutt Tiwari continues to be Chief Minister even today of the newly created state of Uttaranchal in north India.

younger crop of parliamentarians looked towards him, some of them even met him to persuade and advise. With a remarkable mixture of ambition and restraint, Scindia kept himself away focussing instead on making a success in a purely administrative capacity, within a ministerial rank. Yet, he too faced innumerable obstacles which stemmed primarily from a weak regional following and a streak in his own nature which did not entirely conform to the culture of conspiracy and manipulation prevalent in politics. He was, in essence too fastidious and politically too abstemious.

It is almost a miracle, given the weight and stature of so many individuals in the party that the Congress settled for a consensus over a candidate. Rao had stood down from active politics before the general election and in May 1991 was midway to returning home to Andhra. Barely a few months earlier he had undergone a quadruple coronary bypass surgery and he hoped to spend his retirement as a man of letters; poetry and a love of literature were a cultivated hobby. Perhaps it was this illusion of a detachment from politics and thus from an active participation in the politics of the party that so many senior leaders in the party rallied around his candidature. He would be a "safe bet". Alternatively, the distant prospect of a non-Congress alternative emerging to fill the power vacuum may have pushed the hand for some. The Congress was the single largest party in Parliament and fighting for the spoils would have reflected badly in the eyes of the public. What certainly weighed matters in Rao's favour was the return of 87 MPs from his own home regions of South India. This caucus added up to over 40 per cent of the total number of Congress MPs and came from the four southern states of Andhra Pradesh, Kerala, Karnataka and Tamil Nadu. He was therefore the first Prime Minister of India from the South and the first Congress Prime Minister from outside UP. An interesting statistic is that of all the nine Prime Ministers of India between 1952 and 1991 only Morarji Desai[28] and Narasimha Rao were from outside UP.

---

28. Morarji Desai was Prime Minister between 1977-1979. Was previously a Congress leader and was in the governments of both Nehru and Indira Gandhi. Split the Congress to form his own group. A lasting opponent of Indira Gandhi.

Rao was a Congressman of the old school. In generational terms he belonged to the same era as Indira Gandhi. Indeed it was under her patronage and trust that Rao cultivated his career, first in his home state Andhra and in the post-Emergency phase, at the centre in Delhi. He always was the loyal peer, unwavering and constant in his service; straight, simple and cerebral. Rao had successfully groomed himself in the role of an ancillary.

His first experience of politics was in the Telangana Movement of resistance against the Nizam of Hyderabad which eventually ended in the deposition of the Nizam and the integration of Hyderabad State into the Indian Union[29]. Rao became a member of the AICC in 1951 and held several ministerial offices in the Andhra Government becoming Chief Minister of the state in 1971. At the centre he served as Minister for some crucial portfolios in the cabinet including the Ministry of Defence, External Affairs and Home. Under Rajiv Gandhi he also headed the Ministry of Planning, and the Ministry of Human Resource Development, both crucial in that era of reform and modernisation.

Rao had never been a contender for the post of Prime Minister. In the immediate aftermath of Indira Gandhi's assassination when the Congress did have the option to select his age and experience over Rajiv Gandhi's dynamic youth, Rao, with the exception of Pranab Mukherjee, was the only choice for installation as Prime Minister. However, that opinion is inconsequential but it does indicate that as a politician Rao enjoyed both experience and the confidence of the party high command even before he actually succeeded to the post of Prime Minister.

The Party anointed him as its President on May 29, 1991, nine days after the death of his predecessor Rajiv Gandhi. He became Prime Minister on June 21, a full month after the assassination. As he had retired from an

---

29.   The Nizam of Hyderabad wanted to form an independent state after partition, wishing to merge neither with Pakistan nor India.

active political future, Rao had not even contested the election and was therefore not an MP. He returned to Parliament in a by-election in November of that year. Those who had chosen him as their leader had done so after he had satisfied the queries of their own personal ambitions. Their cooperation was guaranteed so long as he remained sufficiently pliable. His example in office over the next five years proved to be far more than a calm interlude. For those who had imagined him as a vestige trailing the coat-tails of the Nehru-Gandhi legacy, Rao had much more to offer than a sterile disposition.

Parliament met for the first time since the dissolution in March, on July 9. In his first address to Parliament, Rao stated:

> We are meeting at a time when the country is facing a difficult situation on various fronts. We must work with urgency, the urgency which the criticality of the situation demands, and work collectively and in a determined manner to face the challenges that the nation is confronted with. In particular, in this House the people expect us to work with devotion, work with single-minded purposefulness and also work with certain dignity. We have to place before ourselves all these expectations of the people, and I am sure, Mr. Speaker, Sir, that under your able guidance we will be able to conduct the business of this House as well as conduct ourselves as the people expect us to.[30]

"The Scholar Prime Minister" as he later came to be known would have to face multiple challenges on many fronts. They would eventually tear apart not only the Congress government but the party in unprecedented turbulence. His muted reflections and natural reticence would invite various inquisitions, but none as vigilant or intruding as those of his own colleagues. P.V. Narasimha Rao had come a long way in politics but he would have to negotiate a travel of a far more arduous strain.

While the role of pack horse had come easily to him, his transformation into the leader of the pack was a greatness thrust upon

---

30. On the occasion of felicitations to the Speaker of the Lok Sabha.

him. No political party takes decisions on the basis of an unadulterated altruism. Rao understood this well, for the pursuit of power is ultimately the criterion against which policy making must be judged. Nevertheless, the voluntary surrender of fundamental political positions to merely perpetuate that power involves the relinquishment of value systems, and with these values goes a little bit of identity. With its cornerstones of identity compromised no political group can hold together, not in government, nor in opposition. With Rao's selection, the Congress leadership did away with a little bit of itself.

A New Congress Government

Narasimha Rao's elevation to the office of Prime Minister is instantly comparable, in terms of the sequence of events leading up to it with the situation which prevailed within the Congress in 1967. Then Indira Gandhi was installed in the premiership owing to the sudden death of Lal Bahadur Shastri, Nehru's successor, in Tashkent[31]. The motivations of The Syndicate, that resolute group of party grandees at the time led by the indomitable Kamaraj were similar to the thoughts uppermost in the minds of Congress leaders in 1991. The new Prime Minister, in either case had to be averse to controversy and confrontation with party colleagues, simultaneously he would have to operate within a consensus of leadership. Individualism would have to be minimised. Unlike Rao however, Indira Gandhi was also the daughter of Nehru in whose lifetime she had already become Congress President[32] and thus recognised by the people and her party rank and file as a leader of stature in her own right. Naturally this was a recognition which even Rao could not possess or cultivate. He took his time to weigh his options, and his likely opponents and announced his government in Parliament on July 10, 1991.

Cabinet formation is always an exercise which involves long and careful deliberation. In India it is further complicated by the precedents

---

31.   Shastri was in Tashkent to negotiate the terms of the cease-fire between India and Pakistan, with his Pakistani counterpart Field Marshal Ayub Khan, after the Indo-Pak war of 1967.
32.   Indira Gandhi became Congress President in April 1959.

of tradition which require proportional representation, in the cabinet and in government of all the major castes, creeds and religions of India. Additionally, it must reflect the geographical diversity of India and maintain a balance in generational composition. In political terms the equations and internal dynamics of a party dictates the level of accommodation of party leaders. For Narasimha Rao the selection of his cabinet was complicated by the discomforting realisation that he was leading a minority government. A corresponding apprehension must have been the presence of several senior leaders, many of whom could have been Prime Minister in his stead. They would naturally have to be appeased and their proteges satisfied. It was not just the potential of events but individuals as well which could prematurely terminate Rao's premiership. He was especially minded to appease Arjun Singh who held a position of considerable influence and strength which in turn was enhanced by his low key role in the scenes of the new succession. Arjun Singh had kept the party united by his own renunciation of the leadership and thus he now became the unspecified but clear deputy to Rao's leaderhip. Along with these not insignificant political considerations the Prime Minister was aware by now of the importance of the various government departments and the role he wished to accord to each one in his tenure, Finance and Commerce being urgently in need of capable handling. The Ministry for Home Affairs required a man in whom Rao could repose complete trust and confidence for the home fires continued to burn.

Rao did not enjoy Nehru's stature which was able to make this selection a more arbitrary practice. Even when his views were contested, which they seldom were after 1952, Pandit Nehru's position in the national psyche disarmed his opponents and caused them to reconsider their challenges. Nor could Rao generate Indira Gandhi's combination of absolutism and popularity which did not require her to appease any constituency within the party, particularly in her later years. In 1991 few even questioned what Rao stood for. Was he a conservative and traditional Congress ideologue as his years and experience suggested, who would continue with a socialistic mixed economy or was he a radical committed to an as yet, undefined reformist agenda?

The challenges were no doubt enormous but the mood of those around him was largely restrained in hostility. Few frankly thought he would complete five years in office and based their attitudes on this presumptive premise. Even these views were carefully voiced, in the corners of Central Hall or within the private retreats of the white-washed ministerial bungalows in Lutyens' Delhi.

Congress had won 226 seats in the general election, which still remained to be concluded[33]. With the strength of its allies inside Parliament the new government could count on the support of 242 MPs. In a house of 543 this did not give it a majority. Narasimha Rao immediately moved for a motion of confidence, in the house on July 12. So far little had happened to justify the need for a vote of confidence. As the Left questioned the move, "why has this confidence motion been called?" In his own mind, Rao wished to "get on" with his job. In his first address to the country as Prime Minister he ambitiously stated that his government was determined to "remove the cobwebs that come in the way of rapid industrialisation". The complications of running a minority government would be best simplified through an early resolution.

Still others took a different line, fully realising the timing of the motion. The BJP leader L.K. Advani in his reply to the motion moved by the Prime Minister asserted:

> Sir, I rise to oppose this Motion of Confidence and I would give briefly my reasons why I am opposing it... Firstly, it is not just a minority Government but it is a minority Government in a truncated House. The elections are not complete as yet. Thirty-six vacancies are still there which means that one out of every sixteen seats in this House is still vacant. Two States are totally un-represented in this House. One is Jammu & Kashmir and the other is Punjab.[34]

---

33. Elections in Punjab and Kashmir had been effectively, "called off".
34. L.K. Advani, then BJP President. July 12, 1991. In the Lok Sabha.

He further elaborated on this view and issued what was clearly a warning to the new administration:

> If you were to closely examine these vacancies anyone would come to the conclusion that if today the difference between the ruling party and non-Congress parties is 242 versus 267 when these vacancies are to be filled, the shortfall would become even larger.[35]

This was a genuine concern which found the support of others in the house, the veteran Communist leader Indrajit Gupta, for instance, who argued that the government had not been constituted long enough for anyone to express confidence in its work, in whatever terms. Simultaneously he represented a substantial section of MPs who were apprehensive about the preliminary indications of the emerging economic stance of the government, particularly with its references to liberalisation. The Prime Minister's motivations stemmed from the urgency to rework the economic complexities which his government faced. In order to move on he had to remove the first and obvious threat of a no-confidence motion being brought against him. In real terms the threat of a no-confidence motion being raised was a distant one and the reason was simple enough. No one wanted another general election, not yet. Stability was construed as the most popular and desirable political condition by an electorate which had witnessed two general elections and four Prime Ministers in two years. The expectations from the government were primarily to provide a stable administration. The burst of successive governments following each other from reign to ruin induced a national frustration in the electorate. Between himself, V.P. Singh and Chandra Shekhar, Rao seemed the strongest Prime Minister, even though he had not led his party in an election but came to occupy his position through an accidental installation. At the same time, it was obvious, as Advani had stated that, once the house was assembled in its full strength the deficit in the government's strength was only going to grow larger. To Rao's advantage

---

35.   Ibid.

he was the Prime Minister in a "truncated" house and one which included a further divided opposition. While the Left parties may have been opposed to the government, their objectives and aims were not the same as the BJP's whom they would have been loathed to support. The government was safe and Rao's confidence motion was carried by a satisfactory division; 242 in support and 111 in oppostion. One hundred and twelve MPs abstained.

With the opposition resolved, the assuring words of Arjun Singh in Parliament would have comforted the Prime Minister's fears about the potential for an offensive being launched from within the party ranks itself:

> ...this Confidence Vote which the Prime Minister has sought will be the beginning of a new political experimentation in the running of the country...[36]

The operative term here is the allusion to "a new political experimentation". This must not be misconstrued as an abdication of Congress supremacy or of the sentiments which invoke that now obsolete state of affairs. Arjun Singh's missives have to be understood in direct relation to the less abrasive advice issued by the Prime Minister himself when he invited the opposition to work with him in a consensus. While they fecilitated the passive participation of the opposition in a more participatory form of politics this "new experimentation" could easily have been signifying the viability of the minority Congress government. What its elders wanted was compliance. Assuredly for Rao, Arjun Singh then added the weight of his own sobering confidence behind the Prime Minister:

> ...and I can tell you that the confidence he has of his party, the goodwill he has of the country will enable him to usher in a new era for this nation which wants to go forward and in spite of all the challenges, in spite of all the impediments it wants a place under the sun for the toiling masses, for the

---

36.   Arjun Singh in the Lok Sabha. July 15, 1991.

poor and the dispossessed. There lies the future of the country and the nation and that future we shall ensure with all our might.[37]

Rao was aware that he required the secure bolster of his party before any other source of support. This was forthcoming because the Congress had to portray a united front to the outside world. In addition, the perceptions about the new Prime Minister were those of a non-confrontationist, consensus builder who was perceived as far too indecisive and politically weak to entertain any independent attitudes on sensitive issues of party political or national importance. An attendant feeling of solidarity also existed, fast diminishing in those early days after the death of Rajiv Gandhi. Above all, Rao's apparent characteristics enhanced the strengths of the other senior leaders in the party. He was not unpopular but he also lacked the following of a mass party base, a source of support which was amply compensated by the large contingent of MP's from his own home turf[38].

His elevation was the reward historically granted to those who have patiently and loyally given their career to the service of their chosen cause. That was also the reasoning of some of his supporters. At most even that brittle bunch could only conclude that Rao deserved to be Prime Minister and the party required his experience. His critics had no issue or concern to voice at this early juncture, though the spectre of a radical economic shift had raised murmurs. Some of them were placated by their inclusion in the 57-member government. Others fell in as sanguine members of a party in power which seldom entrusted its functions to the engines of a collective leadership with plural powers of dispensation.

Yet what guided Rao's thinking in the early days in office was something far removed from the machinations of party politics. It was a concern immediately higher than party management. This was the foreboding of an economic disaster and something not exerted on him by

37. Ibid.
38. 87 Congress (I) MPs had been elected from the southern states of Karnataka, Andhra Pradesh, Kerala and Tamil Nadu alone.

the electorate or through any domestic pressure. It necessitated reappraisal and massive reform because without this rethink, India's economy would collapse. The seriousness and magnitude of the problem did not sink in until he was bluntly informed that India was nothing short of facing a bankruptcy. This urgent situation demanded the inclusion of a new team, and this was the reason why Dr. Manmohan Singh now found himself sitting beside the Prime Minister on the Treasury Benches.

The Emergence of Dr.Manmohan Singh and the New Economic Policy

On the day that Narasimha assumed the office of India's Prime Minister he also made the most crucial appointment of his government. Early on June 21, Rao placed a call to Dr. Manmohan Singh and informed him that he was to join the government as Finance Minister.

Manmohan Singh was not new to the political dimensions of economic management. He had served as an economic adviser to Prime Minister Chandra Shekhar when India had mortgaged its gold reserves to prevent defaulting on its payments. Before joining that administration the soft spoken Sikh technocrat had served as the Deputy Chairman of the Planning Commission during Rajiv Gandhi's term in office. His new job was a profound and urgent entrustment. Ironically it would also dismantle many of the precepts propounded by centrally controlled planning commissions. When Manmohan Singh arrived at the Treasury the fiscal deficit of the central government was a very substantial 8.5 per cent of the Gross Domestic Product (GDP), the account deficit over 3 per cent of the GDP. India had just enough foreign exchange reserves to finance imports for another fortnight and the balance of payments deficit was critically and increasingly amassing. Manmohan Singh understated his difficulties when he jocularly remarked in Parliament:

> Few would disagree that I am one of the most harassed Finance Ministers in recent times...[39]

39.　July 24, 1991 in the Lok Sabha.

If a cricketing analogy may be permitted, the position of the new Finance Minister was that of a night-watchman sent in to open the innings against a hazardous bowling attack on a very erratic and uneven wicket with a volatile crowd around him. He did however possess the complete confidence of his team captain, the Prime Minister himself, which was no inconsequential matter, as events would prove.

Preliminary discussions over what was to be done took place between two people, Rao and the former Finance Minister Pranab Mukherjee. This preliminary brainstorming suggested what both men already knew, India would need another loan from the International Monetary Fund (IMF). The outgoing Chandra Shekhar government had negotiated a loan for $1.8 billion in January 1991 but that corpus was by now exhausted. The crucial, but by no means the only reason for imminent fiscal collapse was the rapid flight of capital being carried out by Non-Resident Indians who withdrew their deposits in an unprecedented but flexible show of national feeling. Adding their weight to the fiscal crisis was the cumbersome baggage of traditional economic management and thinking. These controls and regulations had guided India's economic policy well into the early 1980s and called for the state to play an interventionist, almost a paternalisitic role within a socialistic polity. The many aspects of this form of economics; land reform, fiscal and industrial regulations, subsidies, nationalisation and other controls did not form an inviting proposal for the IMF or the World Bank to intervene with altruistic rescue packages. Reform was necessary. It has been argued that the initiative to reform and the extent of liberalisation pursued by the Rao government were both carried out due to pressure from the World Bank and the IMF. The Left certainly believed this to be true. However the comfort of ideological opposition to such demands by international loan sharks like the IMF, were not available to Dr. Manmohan Singh, who knew only too well how serious the problems were:

> There is no time to lose. Neither the government nor the economy can live beyond its means year after year. The room for manoeuvre, to live on borrowed money or time, does not exist any more. Any further postponement of macro-

39

economic adjustment, long overdue, would mean that the balance of payments situation, now exceedingly difficult, would become unmanageable and inflation, already high, would exceed limits of tolerance. For improving the management of the economy, the starting point, and indeed the centre- piece of our strategy, should be a credible fiscal adjustment and macro-economic stabilisation during the current financial year, to be followed by continued fiscal consolidation thereafter. This process would, inevitably, need at least three years, if not longer, to complete. But there can be no adjustment without pain. The people must be prepared to make necessary sacrifices to preserve our economic independence and restore the health of our economy.[40]

The resulting liberalisation was the most radical effort at policy-making witnessed in India, in any sector of governance. The budget speech was more of a *fait accompli* presented to parliament, and came as a surprise to some of his own party members.

The policy of economic liberalisation was of course a radical shift in terms of ideology and management, even more drastic perhaps was the change in the methods and manners of those implementing this policy decision. Policy making is traditionally seen as a laborious and crawling process in India, movement and development in slow motion. The team put together by Narasimha Rao forced the pace, a necessary progress if real change was to be brought about. The result was a change in the mindset of bureaucracy and industry alike. The ministerial team of Manmohan Singh, P. Chidambaram and to an extent R. Kumaramangalam drafted and re-drafted amendments and proposals. They formulated initiatives and presented alternatives. Assisted in their efforts by Jairam Ramesh, who doubled as an emissary and an adviser and by the bureaucrats, themselves surprised but satisfied by this genuine progress, the ministers ploughed on. The Budget was the presentation of their preceding efforts. These efforts were nothing short of a sweeping change.

On July 1 the Reserve Bank of India (RBI) had devalued the Indian rupee by 9.5 per cent against the dollar. This was at first presented as a

---

40.   Dr. Manmohan Singh. July 24, 1991 in the Lok Sabha. General Budget speech.

routine measure. Rao considered this too steep and sounded out Manmohan Singh on his disquiet. The RBI Governor, S.Venkataramanan and his deputy C. Rangarajan were already moving ahead with their second stage of devalutaion, and this came within two days. On July 3 the RBI devalued the rupee even further, this time by 10.6 per cent against the dollar. Thus in three days the rupee was devalued by over 20 per cent. Manmohan Singh had made his point about how he intended to progress. Within the next few days and weeks a number of changes would be ushered in. These included new industrial and trade policies, restructuring of subsidies, fiscal amendments and disinvestment drives, abolitions of price controls in certain sectors and other reforms and amendments which altered the structure and the dynamics of the Indian economy within the first months of Rao's premiership. More was done in the first few months than would be performed in the next few years, quip observers in retrospect.

Nevertheless the success of the reforms lay in how well Rao could present them to his party. Moreover, not merely his presentation but their acceptance in turn was the necessary condition for their success. Facets of the liberalisation programme, including the Exit Policy, the Industrial Policy and the decision to cut agricultural subsidies met with opposition within the ranks of the cabinet itself. The protests were not just the instinctive reactions of ministers brought up on a vocabulary of socialistic economic programmes, there was an intellectual opposition voiced by senior members of the cabinet like Arjun Singh and Madhavsinh Solanki. Rao had forseen this eventuality and despatched his emissaries to Arjun Singh, to sound him out on the proposals. Very few of the draft proposals had been discussed within a party forum and senior members perceived this with some chagrin. Consequently a cabinet sub-committee was formed and included Arjun Singh, M.L. Fotedar, Madhavsinh Solanki and B. Shankaranand along with the ministers concerned. Arjun Singh had always believed economic reform and economic policies as a whole to be linked to politics, which they naturally were. At a meeting of the sub-committee he stated, "This policy is a very dear departure from the past, it is politically unacceptable." Arjun Singh elaborated further on the need to establish a continuity between the past and the present policy, without completely ruling out the new programme. Alternatively, at the same meeting M.L. Fotedar stated that the policies were anti-Nehruvian, thus displaying an alarming panache for generalisations, a manner which comes all too easily to senior and experienced politicians. This was exactly the kind of instinctive and uninformed opposition which Narasimha Rao had expected. This ignorance and the mentality to argue, merely for the sake of argument without attaching relevant importance to the issues under discussion, met with a measured and apt rebuke from P. Chidambaram:

> This has nothing to do with Nehru or Indira Gandhi. The only nationalisation Nehru did was of the Life Insurance Corporation of India. After that all nationalisations took place between 1970 and 1977. What have these to do with Nehru? Yes, Indiraji said the state must play an interventionist role. This was inspired by the philosophy of Mohan Kumaramangalam, C. Subramaniam, to some extent I.K. Gujral and Mohan Dharia. You cannot attribute it to Nehru.[41]

The objections over continuity were serious enough however because a complete and clean break from past policies would inevitably have been construed as a rejection of the Nehruvian consensus upon which Congress foundations lay. While the new policy could not have come about without the preceding era of controls and state management, critics of the government would have condemned the past record of the Congress without attaching any thought to the realities. Sure enough, the ministers went back to the drawing board and by the time Manmohan Singh rose to speak in Parliament the matter had been settled. His words gave credit where it was due to past leaders and established a chronological course of economic development pursued by the Congress Party. His insertions in the budget speech have been interpreted as mere obeisance, but this

---

41. Palakunnathu G. Mathai and Sujatha Shenoy. As reported in *Business World*, 1991.

ignores the very real contribution made by preceding economic planners to the present pattern of economic development. The Finance Minister, however, made this clear:

> Thanks to the efforts of Pandit Jawaharlal Nehru, Indira Gandhi and Rajiv Gandhi, we have developed a well diversified industrial structure. This constitutes a great asset as we begin to implement various structural reforms... For the founding fathers of our Republic, a public sector that would be vibrant, modern, competitive and capable of generating large surpluses was a vital element in the strategy of development.[42]

This reassurance was meant to pacify, above all, elements within his own party. The following excerpt rationalised the necessity to change without discrediting past policies:

> The public sector has made an important contribution to the diversification of our industrial economy. But there have been a number of shortcomings. In particular, the public sector has not been able to generate internal surpluses on a large enough scale. At this critical juncture, it has therefore, become necessary to take effective measures so as to make the public sector an engine of growth rather than an absorber of national savings without adequate returns.[43]

Similarly he balanced the new liberalisation process with the former system of centrally controlled planning without suggesting the contribution of planning as obsolete:

> After four decades of planning for industrialisation, we have now reached a stage of development where we should welcome, rather than fear, foreign investment.[44]

The issue of subsidies had attracted considerable protest, principally from the leaders who had linked their political careers to the agricultural interest, leaders like Balram Jhakkar and Rajesh Pilot. Without a background in party politics, Manmohan Singh had bluntly asserted his

---

42. General Budget speech.
43. Ibid.
44. Ibid.

intention, to the Congress Parliamentary Party to increase the price of fertilisers by 40 per cent in order to reduce the subsidies linked to them. His case is convincing if one looks at the statistics alone. Fertiliser subsidies had grown from almost Rs. 4 billion in 1979 to over Rs. 40 billion in 1990. The decision led to protests and demonstrations by farmers and inevitably to their representatives in the party opposing the move. A memorandum was circulated, signed by no less than forty Congress MPs criticising the policy. Manmohan Singh, as yet unversed in the levels of inner-party brinkmanship (or perhaps because he was well-versed) offered his resignation to the parliamentary party. Rao turned down the offer and appointed a committee to suggest a way out of the deadlock. The committee stated that the policy would have to be reversed, given the level of opposition to the policy. Manmohan Singh refused to completely relent but agreed to a compromise. The price increase was reduced from 40 per cent to 30 per cent and small farmers were waived through. This episode highlighted the shadow play already in progress in the party to observers outside.

Economic policy had already divided the party into two camps. These were not as rigid as pro-changers and no-changers. Very few, if any party MPs were against the New Economic Policy as a whole. It was the measure of change and the method in which this was brought about which opened a front, albeit in the form of a pressure group against the Prime Minister. He could no longer say with confidence that the whole party owed him their allegiance. Left to mature this feeling could well graduate from the exertions of a pressure group to the intrigues of a dissenting bloc, within the cabinet as well as the rest of the party. For Rao and his Finance Minister however the attendant corollary of comfort lay in what they had achieved. The success of their policy lay in its radicalism and the acceptance of this scale of radicalism by the rest of the party. At least to begin with. The NEP had raised the temperature in the party, but only slightly. The issue which led to a dramatic flare-up had been ignored by the Prime Minister for quite some time.

Congress and the Myths of Muslim Appeasement

Prime Minister Narasimha Rao must have felt uneasy as he retired late on the night of May 9, 1992. During that hot summer night the Prime Minister had met a delegation of Hindu spiritualists at his Race Course Road residence. In normal circumstances the presence of godmen, Swamis and Maharishis is an accepted, even expected attendance in the homes of India's political leaders. This particular group however was not a collection of callers who had arrived to give blessings or cast spells, both of which would have been welcome to the Prime Minister negotiating a tough political existence. As the air conditioning whirred in the background the holy men raised the heat on the septugenarian leader. They were here to discuss a serious matter, the Ram Janamabhoomi dispute which Rao had not addressed since he became Prime Minister almost exactly a year ago. Among the holy visitors were some of the most recognisable faces of Hindu sainthood, figures like Swami Chinmayananda and Mahant Avaidyanath. Their principal complaint was this, "You seem to have no place for Hindus in your mind, all your thinking seems to be centred on minorities." Narasimha Rao, learned Brahmin and experienced politician did not say much. He seldom did.

The Hindu *Sants* and *Mahants* had a justifiable case to plead before the Prime Minister, but their allegation of minority appeasement, Muslim appeasement, in other words, was the result of a problem much older than the Ayodhya matter they had come to discuss.

The myths of Muslim appeasement have been in circulation ever since secularism replaced anarchic sectarianism as the representative character of India's polity and constitution. The same anarchic sectarianism which had led to a partition of India in 1947. The condemnable condition is that secularism has come to mean protection of minority rights alone, while its intention was to keep religion out of the state though not out of community life. Yet no social issue damaged the Congress more than the clamouring and noisy charges of "pandering to Muslim "vote-banks" brought about by the BJP and other elements of the right wing. Inevitably these charges emanated because of political reasons and in turn led to political ramifications. Why? Because like Rao, the Congress leadership remained mute under fire.

For the Muslims of India politics is a means for security. This details a protection of their culture, religious customs and traditions and a prolonged security for a particular way of life. The right-wing and indeed certain proponents of the anti-religion school of thought have argued that this difference in culture and lifestyle somehow makes the Indian Muslims alien to their nationality, even anti-national. Divergent cultural streams and alternative religious practices do not appeal to these proponents of "one culture nationalism". Their rhetoric frequently invites a response from Muslim reactionaries and ultimately the battle lines are drawn between secularists and communalists. This recurring drama meanwhile clouds the realities.

Participation in politics is still not an occupation of the Muslim social mainstream. In post-partition India those Muslims who remained behind had to contend with a situation that did not easily lend itself to their advantage. For a brief period immediately after partition it was felt that perhaps Jinnah's arguments, that in a Hindu majoritarian state Muslims would acquire the status of an oppressed community were true. In such a milieu the offerings of the Nehruvian Congress, its espousal of the causes of secularism, plurality of culture, freedom of religion and equality and Pandit Jawaharlal Nehru's own towering and at the same time comforting image pacified the community. Unlike Pakistan, India naturally progressed to becoming a secular state with a Constitution that guaranteed the rights and privileges of all communities under the law. That is a simplified rationalisation of the Congress-Qaum relationship as opposed to the simplistic argument that typifies this relationship as an exchange of appeasement for votes. It is true that even within the Congress of early independent India a sub-culture of communalism existed inside the party, what contemporary analysts call "soft-saffron" politics. Nonetheless, it did not form the core of the party philosophy as it did, and continues to do, within the more right-wing Hindu nationalist political groups like the BJP. The fact that it existed however at such a primordial level of India's evolution as a state is an indisputable fact. The RSS and Jana Sangh have identified the leaders of this sub-culture as votaries of Hindutva politics. Hence Congress leaders like Purshottam Das Tandon have become more an object of aggrandisement and eulogy within the circles of the Sangh than within the Congress itself. This influence found a rebuke from Prime Minister Nehru of course who regularly wrote to his Chief Ministers and chided them for what he saw as a diseased development. When, in 1949 idols of Ram "mysteriously" appeared within the sanctum of the Babri Mosque in Ayodhya, Nehru immediately recognised the adverse potential of these developments. In conjunction with the broader matter of Hindu revivalism, particulalrly in Uttar Pradesh, the Ram Janamabhoomi issue threatened to rekindle the consequences of communalist politics. Consequences which had meant a partition of the Indian subcontinent only two years ago. Writing to the Chief Minister of UP Govind Ballabh Pant in 1950, the Prime Minister made a forceful and sincere comment on what he feared was a fast moving deterioration for the province:

> I have felt for a long time that the whole atmosphere of the UP has been changing for the worse from the communal point of view. Indeed, the UP is becoming almost a foreign land for me. I do not fit in there......All that occurred in Ayodhya......was bad enough. But the worst feature of it was that such things should take place and be approved by some of our own people and that they should continue.[45]

Nehru had perhaps attempted to nip any possible shift towards the right in the bud. Certainly the Congress did not incorporate Hindu revivalism into its own ideological strands. In the Congress it was a peripheral influence that would sometimes guide the party's vocabulary, and thinking. It continued to be a means towards an end, not an end in

---

45.   Nehru to Govind Ballabh Pant, at the time Chief Minister of the United Provinces (UP). April 17, 1950. Nehru Papers.

itself. By 1992, however, it was apparent that what had so far been a secondary, phlegmatic influence on the party's thinking had now evolved into a principle of pragmatic politics. While they did not wholeheartedly adopt communalism as a conviction of their political beliefs, some influential Congressmen did begin to view it as a doctrine that could be used to shore up a fast diminishing vote base. The story of Muslim estrangement from the Congress Party however did not begin in Ayodhya with the shilanyas as various commentaries have suggested. Nor was this disillusionment ever as complete as academics have advised us. Indeed, right from the days of the Khilafat in 1919, through to the Quit India Movement in 1942, and just after the bloody partition of the Indian subcontinent in 1947, Muslim political association has always been brittle and inconsistent. Jinnah's Muslim League hardly attained sanction or legitimacy within the councils of the Muslim dominated legislatures of Punjab or the North West Frontier in the pre-partition elections to the council. Of the provincial elections of 1945-1946, Patrick French writes:

> Congress won a landslide victory in the elections. They formed the government in all provinces of British India except Bengal and Sind (and Punjab)......In the provinces of the proposed Pakistan, things were as chaotic as ever: it was only in Muslim minority areas such as the United Provinces that Pakistan seemed unreservedly popular."[46]

The politics of separatism were resisted by the nationalist Muslim leaders and their followers. Similarly, the parting of ways between comrades in arms such as Maulana Muhammad Ali and Mahatma Gandhi over questions of Muslim representation all demonstrate the lack of focused support and the basis upon which Muslims have organised themselves within politics. Robinson has argued that Muslims tend to organise on the basis of their faith. Citing Paul Brass, Robinson writes:

> According to Brass, if Muslims organise on the basis of their faith in politics,

---

46.   Patrick French. *Liberty or Death – India's Journey to Independence and Division.* Harper Collins Publishers. India. 1998.

it is because Muslim elites perceive it to be the most effective way of keeping or gaining political power.[47]

He concludes:

> But it seems likely that the ideal of the Islamic community shaped and shapes their apprehension of what is legitimate, desirable and satisfactory political action.[48]

However the evidence for this in modern day India is weak. There has neither been nor exists a pan-Indian Muslim party catering exclusively to the Muslim interest. Post-partition the Muslims of India, and particularly in UP have allowed themselves to be represented by secular leadership within secular party organisations. There are instances of Muslim support for fringe groups like the Majlis-e-Ittahadul-Muslimeen in Andhra Pradesh, led by Salauddin Owaisi or membership of the Muslim League in Maharashtra and Kerala, these however are remote. By and large the support of the community as a whole has been behind secular formations, particulalrly the Indian National Congress. The most notable instance being the large percentage of Muslim support which the Congress received immediately after the Bangladesh war in 1971. Muslims, at 74 per cent supported Indira Gandhi more than any other single community, thus asserting their endorsement of her leadership. By 1998, out of the total Muslim vote only 50 per cent were still voting for the Congress and its allies at the All-India level. However, even this formed a crucial 19 per cent of the entire vote received by the Congress alliance. Whatever the critics of the Congress and particularly of the Nehruvian tradition may say, the Indian National Congress has never worked in partnership with the BJP or any of its previous reincarnations. This is not an abstract illusion. The Congress continues to be the only party of any consequence in India which has never directly or indirectly supported a BJP or Sangh coalition government. Nor has there ever been a partnership linked

---

47. Citing Paul Brass in his essay 'Islam and Nationalism' in *Nationalism*. Oxford University Press. 1994. John Hutchinson and Antony D. Smith (Eds.)
48. Ibid.

through coalitions or alliances. For all their vitriol against communalism and against individual leaders of the Sangh, both the SP and the Left parties were in partnership with the BJP in the 1989 Lok Sabha election. Their willing participation in a joint alliance with the BJP under the aegis of the National Front led to the eventual spawning of BJP MPs, their numbers rising from two in 1985 to 82 in 1989. Clearly anti-Congressism had got the better of anti-communalism. Mulayam Singh Yadav, the now vociferous anti-BJP socialistic leader of the SP cannot escape the verdict of his own (largely sympathetic) biographers who conclude, with some regret it would appear that:

> Devi Lal and Arun Nehru masterminded the Janata Dal's alignment with the BJP. Mulayam Singh was against any such tie up but decided to remain neutral. These alignments proved beneficial for the Janata Dal in the short run, but the rigid attitude of the BJP gave an indication of the problems ahead.[49]

Ayodhya and the entire conundrum of the Congress stand on the issue was merely a final arbitration on the prolonged dispute within the community over who represented their interests in the political domain. Thus we can identify it as a catalyst rather than the genesis of the divergence between the Muslims and the Congress Party. Assembly elections held in 1994 soon after the fall of the Babri Masjid, in Karnataka and Andhra Pradesh, were a resounding defeat for the Rao government. Similarly in 1998, the Congress would not win a single parliamentary seat of the 85 in UP. Politicians and analysts have often viewed these developments, between 1989 and 1998 as a Muslim backlash against the Congress Party. Perhaps the statistics credit that theory. However we have also seen a growth and radicalisation of anti-Congress secular forces in this period who have emerged as alternatives to the party of dominance in the eyes of the Muslim community. There are various reasons for the disenchantment with the Congress and they can be assimilated into four

---

49. Mulayam Singh Yadav – *A Political Biography*. Ram Singh and Anshuman Yadav. Konark Publishers. 1998. New Delhi. The alliance benefited the BJP far more than it did Mulayam Singh's Janata Dal, opening the doors for its subsequent ascent to power.

generic sections which in turn constitute the failure of the Congress Party to sustain its Muslim vote-bank. They can also explain why the Muslims increasingly opted for non-Congress alternatives wherever the Congress was not engaged in a head on fight with the BJP or other Sangh associates.

The first is a genuine complaint against a lack of development of the community. While sufficient importance has indeed been accorded to Urdu it continues to be viewed, unfortunately, as a language exclusive to the Muslims of India. That, however, is a superficial engagement of the issues which obstruct the progress of the Muslim community at a national level. The facts are a painful indictment for the Indian National Congress which has always claimed to champion the cause of the minorities and Muslims in particular. They blow a clear hole in the rhetoric of the BJP which has challenged the few policies which the Congress has brought about. The situation is summed up in a report prepared for the National Council for Applied Economic Research (NCAER) in 2000 which states:

> A review of the existing literature on Indian Muslims suggests a poor human development status for the Indian Muslim. Widespread illiteracy, low income, irregular employment implying thereby a high incidence of poverty, are some of the indicators pointing towards a low level of human development for the Indian Muslims.[50]

The second cause for Muslim disenchantment with the dominant Congress establishment has been a lack of representation and consequently the apparent disinterest in promoting Muslim representation in the mainstream of national and public life. Whether in the armed forces, the civil service or other sectors of public sector employment, Muslims have fared miserably. The National Commission for Minorities concludes:

> The enormous Muslim population of India is terribly under-represented in all public services both at the national and state levels. Their presence in

---

50. "Differentials in Human Development: A Case for the Empowerment of Muslims in India." Prepared for the Programme of Research on Human Development of the National Council of Applied Economic Research. New Delhi. Azra Razzack and Anil Gumbler. In addition the report provides detailed statistics and case studies.

general educational institutions of the country is also much below their population ratio–and is found nil. Educational backwardness is both the main cause and the inevitable effect of under representation of the Muslims in public employment and resource generating bodies…[51]

This lack of representation is more acutely highlighted in the political arena where Muslim participation is negligible. The percentage of Muslim legislators elected to the Lok Sabha in 1991 and 1996 was a mere 5.15 per cent and 4.97 per cent respectively. An insignificant proportion, in terms of representation of 18 per cent of India's total population. Even in the AICC the number of Muslim office bearers fell from 61 in 1981 to around 20 at the beginning of the decade under study.

The third causal factor for a loss of faith in the Congress leadership was the inability of the Congress Party to articulate a counter-response to the charges of appeasement constantly made by the Sangh Parivar. These coupled with the stereotypical imaging of the Muslim community further emboldened forces of sectarianism to press their charges of Muslim appeasement, and get away with it.

In 1992, almost everyone had a view or rationale on the Hindu–Muslim relationship. The Ayodhya movement had created fissures that in equal measure required either deepening or dissolving, depending on which side of the divide one stood. One of the dividing tactics was the construction and publicity of racial and communal stereotypes, the propagation and repropagation of which had a vital and dangerous role to play in further antagonising already strained relations between the two communities. That same year the Indian scholar Asghar Ali Engineer wrote in his book *Communal Riots in Post-Independence India*:

An average Hindu's prejudice against the Muslim community is because of his misconceived perception of firstly, the attempts made by the Muslim rulers in medieval times to destroy Hindu culture; secondly, the separatist role played by the Muslims in the freedom struggle; thirdly, their refusal

---

51. Ibid.

to modernise themselves and accept the uniform civil code, family planning, etc. and finally, their having extra-territorial loyalties.[52]

One can easily identify these four assertions made by him here and they do represent correctly the misconceptions and misunderstandings in the Hindu mind about their Muslim compatriots. There was a dire need for an aggressive response from the Congress to this strategy, especially in the run up to the events which led to an electoral polarisation in 1996 and in the various regional elections between 1991 and 1998. None was forthcoming. Few realised, or acted against such tactics which did as much damage to the cause of the Congress as they did to the Muslim community. If the Muslims of India were appeased or privileged or patronised, the appeaser and patron was the Congress in power. That was the logic of the BJP the constant and varied propagation of which the Congress was unable to prevent. In the northern states where the BJP rode into power on the back of this polarisation of the Hindu vote the Congress appeared meek and almost the guilty party. Its leadership did not challenge the accusations made by the BJP and its Hindutva allies of pandering to the Muslim vote-bank. There is little evidence to support the various myths produced by the BJP and other right-wing forces that the Congress has appeased Muslims in exchange for their votes, as we have already seen. No empirical data can be or has been furnished to credit such theories. Whatever is available demolishes these precepts. Lamentably for the Congress Party, it was neither prepared nor willing to rebuff these arguments. Its septugenarian leaders in fact played right into the hands of the BJP leadership and instead of countering their postures began to compete with them by practising the politics of majoritarianism. This is what led to the fourth and final causality that eventually severed the relationship between the Congress and the Muslim electorate. The accommodation of the right-wing. Indira Gandhi had successfully competed with the right-wing through her association with symbols of Hinduism, in garb, in language and sometimes through action. She believed she could disarm the Hindu-right by adopting their postures

---

52. Cited in *Jinnah, Pakistan and Muslim Identity: The Search for Saladin*. Akbar S. Ahmad. Routledge. London. 1997.

as her own as she had done in the early 1970s with the Left parties. Her critics argue that:

> The move to the right was also probably based on a curious belief by Mrs Gandhi that only she (and her son) stood between India and serious communal strife. So, still more curiously, she apparently believed that, by catalysing communalist sentiments, by becoming the main mouthpiece for Hindu communalism, she was protecting India from the dangers of it. She appears to have rationalised this dangerous quest for short-term political advantage by concluding that communalism was safe only in her hands and that by taking it up, she could disarm it as she had disarmed leftist sentiment after 1969.[53]

The logic of Indira Gandhi's posture may not appeal to many, however the motives were clearly the result of an authoritarian secularism by which she decided that as long as she was at the helm of affairs the communalisation of politics could be controlled and eventually curbed. Dangerous though it may appear, such a motive was still the result of an instinctive commitment to secularism, personally. Rajiv Gandhi pursued the same course though less successfully. He was willing to accommodate both the Muslim right, as was apparent in the Shah Bano controversy as well as the Hindu right through the official patronage he extended to the shilanyas at Ayodhya. Yet even then, he too felt that by retaining these actions with himself he could counter the right-wing whether Hindu or Muslim. For Narasimha Rao, events centring around the town of Ayodhya in central UP would reverberate with a ferocity unknown to any of his predecessors. At no juncture in the politics of the Congress Party is the interaction of hesitation and lack of purpose more pronounced, or its political consequences as important as it would be in this period. The resulting shock would be so absorbing and so absolute that the Indian National Congress, the party of Mahatma Gandhi, Pandit Nehru and Maulana Azad would be extinguished in its former bastion of Uttar Pradesh. From Muslim appeasers, Congressmen would appear as sectarian apparatchiks and people would ask, "Whither Nehru?".

---

53. James Manor in his paper Parties and the Party System in *Parties and Party Politics in India*. Oxford University Press. New Delhi. 2002. Zoya Hasan (Ed.)

A Period of No Confidence

The Costs of Appeasement and the Babri Crisis – Assemblies in the South – Factions and Friction - A Letter of Resignation

The Costs of Appeasement and the Babri Crisis

By 1992 political logic and motivations had ceased to be operative in the minds of the Congress Party leadership. Narasimha Rao's actions over Babri, though he argued a persuasive case citing the limitations of constitutional technicalities, cemented a perception among Muslims that the Congress no longer remained the pan-Indian, secular party it once was. A simplistic argument yes but one which was reinforced by consequent developments and eventually transformed into an axiom in the minds of the Muslim electorate. Particulalry so in UP where Mulayam Singh, himself culpable on many counts, used the opportunity to garner the eroding vote of the Congress Party. The fact that the Babri Masjid fell during the tenure of a Congress government at the centre was enough for the Muslims to make up their minds about the Congress leadership. It no longer appeared to safeguard their community interest. While the confusions wrought the community, Mulayam Singh Yadav had already deepened the divide by taking action against BJP supporters who gathered in Ayodhya. Karsevaks were shot dead and rumbustious speeches were made to "enlighten" the Muslims of UP about the record of Congress governments, past and present. The result was a polarisation of Muslim votes towards the SP and of the upper castes towards the BJP. It was a repetition of the patterns in Bihar where Laloo Prasad Yadav had arrested L.K. Advani in Samastipur thus bringing his rath yatra to a close but fuelled passions in the process.

On December 6, 1992, thousands of Sangh "volunteers" under the aegis of their national leaders supervised and participated in the destruction of the 16th century Babri Mosque at Ayodhya. No intervention was made by the police and paramilitary forces in and around the site. The 'official' description of what happened was later relayed by the Home Minister S.B. Chavan in the Government's White Paper on Ayodhya. It stated:

> On December 6, 1992, initial reports from Ayodhya indicated that the situation was peaceful. However, between 11:45 and 11:50 hours about 150 karsevaks suddenly broke the cordon and started pelting stones at the police personnel. Equally suddenly, about 100 karsevaks broke the RJBBM structure. About 80 karsevaks climbed the domes of the structure and started damaging them. At 14:40 hours, a crowd of 75,000 karsevaks surrounded the structure and many of them were engaged in demolishing it.[1]

A makeshift temple was hastily installed where the mosque had earlier stood. Almost immediately afterwards, communal riots broke out throughout the country. In Bombay[2] the riots assumed unprecedented dimensions and the role of the Naik government in the state and a strong representation at the centre called into question the Congress' strength, indeed willingness, to pacify the violence led by the Shiv Sena.[3]

Congress MPs, immediately sensing the furore and shift away from the party awaited some "heads to roll" in the aftermath of the Babri demolition. As news of the tragedy filtered back to New Delhi, Congressmen in the capital expected Rao to dismiss the Home Minister or persuade him to resign. Other resignations were expected too, particularly from senior Muslim ministers in the government. No one resigned and the idea of someone taking responsibility for the failure did not enter the minds of the high command.

The unwillingness to act upon the incompetence of his own ministerial colleagues signified not merely weakness and indifference in

---

1. Government White Paper on Ayodhya. 1993.
2. Now pretentiously called Mumbai.
3. The Defence and Home portfolios in the cabinet were both held by Maharashtrians, Sharad Pawar and S.B. Chavan respectively. Chavan was later felicitated by the ultra right-wing Shiv Sena whose invitations he accepted unrepentantly.

Rao but more alarmingly raised questions about complicity in the act. As so often happens in politics while radical action and strong arm tactics in situations of mild misdemeanours can attract dissent and retribution, the converse is equally detrimental. Studied silences and indecision in the event of monumental mismanagement is likely to attract vexation and dissonance of a far higher degree. Moreover, the discursive politics on display in the immediate aftermath of the Babri demolition emboldened Rao's critics and others nursing apprehensions or ambitions in varying measures. The strategy, if such a muddled parody of a response from the Congress Party can be dignified by that precise term, was to turn the tables and present the Congress leadership as a victim of the right-wing's deceit.

Even this approach was mismanaged from the very beginning. While Narasimha Rao confidently asserted, with some justification, that the entire demolition was a planned exercise, the Union Home Minister S.B. Chavan, the man 'in-charge', stated that it wasn't. When confronted by these contradictions the Home Minister added that the commission of inquiry would probe the matter. Critics were less sparing about Rao than they had been about previous Congress governments:

> Under Narasimha Rao, the Congress for the first time in its history organised a de facto alignment with the BJP (before the destruction of the Babri Masjid) to stabilise its rule at the Centre. This further legitimised Hindutva politics and encouraged the forces of political Hindutva in its Ayodhya campaign. Indirectly, the Congress bears a great deal of the blame for the destruction of the Babri Masjid. It could see what was coming, could have done much more to prevent it, and to legally and politically punish those responsible for these communal crimes, including the unleashing of widespread anti-Muslim pogroms that followed in the wake of the demolition. That it did none of these things reflected its inordinate concern not to go against what it perceived were pro-Hindutva sentiments among Hindus. The politics of expediency and cowardice were of greater consequence than any politics of principles precisely because the old Congress ideology had ceased to have any guiding relevance.[4]

---

4.   Achin Vanaik. *The Furies of Indian Communalism – Religion, Modernity and Secularisatio*
    Verso Press. London. 1997.

Having-absolved itself of any responsibility and in order to demonstrate strength, the Rao government arrested some BJP leaders and dismissed the three BJP state governments in Himachal Pradesh, Madhya Pradesh and Rajasthan. It proved to be a case of too little too late. The terms of the relationship between the Indian National Congress and the Muslim quam had been drastically altered. In UP, which was the focus of this entire degeneration, the Congress would not even remain a significant political force any more. This event proved to be a body blow whose ramifications were felt without delay on the body-politic of the Congress Party. A chain reaction of events followed, both within the party and imposed by events from outside which claimed as its first casualty, the confidence of many of its senior leaders. The electoral costs would be borne in forthcoming contests.

The debacle over the Babri Masjid issue symbolised much more than the physical destruction of a monument in the minds of the massive but introverted majority of India's secular population. The inaction of the Congress Party and Rao in particular motioned towards the coming of an era in Indian politics which would be bloodier, more unstable and more traumatic than that of preceding years. By seeking to arrest disorder and social disharmony through delay and inaction, Rao succeeded in pushing away the prospects of a dialogue between the parties concerned. Simultaneously, his initial discussions, which some Hindu seers may have perceived as assurances, were discontinued midway, thus leaving in the lurch a substantial group of people involved in the Ayodhya movement. Subsequently, Indian society was divided more deeply and more permanently than ever before as a result. That has been the success of the BJP and its allies. A debate over secularism and what fundamentally constitutes plurality and diversity in a country of India's social expanse would have been a welcome exchange between secularists and their favourite bedfellows the communalists. Alternatively, stringency and confrontation between two ideologically different groups scuttled the potential for this dialogue. No one remained passive or neutral. The Congress which under Rao had sought appeasement and accommodation was the first victim of this new political polarisation.

Assemblies in the South

For the central government Assembly Elections are often a litmus test to gauge public opinion and form readings of present and emerging political trends. Alternatively, they have the same value in terms of warnings as by-elections. Their results induce an acute sense of foreboding, they represent the auguries for a General Election. The winter of 1994 provided just this opportunity for the Narasimha Rao government in the form of regional elections to the state assemblies of Sikkim, Andhra Pradesh and Karnataka. For Narasimha Rao the elections in Andhra Pradesh and Karnataka possessed a special significance. Rao belonged to the south and had served a brief term as Chief Minister of Andhra Pradesh in the 1970s. He was the first Prime Minster who belonged to southern India. In the weeks leading up to these elections, Rao had publicly declared them to be a matter of personal prestige. His election speeches, particularly in Andhra, demonstrated a combative mood and could be admired for their boldness. In the aftermath of the elections, they would be damned as hollow rodomontades. For Rao however, this was no time to appear philosophical or to express conciliation towards the elements of dissidence rising within the party. A victory in the south would provide him strength on many fronts and much needed vigour to carry on as Prime Minister in the face of rising challenges from senior leaders like Arjun Singh and from the dissatisfied backbench in Parliament. Of the entire Congress members in Parliament, most had been elected from Andhra Pradesh and Karnataka alone. It was this rather substantial caucus which had backed Rao as Prime Minister in the uncertain days of May and June 1991 and had since reinforced his position within the parliamentary party. In order to retain their confidence he had to express to them, above all, that their future was secure under his leadership. A victory could in turn presented as a favourable referendum on the three years of his government and trumpeted as a positive response for economic liberalisation and the New Economic Policy introduced in 1991, which had its critics even within the Congress. N.T. Rama Rao, the colourful and popular TDP leader of Andhra Pradesh had challenged the reforms in his election speeches and made the subsidised rice scheme one of his party's manifesto commitments. Yet one cannot doubt that Rao and his closest aides, in the PMO as well as at the AICC and in Parliament did in fact expect to win these contests or at least to secure some fundamental approval for themselves through them. Had this not been the case, Narasimha Rao would have cultivated the longest possible distance between himself and elections to regional assemblies. It was possible to do so. The Prime Minister could easily have portrayed himself as a statesman straddling the diplomatic stage abroad and the platform of economic reform at home, too occupied and distant to care about Assembly elections in a few regions of India. Moreover, he could have delegated this responsibility to other senior leaders who, had defeat been apparent, would have perished politically. Nonetheless that the Prime Minster took it upon himself to strategise and execute the entire election programme, right from the distribution of tickets down to the often chaotic and relentless campaigning in these states is evidence that he expected a good result. It was also an attempt to take on the growing dissidence through confrontation rather than appeasement.

When the results began trickling in on December 9, Rao was closeted in his Race Course Road residence in Delhi with some of his inner circle. A 15 per cent swing against the Congress had reduced it to a rump in Andhra Pradesh. N.T. Rama Rao's TDP had swept the state massively. Of the 294 seats, Congress retained only 26, a loss of 157 seats. The TDP secured a landslide of 253, a gain of a hundred and sixty. Narasimha Rao's own son, Dr. P.V. Ranga Rao lost his seat, of the nearly 40 ministers of the Congress government only three were re-elected. The results from Karnataka did not provide any breathing space for Rao and his loyalists. It was a similar performance, a massacre in political terms.

Here too the Congress faced a nearly 15 per cent swing against itself. The proportion of losses was equal to if not more than those suffered in Andhra Pradesh. The party lost 141 seats being reduced to a paltry 35 in an Assembly of 224. The added insult to this injury was the performance of the BJP, a party with relatively no presence in Karnataka before, which won 40 seats on a 21 per cent swing in its favour, five more than Congress. The Janta Dal (JD) would form the government, with a precarious majority of 3. The united JD had won 116 seats on a 2.7 per cent swing towards it. It was an indication of the Congress Party's dilatory approach to regional politics at the time that the disparate and often disengaged elements of the JD had come together as a united front to contest these elections. The Congress was doubly decimated. Rao's first reaction was characteristic, "It is indeed a storm," he observed weakly to a party MP who was with him when the results had become clear. His mind must have turned to the meetings of the Congress Parliamentary Party and the CWC slated for the next day. Meanwhile, the backroom boys, V.C. Shukla, Bhuvnesh Chaturvedi and others had recovered from their initial shock and got into a damage control exercise. As can sometimes happen, the defences they began to prepare were required more urgently to protect the Prime Minister from his own colleagues and inner-party intrigue than from any external political threat.

Paradoxically, the first threat they identified was Sonia Gandhi, who herself was satisfied to observe rather than participate in any move against Rao. Since Rajiv Gandhi's death in 1991, she had cultivated a very low profile. Her association with political leaders was purely a personal one. However this circle of confidantes included among them personalities like Arjun Singh and Rajesh Pilot, front-runners for dissidence. Her motivations for keeping political contacts in the party were far from the factors of destabilisation as Rao may have suspected. She was and remained an outsider with channels within the party which kept her informed and advised her about issues in a period of her life which was acutely vulnerable. While some dissident leaders may have given off a sense of being "backed" or supported by Sonia Gandhi in their activities she herself did not provide this support. For the suspecting inquisitors of Rao's inner circle her own motivations were of secondary importance. What was urgent was to minimise all voices of discontent. The task of identifying the causes of the party's defeat did not require much effort and appears to have been referred to in passing. The endeavours of the Prime Minister's coterie were singularly devoted to resisting party obloquy from the ranks of the Congress and the supposed threat from Sonia Gandhi.

Factions and Friction

The highest echelons of the Congress Party met on December 10 at the CWC meeting in the AICC headquarters. This was followed by a session of the Congress Parliamentary Party, presided over by the Home Minister S.B. Chavan. The mood was tense at both these sittings. Arjun Singh, backed by other leaders from north India queried the point of having a CWC meeting to express faith in the Prime Minister so frequently. That after all was the stated purpose of this exercise. Both N.D. Tiwari and Rajesh Pilot supported him. Pilot voiced his concerns over the causes of the defeat which he identified as a weak strategy against corruption and the alienation of the Muslims from the Congress. N.D. Tiwari for his part likened the loss of Andhra Pradesh and Karnataka to the reverses suffered in UP earlier and described the defeat as part of a "crisis on a national scale". Rao listened to these voices but did not contradict them, even silencing those who bobbed up and down trying to succour him. This strategy of appearing conciliatory from a position of weakness did not cut much ice with the dissidents, now slowly grouping around Arjun Singh and Rajesh Pilot. Tempers were displayed later that day at the meeting of the parliamentary party when some MPs took offence to Chavan's statement that the losses in the south were similar to the defeat suffered by Indira Gandhi in 1977. To this several MPs responded strongly and asked the Home Minister to cease drawing such comparisons. "No one should compare himself to Indiraji," said Suresh Pachauri, a Rajya Sabha MP from Madhya Pradesh. Chavan's statement was omitted from the minutes of the meeting.

Since 1992, fissures had developed within the Congress on a scale which made a split likely, even inevitable. Rao had appointed Arjun Singh as the Chairman of the Cabinet Committee which was preparing the White Paper on Ayodhya, outlining the government's response. Singh, however, resigned his position in January 1993 saying that the government's response was not adequate enough. He reiterated this concern in February 1993 when the White Paper was finally laid before Parliament. Since then, through the AICC session in Surajkund and within meetings of the CWC, Arjun Singh, his supporters and sympathisers had made life uncomfortable for the Prime Minister. The latest round of assembly elections only emboldened them further. The prolonged attrition between Narasimha Rao and Arjun Singh also created a space for people who did not see themselves as part of either "camp". This motley collection was made up of MPs and leaders who owed their positions of influence to Rao but were not overly sympathetic to his cause. Simultaneously they did not belong to the faction led by Arjun Singh, some even bore grudges against him. This group was leaderless, although it can be argued that at one stage Rajesh Pilot did seek to portray himself as its leader. However the composition of this caucus, which at one point comprised almost 50 MPs of the Congress Party was too diffuse, both in the number of personalities as well as in their variation of interests for it to have existed as a solid block. Consequently it could not effectively negotiate with the leadership or bargain over ministerial positions. Although only a few days after the CWC meeting of December the 10th, a substantial number of MPs met at the residence of the Minister of State for External Affairs Salman Khurshid to discuss their position. No minutes exist of this meeting, however, it is clear that the intention of this group was to alert Rao of its neutrality but at the same time draw his attention to their demands which would be voiced individually. The stated intention of this sub-group was the all too familiar but ambivalent totem of 'party-revitalisation'. Certainly this was no entrenchment of opposition to Rao nor was this formation a flank of defence for the now dissident Arjun

Singh. The manifest objectives of this group were spelt out by Rajesh Pilot when he stated to the *Sunday* magazine, "Our job is to strengthen the party and to raise issues like its pro-poor image, welfare of the weaker sections and restoring the confidence of the minorities." Taking this line however had its drawbacks too for Arjun Singh had expressed, perhaps more sharply, exactly the same reservations at various meetings of the CWC. It is therefore plausible to suggest that in character this new section was more of a pressure group within the party that sought to draw maximum advantage from a weakening Rao. It is not sufficiently clear how far they succeeded but they did register their presence enough for Rao to take notice of their activities from then on.

Within these emerging faultlines, Sonia Gandhi is not visible. None of the trenches rapidly emerging within the Congress battlefield could wholeheartedly claim that she was a presence in their camp. Definite attempts were made arbitrarily, by both Arjun Singh and Pilot's "Young Turks" to attach her support to their respective causes but from 10 Janpath there was no indication which could be construed as an extension of support. While it could not have suited Narasimha Rao, as Prime Minister, to acknowledge Sonia Gandhi in a capacity of leadership, the other factions used her as a bogey with which to exert their combined pressures upon him.

A Letter of Resignation

On December 24th, Arjun Singh submitted his resignation from the Council of Ministers. Apart from the dynamics and proceedings of this episode in particular, it would serve well to identify what in the first instance are the causes of dissent and deviance in a political organisation.

Olson wrote that:

> ...Unless the number of individuals in a group is quite small, or unless there is coercion or some other special device to make individuals act in

their common interest, rational, self-interested individuals will not achieve their common group interest.[5]

Several perspectives can be used to study and explain the causes and consequences of deviance in a political organisation, the primary one being the justice perspectives. Within this is the element of perceived powerlessness as a cause for deviance, unfair treatment, the norms and situational factors like changes in organisational structure as causes along with the personal or psychologically-oriented causes. In conjunction with the justice perspective, we can also observe the equity perspective where the focus is on the fairness of outcome. If the outcomes or the perceptions about these are inequitable, individuals will be motivated to act negatively. In political parties coercion is used in tandem with other "special devices" which can include systems of reward, which amounts to buying off the opposition. In the Congress Party this has often meant a bureaucratic promotion to a higher level. So while it made sense for Kamaraj and The Syndicate to elevate Indira Gandhi to the office of AICC President in 1967, the same practice could not be applied by Narasimha Rao with regard to Arjun Singh nearly thirty years later. What occurred was more a dysfunctional consequence of having a leadership which is too centralised and bound by excessive norms. Singh's calls for greater "inner-party democracy" were by implication an attack on Rao and were in fact justified since he had won his election to the CWC by the highest number of votes gained by any member. However, grievances as a whole are rarely addressed, normally they are either suppressed or else ignored as the party has to choose between allocating resources to deal with these grievances and other factors. Unaddressed, they are likely to escalate into some form of dissent. In the same vein, this dissent can emerge as a response to the way that change is introduced into an organisation. Long entrenched party leaders become apprehensive of their position within the party when there is talk of "organisational reform" or "structural changes". Thus change meets with resistance from the very forces responsible for its introduction. In the Congress this has been one of the fundamental reasons

---

5.   Magnur Olson on parties and party organisations.

why strategies for change are neither conceptualised nor, therefore, implemented since established leaders resist any change which may appear (in their view, threaten) to construct alternative power bases or lay new lines of control and influence. This self-preservation, as opposed to motivations which enhance the group, undermines organisational commitment and leads to factionalism. As a result, internal tensions are added to the already overwhelming external opposition to the party. Ultimately coercion has to be applied to correct this and that is a measure, like reward, which must be economically and sparingly used in politics. Members of a political group have several reasons to deviate from groupthink on reasons as broad as party philosophy and ideology to specific issues and policies. These can arise from genuine grievances which according to expectancy theories do not meet with an individual's criteria of private success, or they could be an excuse to leave an organisation whose body of influence may not appear to be successful facilitators of either policy or the dissident's own prospects. While the method of how this deviance is played out can assume many forms, in all cases the leadership has to either evolve consensus through persuasion or apply coercion through punishment in order to maintain control. This is the course Narasimha Rao was forced to adopt following the resignation of Arjun Singh from the cabinet.

Down and Out in Uttar Pradesh

The Deficit Vote - Bank – Fireworks in Amethi – 'My Kingdom for an Elephant'

The Deficit Vote-Bank

The impact of the Babri Masjid Ram Janamabhoomi controversy and the subsequent demolition of the mosque changed the face of politics in Uttar Pradesh forever. In the General Elections of 1996, this change would be played out as a loud and clear death knell for the Congress Party in the state. Out of the 85 seats to Parliament from UP the Congress only won 5 and the percentage of the Congress vote fell to a dismal 8 per cent.[1]

By 1990 the Ram Janamabhoomi[2] movement had reached a crescendo during V.P. Singh's premiership of his resistance to the movement generated by the BJP and its affiliated organisations forced them to withdraw the support of their 82 MPs to his government. Political erudition had prompted Singh to create his own mechanisms to disarm any possible backlash against himself. He proceeded to do so now by digging up the Mandal Commission Report, a document like any one of the countless others drawn up by governmental and inquiry commissions which, in normal circumstances, seldom see the light of day. Nevertheless, the decision to implement the recommendations of the Mandal Report created and in some cases revived fissures of caste sectarianism never witnessed in India previously. For the first time in its history, India was simultaneously divided along cleavages of caste and communalist politics. For a while it did seem that the daily news and debates generated by Advani's Rath-Yatra or the Sangh's pronouncements on the temple issue had been pushed into the background. Students and youth organisations

---

1. So long lasting was the impact that in 1998 the Congress won not a single seat out of the 85. In 1999 with Sonia Gandhi as President the party did win 10 seats and the vote share climbed to 18 per cent.
2. See preceding chapters. (Ch. 2:7)

carried out protests all over the country and the capital New Delhi witnessed daily lathi charges and crackdowns on these protests. Many immolated themselves to draw attention to the perceived and real injustices of the Mandal recommendations. The Congress, meanwhile, spoke about justice, of needing to maintain an equilibrium between qualifications and receiving reservations. V.P. Singh was criticised as opportunistic and manipulative. Such discourse however was overshadowed by the rise of new forces, particularly in Bihar and Uttar Pradesh. Mulayam Singh Yadav, Ram Vilas Paswan, Sharad Yadav and Laloo Prasad[3] all came to prominence in this period as vociferous proponents of the new found cause of social justice. Each represented specific constituencies and spoke of exactly what those social groups wanted to hear, in a language they would understand perfectly. Thus V.P. Singh created an entire second generation leadership which had a particular issue to stand for. Not since the late 1970s, in the aftermath of the Emergency, had such a combination of strong non-Congress personalities emerged.

Had V.P. Singh anticipated the direction the Ram Mandir movement would take or was his "Mandal politics" a genuine and sincere effort to grant equality of opportunity to the former "untouchables"or Dalits and the backward castes of India? One argument would suggest that the entire policy on reservations in public sector jobs was a general defence mechanism to ward off any potential offence against him. No political party in India, no matter how deep their suspicions about Mandal may have been, has stated on record that they are opposed to the policy of reservations. The Congress, as the principal opposition at the time, did periodically criticise the motivations behind V.P. Singh's decision but never condemned the policy. The resolution of the CWC on the matter stated:

> The evil of caste-based discrimination has plagued our society and our
> civilisation for centuries. It was with a view to ridding our nation of this

---

3.   All these leaders are political proteges of the socialist leader Ram Manohar Lohia. They now head their own disparate political groups in UP and Bihar.

evil that our Constitution pledged equality and fraternity to all our citizens and proclaimed the abolition of all discrimination based on caste...The founding fathers of the Constitution deliberately used the word 'classes' and not 'castes' because they were fully conscious of all the many dimensions of backwardness....It was no part of their purpose to perpetuate caste divisions, caste consciousness or even caste awareness in our society."[4]

On the other hand, the Congress stood alone against forces which swore by Mandal, they were pronounced and highly vocal in their utterances for its support. The BJP, the emerging "dark horse" did not need to do any such thing or even involve themselves in the issue. The Ram Mandir movement had generated nationwide support for their cause, though their supporters may have varied in their zeal. Their vote-bank was assured and steady. The battleground for the next general election was being created in the "Hindi-belt" of Uttar Pradesh and Bihar. Faced with such a situation, Congress elders met in their committee rooms at the AICC headquarters in New Delhi, preparing drafts and re-drafting them to issue to the press and whoever was prepared to listen. Think-tanks were created to come up with "ideas" as nervous leaders floated between motivation and musings. The Youth Congress was restless too, many began to take sides with the various groups at war with each other throughout the country; Mandal or anti-Mandal, anti-Hindutva or pro-Hindutva. Thoughts on how to retain the slipping "vote-banks" in UP and Bihar were stone-walled by reality. The situation in the rest of the country did not present a threat to the party's prospects at the next general election. Of course, it must be remembered that this was a time when the BJP was still considered an "untouchable" party by most, although tactical alliances and seat adjustments in UP and elsewhere had helped it grow from 2 seats in the Lok Sabha in 1984 to 82 seats in 1989[5]. However, in the larger course the matter of forming state-wide alliances based on

---

4.   CWC resolution. New Delhi, August 1990.
5..   In 1998 the BJP won 182 of the 545 seats to Parliament thus becoming the single largest party in the house. The number of seats stagnated and remained the same in the 1999 General Elections.

varying levels of anti-Congressism had not yet come into play. The Congress was still the only national party with a presence in every district in the country and still possessed a strong enough organisation capable of carrying through an election on the strengths of its infrastructure. The personality of the leader too was of crucial importance. However much the "party high command" may have dithered and floundered, Rajiv Gandhi had revived public goodwill for himself and for his party by appearing personally confident and confrontational. Like his mother before him, he had also become increasingly visible and accessible on the scenes of the tragedies which played themselves out in this tumultuous period. Yet even the force of his personality and the appeals of sobriety generated by the Congress at this time could not halt its decline in Uttar Pradesh.

Uttar Pradesh is India's most populous state with a recorded population of over 140 million. It is considered the repository of India's political power not simply because it sends the largest number of MPs to the Lok Sabha, which is 80 of the total 545 seats, but because the state of politics at the centre mirrors resolutely the political circumstances of Uttar Pradesh. Socially too, Uttar Pradesh is a highly divided region, where caste and creed lie at the centrality of public and social life in this province. Zoya Hasan writes of UP:

> It is also the chief locale for the transition to a post-Congress polity, and it is the pivotal site of contestation between non-Congress groups. Inter-caste conflict, assertive lower castes, and Hindutva politics all manifest themselves in UP. Potentially, the most radical challenge to upper caste hegemony, the outcome of which would affect the overall structure of social inequality, is taking place in UP. The way in which conflicts between castes and communities are played out in UP will influence the course of democratic politics in north India and alter the ways of wresting and sustaining political power at the national level.[6]

This description, not only of the existent social milieu of Uttar Pradesh

6. *Parties and Party Politics in India.* (Delhi: Oxford University Press.2002). Zoya Hasan (ed.)

but of the long-term bearing which these factors are going to impose upon the national polity is sufficient evidence to suggest that whoever controls UP holds a crucial stake at the centre too. Balkanisation along caste and communal lines is absolute. Even within such broad groupings like the upper castes, differences exist between Brahmins and Rajputs, each seeking greater control over the other. In politics, that influence is sought over day-to-day policy making and implementation. Similarly sub-castes within the larger group of Backward Classes will often compete with each other within politics as well as over resources. A culture of competitive, regressive nomenclature has developed in UP within which, it is remarked, social groups are actively competing to remain "backward", and more recently, "most backward" in order to avail themselves of opportunities like reservations and other social benefits.

The strength of the many regional parties, and particularly the Mulayam Singh-led SP lies in identifying castes or social groups which they can ally together and thus create a combination as their support. The SP, for example, appealed post-Mandal to the Backward Castes and OBCs (Other Backward Castes) by their support and espousal of "social justice". Simultaneously, Mulayam Singh proclaimed his protection for and patronage over the Muslim community through strongly worded speeches and what his supporters call "decisive action" against the BJP in the state, in the wake of the Ayodhya movement. He successfully portrayed the Congress and BJP as brothers-in-arms against the minority community and as sharing an *esprit de corps* on the question of the Babri Masjid. The creation and cementing of such sectarian combinations, otherwise odiously disguised under the pseudonym "social engineering", replaced the Congress as the representatives of these diverse social groups. The Congress, on the other hand, merely issued weak protests.

Of the multiple caste segments of the state's society it is the Scheduled Castes and Muslims who comprise the largest single groups at 21 per cent and 17 per cent respectively, the Brahmins are not far behind at 13 per

71

cent[7]. All three comprised the core vote-bank of the Congress Party since Independence. All three were now part of movements led or represented by political formations other than the Congress Party. The Dalit resurgence, powered by the ideologies of Dr. Ambedkar[8] had found new propellers in the dramatic duo of the BSP, Kanshi Ram and Mayawati. The monopoly of the Congress over the Dalit vote-bank was broken by their new assertion of power for the Dalit community represented by members of the Dalit community. For them the Congress hereby became the Manuvaadi Party, or the party adhering and propagating the values of Manu's caste system, which placed the Dalits outside the fourfold varna or caste system, uncharitably naming them the Untouchables. To suggest that from Independence right upto the early 1990s the Congress merely used the Dalits as one of its many social supports for electoral purposes would be unfair. In every event, there does occur some exchange between social groups and the political formations which seek to represent them. Dalit leadership within the Congress was cultivated both by Indira Gandhi and later Rajiv Gandhi. Babu Jagjivan Ram, until he left the party in the late 70s, symbolised to some extent, Dalit representation in the establishment. Although appointments of other Dalit leaders, like Mahavir Prasad, as PCC Presidents occurred much later. Similarly in terms of policy matters too, Indira Gandhi's anti-Zamindari[9] programmes were intended to percolate empowerment to disadvantaged groups. These, however, could not match the aspirations of the Dalit community as a whole to be represented by groups from within the community itself.

For the Brahmins and other upper castes, principally the Thakurs or Kshatriyas, the BJP's identification with religion and religious symbols

---

7.   This 13 per cent is in turn 40 per cent of the total number of Brahmins in the country. Their highest density on a national scale.
8.   Dr. B. Ambedkar is regarded as the father of the Indian Constitution. Nationalist Congress leader who preached reform for the Dalit community.
9.   The Zamindari system was technically a landholding system incorporated by the Mughals and subsequently readopted by the British which allowed landowners to collect rent on behalf of the authorities from the peasantry who tilled the land. Socially the Jagirdars, Taluqdars and Zamindars are comparable to the Junkers of Prussia or similar feudal patriarchs.

and values, its obscurantist but utopian drive towards Ram Rajya, or Rule of Rama, delivered to them a political platform unadulterated with other concepts like secularism. Although the Congress never had a dearth or vaccuum of upper caste leadership within UP, it is evident that merely representing groups through personalities within the power circuit was not going to be enough. Kamlapati Tripathi, H.N. Bahuguna, V.P. Singh, N.D. Tiwari and Vir Bahadur Singh, all Congress Chief Ministers of UP and all either Brahmin or Thakur were recognised leaders of their respective communities. (N.D. Tiwari, of course, continues to be the Chief Minister of the newly created state of Uttaranchal.) However, the BJP revivalism replaced their appeal and acceptability with concepts that could not be defined by politics alone. It was to this illusion that the upper castes were drawn, away from the Congress and into the BJP. Most importantly, however, is the need to recognise the strategy of tactical alliances which the BJP devised right from its inception. More than any other factor in the entire sequel of events which led to the establishment of BJP supremacy it was their ability, at crucial junctures, to form alliances in state after state, thus acquiring new ground which covered the Congress retreat. Nonetheless the social space within the BJP was uncrowded by any vast "rainbow coalition" of multiple caste and community representation, as it was and continues to be within the Congress. For the BJP at the time, and to some extent even presently, this seemed a welcome opportunity for them to exercise their own political interests within the broader body politic.

The Muslims, feeling more alienated than ever before due to the accommodative spirit shown by Rao and senior members of his government like Home Minister Chavan[10], aligned themselves increasingly with forces hostile to and in competition with both the Congress and the BJP. The principal beneficiary of this electoral migration of the Muslims from the Congress was Mulayam Singh Yadav, in Uttar

---

10. The Home Minister was not averse to sharing the platform of various right-wing parties and organisations affiliated to the BJP. Similarly his disastrous management of the Babri Masjid-Ram Janamabhoomi controversy led to the subsequent demolition of the mosque.

Pradesh. In states where no third alternative to the Congress and BJP existed, the Muslims persevered with the Congress. This was true of states like Madhya Pradesh where such political realities and the presence of a strong, and vocal secular leadership under the aegis of Digvijay Singh, Madhavrao Scindia and Arjun Singh[11] managed to retain minority goodwill.

The dual combination of casteism and communalism created a political residue which was too complex and too modified by circumstances for even the best minds of the Congress to comprehend. Far from being able to take advantage of the new scenario, the Congress proved incapable of even understanding the political fallout, still less the meanings of these issues. This was generally true of the Congress reaction to national politics, for example in Gujarat where the KHAM (Kshatriya, Harijan, Adivasi, Muslim) combination did not prolong itself towards effective fruition. It was particularly true of Uttar Pradesh. When UP went to the polls in 1991 the political scene in the state was dominated by three broad and unequal fronts; the BJP, the non-Congress oppostion and the Congress. The political cake baked here by the Janata Dal and the BJP comprised two recipes whose ingredients were unfamiliar to the Congress; casteism and communalism. The Congress unable to contribute to this cake now grappled to take a bite. The best example of this attempt was the call for Ram Rajya[12] and the opening of the locks of the Babri Masjid and the subsequent shilanyas[13] at Ayodhya to inaugrate the 1991 General Election campaign. The Congress did bite, but toothless and weary it could not chew. The assassination of Rajiv Gandhi in the course of the campaign was a double blow because, in opposition, he had begun to show an understanding for the issues at play. As Prime Minister this may

---

11. Both Arjun Singh and Madhavrao Scindia were expelled from the Congress by Narasimha Rao and formed their own parties.
12. The Rule of Ram, an aphorism for a Golden Age symbolised by the reign of King Ram whom many Hindus revere as God. He was born and ruled in Ayodhya, allegedly on the spot where the Babri Mosque once stood.
13. Foundation laying ceremony.

have translated itself through a political will to act. His death left the party in UP confused and rudderless. From then on the political strategy of the Congress was based on simply reacting to events while the party's opposition generated them. The details of the Ram Janamabhoomi-Babri Masjid conflict and the position of the Congress in that episode have been deliberated upon in earlier chapters. Nevertheless, the dynamics of Congress "positioning" on this issue demonstrate conclusively that mere reactions to events, as opposed to initiatives, were the order of the day throughout this unsettling period in the state's social and political history. As subsequent chapters will show, for the first time in its history, the Congress would need the support of other regional parties like the SP and BSP, as crutches to keep it going. In 1993 it would ally with the government of Mulayam Singh. The tactics of forging alliances would be repeated in 1996 too, this time by engagement with the BSP. Alternatively, it would offer its own support to such parties to remain visible in the clouded and tumultuous scenery of UP politics, as it did to Mulayam Singh Yadav in 1993.

Fireworks in Amethi

On the evening of August 23, 1995, passengers waited in the departure lounge of the domestic terminal, Indira Gandhi Airport in New Delhi for the Indian Airlines 5 pm flight to Lucknow. The monsoon had receded, the weather was clear enough but there was a delay in departure. Not unusual. Once the passengers had taken their seats the plane waited for a few more minutes. A few passengers looked at their watches, delays of a few minutes were usual on domestic flights. Only those on the "port side" even noticed the short convoy of VIP vehicles, their red sirens buzzing, making their way across the tarmac towards their aircraft. Once more they were not surprised, VIPs were often flying to and fro between Delhi and Lucknow, the capital of the politically volatile Uttar Pradesh. In a few moments the aircraft began taxiing down towards the runway. Most of them remained unaware that accompanying them was the most sought after personality of Indian politics. The "aloof and reserved" Sonia Gandhi, as the press called her. The most prized possession of vast sections of the Congress Party, prized yes but unpossessed. The widow of former Prime Minister Rajiv Gandhi, whose every public appearance sent a flutter down the speculators of power politics in India, whether in the media or within politics. Sonia Gandhi, whose every utterance would make politicians and journalists draw meanings and construct parallels, even when neither were intended. She in turn was accompanied by her daughter Priyanka, her secretaries Vincent George and Pulok Chatterjee and members of the elite Special Protection Group (SPG). Their destination was Rajiv Gandhi's parliamentary constituency Amethi[14]. The stated purpose; to flag off the Lifeline Express, a hospital on wheels sponsored by the Rajiv Gandhi Foundation[15]. While the aircraft traversed through the skies towards the UP capital the scene at Lucknow's Amausi airport was reminiscent of another age. Not less than 15,000 Congress Party workers jostled for space, outside the airport, within the arrival lounge and on the tarmac. Leaders of every faction and offshoot of the party were there, jostling among the restless, pulsating throngs of human expectations. Some, like the Chief Minister of Madhya Pradesh, had flown down especially for the event from outside Uttar Pradesh. Others, like N.D. Tiwari, who had left the mainstream Congress four months ago to form his own All India Tiwari Congress[16] exchanged pleasantries with his *bete noire* Jitendra Prasad, the UPCC chief, his presence accepted as normal in the heat of the moment. By the time the Indian Airlines flight touched down on the runway, party workers and leaders, sycophants and dissidents at large, had all broken through the weakly asembled security barriers. Leaders, their seniority and rank disregarded by ordinary party foot soldiers, were pushed aside as Sonia Gandhi, followed by her daughter appeared at the top of the ladder. The SPG quickly formed a human cordon

14.   Rajiv Gandhi's former parliamentary constituency, was earlier represented by his father, Feroze Gandhi and brother Sanjay Gandhi.
15.   The Rajiv Gandhi Foundation (RGF) is a non-political organisation which is engaged in the promotion of social and welfare activities. Based in New Delhi.
16.   N.D. Tiwari had formed his own party after serious differences with Prime Minister Narasimha Rao, primarily over his handling of the Ayodhya crisis. Other leaders in this group included Arjun Singh and Mohsina Kidwai.

around them and escorted them, as fast as possible towards the waiting cars. Bouquets, holding hastily written notes, were thrown at the mother and daughter, a lucky few did even get close enough to present theirs. Many leaders were adamant to introduce themselves to Priyanka Gandhi and lost time arguing over the excessive security details with the SPG commandos when they came too close. Sonia Gandhi herself took her time to acknowledge the greetings of those she recognised, they took this to mean silent approval from 'Madam' for their personal causes. A little after 6:30 pm the carcade took off towards the VIP entrance leaving behind a scurrying mass of Congressmen and women looking for their own cars among the hundreds of buses, jeeps and vehicles that litterred the jam packed car park. Even outside the airport, along the road which sped out of Lucknow towards Rae Bareli and Amethi, party workers waved flags, policemen lined the route. Not even the Prime Minister received such a welcome, but then this was Uttar Pradesh; the karmabhoomi[17] of the Nehru-Gandhi family, the erstwhile fortress of Congress power and prestige, welcoming one of its own.

Amethi is barely 150 kilometres from Lucknow. It straddles the eastern edge of the former kingdom of Awadh and the western verge of Purvanchal, or eastern Uttar Pradesh. The cavalcade made slow progress, but that was expected. At regular intervals, villagers and party workers from the rural districts waited for the convoy. Sonia Gandhi would oblige each of these small groups, accept their flowers and greetings and carry on. It was nearing midnight before Amethi was reached. Meanwhile, back in Lucknow, anxious politicos were telephoning their masters in Delhi and reporting the scenes with the relish and hyperbole which comes all too easily to Congressmen. Prime Minister Rao's own trusted inner-circle, comprising Bhuvnesh Chaturvedi[18] among others moved between restlessness and passive confidence as they weighed in their own minds

17. Land of one's *karma* or occupation. The term also has connotations of ancestral home, *et al.*
18. Bhuvnesh Chaturvedi, MP attached to the Prime Minister's office.

Sonia Gandhi's motivations and movements. The general mood in New Delhi was one of apparent indifference which hid apprehensions of another kind. No one knew what 'Madam' was playing at. There was another group too at this time, formed by the coming together of two sub-groups within the party who waited for news to trickle back from Lucknow through their private sources. This was a caucus of the silent Sonia supporters within the cabinet, people like Rajesh Pilot[19] and Salman Khurshid[20]. While they themselves were not necessarily anti-Rao they were joined by leaders whose dislike for Rao exceeded their apprehensions for Sonia. This emerging group was one being watched by the Prime Minister's coterie, who sought to nip any possible revolt in the bud. Her short visit to Lucknow had drawn sharp divides within the cabinet. So far she had not utterred a single word. Tomorrow would be another day.

Sonia Gandhi's programme for the next day listed only two items. The first was the flagging off of the Lifeline Express and would be attended by officials of the Rajiv Gandhi Foundation and the Sanjay Gandhi Memorial Trust. The second, and the one which became the centre of gravity for hovering Congress leaders, was the public meeting slated for the afternoon at the Ramlila Grounds. While the entire visit to Amethi had been meant to be apolitical, the purpose being a social one, the atmosphere generated, first at Lucknow Airport and then back in the corridors of power in Delhi was one conducive to nothing but power politics. So, while no politicians had been especially invited, not even Rao who was chairman of the Sanjay Gandhi Memorial Trust, a sizeable number did turn up. Presumably so their cards would be marked approvingly, if and when Sonia Gandhi was to assume a leadership role in politics. Their attendance could be ascribed to political prudence or, some would say an element of sycophancy. Alternatively, it could be presented as a challenge to the leadership of Narasimha Rao, already unsteady after Arjun Singh and N.D. Tiwari had split the party in May.

---

19.   Minister of State for Internal Security.
20.   Minister of State for External Affairs.

Evidently, all those who attended the meeting, and many who didn't, readily accepted the leadership or at least the presence of Sonia Gandhi as a normal prerequisite for their own survival and for the survival of the party. So, while the crowd grew restless, it was joined in turn by Mohsina Kidwai, Balram Singh Yadav and Congress Legislature Party leader in the UP Pramod Tiwari. Those from outside Uttar Pradesh included Digvijay Singh, Suresh Pachauri and Kumaramangalam. Gandhi family loyalists and trustees Rameshwar Thakur, Secretary of the Sanjay Gandhi memorial Trust and Satish Sharma, who was also the MP for Amethi at the time, were allowed the privilege of sharing the dias with Sonia Gandhi and Priyanka. The stage was set.

Sonia Gandhi began by making "polite conversation" with the public. The first few passages of her speech were predictable enough. She spoke of the importance of Amethi for her family, and, in turn, her family's love for the region and its people, how happy she was to be there and similar non-controversial lines. The assembled Congress leaders followed every word of what was being said, some of them waiting for the fire in her belly to find utterance, others, and they were in the minority, hoped that she would continue in this vein and not embarrass them or their government by saying anything provocative or controversial. They were to be disappointed. As soon as the formal pieces of the speech were over, Sonia Gandhi launched a not too subtle attack on Rao, his government and their policies. What she said would alter the balance of power and prerogative within the party and divert the course of Congress leadership forever:

> The principles and ideals to which Jawaharlal Nehru, Indira Gandhi and my husband devoted their lives are being tested today, divisive forces are gathering strength.

In the political and social context of the day the said "principles" were without doubt elements of the Nehruvian consensus and secularism in particular. Thus the "gathering strength of divisive forces" was no doubt a pointed attack on the BJP and its affiliates who had grown bolder and strong with Rao's soft tactics of appeasement. What she had done was added the weight of her words behind those who had already risen against Rao on matters such as these.

Sonia Gandhi then continued to speak on a subject everyone had expected her to raise at some juncture, the assassination of her husband Rajiv Gandhi:

> You can understand my anguish. My husband has been dead for four years and three months, but the inquiry into his assassination is moving at such a slow pace.

While this may have been a political issue for some, she had the privilege (if it may be called that) to address the assassination probe from a personal perspective too. Her cadences were balanced with an element of the bellicose, the pauses perfect, equipoise was flashed in abundance and her words fell like seeds on a fertile and awaiting soil. In terms of sustaining evocations and empathy the speech was a masterpiece holding the attention of the crowd and moving its emotions.

In a single delivery, Sonia Gandhi had dismissed the Rao government as far as the assembled gathering was concerned. The dissidents in the Congress Party and those outside, like N.D. Tiwari, had found a new patron. The balance between sentiment and complaint and the feeling of hurt and injustice reflected in her words found favour with almost every party worker who heard that speech as well as those who would hear of it over the next few days. They in turn would now join the bandwagon of dissidents clamouring for Rao's dismissal. Her speech in Amethi provided the occasion when she found her political voice. Nothing she said was opposed, nor was it crafted in a way which could attract derision or criticism, certainly not from a Congress government. The matter of Rajiv Gandhi's assassination was at the time and continues to be a serious issue with Congressmen. The speech therefore exposed Rao to questions from within the party too. It did not attempt to dislodge him but in the eyes of the Congress Party, it signalled the presence of a figure willing to make a stand for issues which as fundamentals of Congress thinking had been challenged. Babri had torn apart the party's secular thinking, the right-wing and extremist organisations had been appeased in an unprecedented manner. She had given the Congress a cause and, more importantly, had finally discovered one herself.[21]

"My Kingdom for an Elephant"

The year 1996 was an election one. The Narasimha Rao government had completed a full five years amidst gloom and predictions that he would not last. However, his tenure had been far from comfortable for him or his party. Very few members of the cabinet remained "cloud free" from the maelstrom of corruption which broke out[22]. Vertical and horizontal splits in the state Congress units of Tamil Nadu[23], Uttar Pradesh[24] and within the central organisation itself deprived the party of both organisational strength and recognised faces. The Congress in Uttar Pradesh had seen a steady haemorrhage building up within the state unit which vacillated between numerous support systems and survival strategies to counter the continual erosion in its support base and a corresponding ascendancy among its rivals. The state of affairs was such that without fighting the election *en alliances* with another party the Congress was unlikely to succeed in any measure. The resulting fear psychosis among the Congressmen of Uttar Pradesh led to a voluntary forfeit of this prime electoral estate. Jitendra Prasad entered into an alliance with the BSP on terms which are best described as humiliating for the Congress Party. Of the 425 seats under contest the Congress agreed to fight on a mere 126 seats, giving away 299 to the alliance. How the division

21. Reacting in an uncharacteristic combative style the Rao Government lodged a plea in January 1996 (subsequently dismissed) with the bench looking into the Rajiv Gandhi assassination case, pleading that the Special Investigation Team (SIT) could not provide their files to the Jain Commission, investigating the case.

22. The Jain Hawala scandal had implicated over half the cabinet on allegations that they had received payments and commissioons from a businessman R.K. Jain. See subsequent chapters.

23. The Tamil Congress leader G.K. Moopanar had formed his own Tamil Maanila Congress.

24. N.D. Tiwari formed his separate All India Indira Congress Tiwari AICC (T).

and distribution of this imbalanced and thoughtless agreement came about is a mystery. It was, nonetheless, a gesture which symbolised the pitiful and final position of the Congress in Uttar Pradesh, the election was fought on the terms of a resignation. Political developments in Uttar Pradesh have always been vital to the assessment of party political positions in the rest of the country. The act of submission committed by the Congress leadership in the 1996 Assembly election symbolised most succinctly and truly the form of politics now being pursued by the Congress Party. It was nothing short of electoral euthanasia for the party to give way of such a magnitude to a relatively new political group, the BSP. Nonetheless, there have been arguments justifying the decision to form this alliance as well, and they are in themselves the repositories of defeatism and decline within the higher reaches of the Congress at the time. For whatever they are worth, these views submit that without an alliance the Congress would struggle to reach any level of comfort, that it would barely survive. Moreover, in the prevailing milieu no other party was even willing to join hands with the party, fighting the elections alone, the proponents hypothesise would have been suicidal. This however, is not the view of the die-hard party activists and many senior leaders of the party such as former UP Chief Minister Narayan Dutt Tiwari, whose differences with the party high-command forced him and Arjun Singh to float their own Tiwari Congress in the same year. To them, Uttar Pradesh has always been the Camelot of the Congress Party. It was along the Ganges that the early Congress found its voice. It was in Awadh that the Independence movement matured into a campaign of mass mobilisation. At the same time the leadership of the Congress Party had always been drawn from Uttar Pradesh, Allahabad being the home of the Nehru-Gandhi family. Consequently, the party had always relied on its vast strength in the state which until now had been forthcoming. Thus a blend of nostalgic evocation and romantic illusions of superiority led many Congress workers and some leaders to view the alliance with the BSP as a sellout or at the very least a blow against a position of previous pre-eminence. For the largely upper caste leadership of the Congress in the state, the ignominy of having to now bear the blue flag of the BSP, stamped with their party symbol of an elephant, was a case of adding insult to injury. Piqued and frustrated, many workers turned away. Others left the party ranks and joined other political groups to safeguard their own community and group interests. The party of Nehru and Indira, inheritors to a grand legacy, had been humbled into a collection of political paupers begging for aid from newly emerging groups. Some party workers alleged that Narasimha Rao, himself belonging to the South and therefore ignorant, or perhaps wantonly, had scuttled the importance of the north in the Congress Party. This is perhaps a little far-fetched. However, that was the nature of the feelings of many grassroot activists.

With the alliance, the Congress presence in 70 per cent of Uttar Pradesh disappeared overnight. In the corresponding general election of that year the party would win only five of the eighty-five seats in the state. The strategy did not work, but no one was even aware of the intent of this strategy.

The last word on the issue must go to the man at the centre of circumstances, the UPCC President at the time, Jitendra Prasad, who stated in retrospect:

> I was sent to UP at a time when many senior leaders had deserted the Congress and the organisation was in great disarray. I am happy they are back in the party now. In those difficult times there were two elections, one for the Lok Sabha and one for the state assembly. In the first, we retained the previous tally and in the second, we won a few seats more than we had in the previous election. What more could I have done in times like those?[25]

This was a reasonable response to the objections raised. However, it meant little to the party workers in the state. For them the kingdom had dissipated, the erstwhile rulers now looked for support from those who had for so long been subordinates in their empire.

---

25. In *The Times of India*. October 2000.

An Unhappy Ship

Sleaze and Scandal and the Hawala Windfall – The Eleventh General
Election, Staying Afloat, But Losing It – Narasimha Rao Comes to Grief

Sleaze and Scandal and the Hawala Windfall

Political power and abstention from the riches derived from that
political power do not easily go together. For the Congress Party to indulge
in the restraints of Gandhian values on one hand and practise precise
realpolitik on the other has proved to be a very hard act to follow. Perhaps
this is why some of its members find it enormously difficult to live upto
the self-imposed and sometimes ridiculous standards of 'simple living and
high thinking'. Shortly before Independence in 1947 no less a figure than
Mahatma Gandhi had called for the Congress to give up its political
bearings and dedicate its organisation to social causes. Michael Edwardes
writes:

> He (Gandhi) was also worried by the behaviour of many Congressmen
> who, it was reported to him, were taking bribes from businessmen to get
> them licences, profiting from black market activities, and putting pressure
> on top civil servants to arrange appointments and transfers for their
> friends. Gandhi put forward the startling suggestion that Congress should
> dissolve itself and form a Lok Seva Sangh or Servants of the People Society
> instead.[1]

With the establishment of a democratic republic and the creation of
a competitive political system, the leadership of the Congress could not
find itself able to accommodate the idealistic virtues of the Mahatma and,
instead, it reinvented itself as the world's largest, and perhaps most
successful, political party. If political parties are a reflection of the society
they represent then a decline in the value systems of its political culture

---

1.   Michael Edwardes. *Nehru. A Political Biography*. The Penguin Press, 1971.

was only inevitable for the Congress. Forty years after independence the social competition for economic resources was so intense and so dependent on political patronage that 'sleaze' in the 1990s was a slur not merely for the political establishment but a defining attribute of India's newly emerging, economically empowered middle classes. In such a situation one might expect the allegations and outbreak of corruption in high places to be a trivial social occurrence. A natural reflex of a society in economic transition. It was not so. When the bubble finally burst in early 1996, the long presumed realities found resonance in actual events. Financial corruption, which incidentally is the only cross upon which the Indian public finds it fit to crucify individuals, was never before so exhibited and speculated upon, as it was by the middle of the 1990s. Strange then that the Indian media should marvel at its own squalor, for the spectators to this drama of degradation were as much responsible for the state of affairs as the protagonists in the scandals themselves. The perspective of inquiries is a very wide one. Exhaustive analysis into who made how much money and why the revelations occurred when they did and the motivations for corruption have been made. Nonetheless, while these were all due very few studies have assessed the reasons as to why these successive scams received as much publicity as they did? Some of the answers have been mentioned earlier, that the presumptions about financial corruption became realities of serious proportions for the first time since independence. Moreover the alleged involvement of such a large gallery of senior political figures was also a new phenomenon. Finally, the outbreak, coming as it did in an election year was bound to attract the attention, contrived or genuine of both, of a normally easy going Indian public and an otherwise tempermental media. Indeed, was the strategy to grant innumerable lines in the press to this most unappetising portrayal of Indian public figures an attempt by the Prime Minister to portray his own figure as a corruption busting champion? After all, the CBI had sat on this particular case from March 1991, when it was first opened during the term of Chandra Shekhar, until 1994.

The Narasimha Rao government had been plagued by the spectre of sleaze for most of its tenure. Scams rolled off the tongue more easily and more regularly than did some of the names of those involved in them. Harshad Mehta[2], the sugar scam, the irregularities in the Enron deal and other similar nuisances popped up and down like backbenchers in a debate. These scams, however, merely set the stage for what was coming towards the end of the government's term of office in 1996. On January 16, 1996 the Director of the CBI, K. Vijaya Rama Rao, chargesheeted seven politicians in the long brewing Jain Hawala case, *ein kolossalische skandal*, if ever there was one. In addition, he also sought permission to frame charges against three members of the Rao cabinet, Madhavrao Scindia, Balram Jhakar and V.C. Shukla. The background to what became known as the infamous Jain Hawala scandal is complex but its political implications hinged upon payments of cash delivered to politicans by a triumvirate of brother temptors S.K., N.K. and B.R. Jain between 1989 and 1991. It was alleged that these payments amounting to a total of Rs. 59 crore were made in exchange for favours in that period. Ominously, each time that Jain made a payment he recorded the details in a diary. These precious notebooks in turn became the main source of evidence for the CBI investigating the case. What must have been particularly upsetting for the Prime Minister was the arrival, in a curious and almost orchestrated manner, of a series of revelations, allegations and random diatribes against his own person and high office. Harshad Mehta, the most visible face of this culture of greed claimed to have delivered money to the PMO himself. Shailendra Mahato, Member of Parliament of the JMM, informed a press conference that he had received a bribe of approximately $130,000 in 1993 from Rao to vote for the Congress government in the vote of confidence that year. The Lakhubhai Pathak Cheating Case was yet to unravel itself fully but the early indications could not have delivered any comfort for Narasimha Rao. Additionally, Jain's testimony to a CBI

---

2.   Stockbroker and securities man. At the heart of the stocks scam, alleged he had paid suitcases of money to the Prime Minister himself. It transpired that the money was paid to Sitaram Kesri as political donations and was subsequently used in elections. This called into question the methods by which political parties are financed, rather than unearthing any 'nest of corruption.'

Superintendent of Police on March 11, 1995 claimed that money worth Rs. 3.5 crore had been paid to the Prime Minister's office through intermediateries in 1991. Since the CBI investigation worked only according to the contents of the by now infamous 'Jain Diaries' neither the Prime Minister nor others implicated in this particular testimony were charged. As the diaries were deciphered, a corresponding count of rolling heads within the government, the Congress party and even the opposition began. L.K. Advani, at the time Leader of the Opposition in the Lok Sabha, was named and immediately offered to step down as a Member of Parliament until the enquiry was over. Other likely targets for political reasons, the duo of Arjun Singh and N.D. Tiwari, both of whom had resigned from the government in 1994, were also named. Subsequently expelled, Arjun Singh formed the Tiwari Congress with N.D. Tiwari. The entire scandal had its absurdities too. With the implication of Madhavrao Scindia not only did the level of ministerial competence within the Cabinet suffer a blow but the charge itself left much to be desired as indeed was the case of L.K. Advani. Analysis of the diaries revealed nothing as far as Advani was concerned, his name figured on a list marked 'POE', or political expenses. However, this information does not tally with the otherwise immaculate figures in the Jain diaries.

Nor were the Prime Minister's confidantes spared. V.C. Shukla, one of Rao's backroom boys and Minister for Water Resources was apparently woken up en route, in his train compartment in the middle of the night, to be told that he had been chargesheeted by the CBI. Furthermore, the growing list of those under a cloud brought within its shadow the Independent Arif Mohammed Khan, erstwhile Congressman but in the present circumstances of minimal political significance. The favourite Finance Minister of non-Congress regimes, Yashwant Sinha, himself rather a dull figure who was condemned more for mortgaging India's gold reserves as Finance Minister under Chandra Shekhar, than for his implications in the Jain case. The portly socialist leader Sharad Yadav of the Janata Dal of Bihar and, of course, the now famous and rather dramatic Madan Lal Khurana. Other ministers and figures of the Congress who faced investigations in other cases included the wily Sukhram. Police raids on his various homes were more likely to generate stashes of cash than not. The telecom scandal in his ministry had discredited the already fast fading façade of Gandhian restraint of most Congressmen.

So how indeed did such a motley collection of supra-entities come together as culprits (or victims) in this great graft? Moreover, did S.K. Jain really pay such a wide gallery of political leaders in order to secure himself a Rajya Sabha nomination? What indeed was the Prime Minister's role in this ultimately messy and crude state of affairs?

Piqued and frustrated by the slow progress in the case, Justice Verma whose bench came to hear the case, decided that the CBI would report directly to the Supreme Court. This example of 'judicial activism', taking power away from the executive in a matter involving investigative agencies did sound a positive step in the otherwise faltering system of justice, particularly in this case. When the Prime Minister declared loftily that 'the law should take its own course', Justice Verma sought to interpret this literally and thus on March 1 came the direction to the CBI to be responsible to the Supreme Court Bench. Commenting on this development, N. Ram observed, "There has been an immunity attached to powerful politicians. For the first time this has been broken through this extraordinary intervention of the Supreme Court."

In response to pressure from the Opposition, on March 8th the Prime Minister arrived at the Lok Sabha and was consistently heckled, he made a short speech, all of which was his reaction to the Supreme Court judgement. Within the span of a minute, he began and ended it:

> The Supreme Court order fully accords with the government's view as to how the CBI should act in this case. The Supreme Court has asked the CBI not to do something which the CBI has not done, is not doing and will not do.[3]

---

3. Prime Minister Narasimha Rao. March 8, 1996. Lok Sabha.

When asked to quit as Prime Minister by a more than usually vociferous Opposition, he responded sombrely:

We don't quit. We just carry on doing our job.

That was all that the Press and the country got to hear from the Prime Minister in those fast paced and dramatic days. His critics were quick to attribute several motivations to Rao. Most argued that he had brought the cases against his own colleagues and the opposition in order to mitigate the sting of the opposition parties in the forthcoming elections. L.K. Advani had announced in January that "...corruption would be high on our agenda for the polls." The consistent battering suffered by the government through the misdemeanours, alleged or real, of its leaders created a compulsion to appear to be decisive and ready to confront corruption. Perhaps the Prime Minister overdid himself because in his attempts to appear a crusader against corruption, he could not conceal his role as an avenging leader of the pack who is incensed by those hounding him within his own group. Thus Rao's visible opponents within the Congress were lined up with loyalists and 'friends' in order to provide some credibility to this persecution of his enemies. The objective of eradicating opposition rather than the deliverance of justice became the single most important feature of this long drawn and finally pointless controversy. Consequently, events became inflicted with what Alan Clark once termed 'a forfeiture of respect' for the Congress Party and the political class as a whole.

For a party which prides itself in and sought to emulate the fundamentals of a Gandhian world view the 'low and dishonest decade' of the 1990s proved too embarrassing and difficult to handle. Images of Congress leaders and subsequently of Prime Minister Narasimha Rao himself, parading in and out of court fighting off charges of corruption were a jarring and unwholesome exhibition of political corruption. They were particularly painful to watch for those countless, sincere and hard working party workers who, despite the prevalent cynicism about politics in the country, still bear the party flag and struggle in the way of their predecessors. Their numbers receded further.

The Eleventh General Election, Staying Afloat But Losing It

The summer of 1996 was one of the hottest in recorded history. In New Delhi the near ballistic temperatures were accentuated by the soaring political heat as India approached its Eleventh General Election in May. Members of Parliament could be found at their respective 'watering holes', comforting their prospects over refreshments and gossip before they would have to cover ground towards their constituencies and campaign trails. Hotels like Claridges which break the endless monotony of government bungalows in Lutyens' Delhi were teeming with political commentators and their patrons who preferred the anonymity of these huddles to the more public hospitalities of the Press Club of India. Far more private discussions between friends and allies took place, *en petit comité*, in the enclosures of political bungalows along the still lush avenues of New Delhi. At these meetings political heavyweights and nonentities alike laid their stalls before whoever they pleased and transplanted their outlooks into pages of newsprint for the following day.

Congress MPs were no exception, indeed they led the way in private strategising, reminiscence and generally holding forth. The divergence of opinion — as to what prospects lay ahead of them — was wide and gradually widening. The overwhelming confluence of interdependent negative factors submerged any potential for meaningful strategy sessions within party circles. Ideological disarray, dissonance within the leadership, disorientation among the party workers and the voluntary organisations and a growing public disenchantment with its internal power plays made themselves diktats to the mood of the average Congressman. And yet, despite the surrounding trappings of power (Congress ministers still had the use of their government infrastructure), there were no delusions this time about the impending gloom. The party's mood was decidedly pessimisstic with individual candidates and leaders concerning themselves with the balance of probabilities in retaining their own constituencies. The Prime Minister's Office was by no means oblivious to this mood and his lieutenants began to 'take out insurance' in order to succour his survival in the post-election scenario, whatever the order of the results may have been. Political chamberlains of Rao, senior colleagues like S.B. Chavan, G. Venkatswamy, Devendra Dwivedi and Bhuvnesh Chaturvedi set to work on the regional satraps who were expected to bring in the new batch of MPs in the aftermath of the election. They travelled to Bhubaneshwar to bring round J.B. Patnaik, already a loyalist and climbed steeper towards the north to placate Virbhadra Singh in Himachal Pradesh. Others forayed deep into Madhya Pradesh to sound out Digvijay Singh, already in the whirl of the campaign. Still more eager ones traversed West Bengal to muster up pledges of loyalty from the disparate Congress groupings in that state. Harcharan Singh Brar of Punjab was advised to keep strict control over his batch. These missions could not have included the promise of reward nor temptations of power at the centre for no one believed that Rao was heading for a second term. The objectives were three fold. Primarily the PM's men were saboteurs who assured his regional bosses that in the post-poll Congress there would be no alternative to Rao as Party leader. This aspect of their mission was to forestall any attempt by regional heavyweights to transfer their loyalties (and thus their flocks of newly elected MPs) to possible challengers. Their second aim was of assurance, that with the control of the party as a whole, their demands at the party political level would be accommodated by a more amiable Rao. Finally the residual reminder of unredeemed pledges, 'you owe it to the Prime Minister...' were by no means an insignificant ancillary to the larger justifications for supporting Rao.

The political environment and particular events leading upto the election could not have provided any comfort for Rao or his loyalists either. The Cabinet was divided over Kashmir and the course of action to be pursued there. There were serious queries, among members and erstwhile members of the Cabinet, regarding the presentation of economic policies, in particular the 'anti-subsidarian' aspects of government spending which (according to Rao's critics) had alienated farmers and agriculturists. Moroever, the deluge of communal sentiment in the country had still not been swept away and the BJP, as yet unaccustomed to power at the centre, was then still a keen advocate of Hindu revivalism. No attempt had been made by the Rao government to arrest deteriorating social tensions in states like Uttar Pradesh and Bihar. Nor did the party leadership attempt to read the mind of its own state unit in Tamil Nadu where the "softly-softly" approach towards Jayalalitha and her AIADMK was drawing active criticism from hitherto loyal state leaders. Now the state unit split. Led by G.K. Moopanar, experienced, abrasive and certainly a man of considerable influence, the newly formed Tamil Manila Congress took with it a considerable support base of the Congress in Tamil Nadu. In his endeavours he was joined by the adroit P. Chidambaram and other senior state leaders like M. Arunachalam and S.R. Balasubramaniam. In the weeks leading upto the split they had all pleaded with the party high command in Delhi to snap its ties with the AIADMK. Frustrated in their hopes to persuade the central leadership to consider their demand, Moopanar was left with no choice but to form his own party. As the TMC formed an alliance with the DMK, Congress supremacy in the South appeared to have taken its heaviest blow yet.

In the midst of these developments the spectre of sleaze had become a platform for those advocating a change in government, not as durable as V.P. Singh's campaign of in 1989 perhaps but just as potent. Unlike the Bofors scandal, reserved now for occassional exhibition, the drizzle of scams washed the credibility of the Rao Congress far away from the political shoreline. The government's response had consigned its complaints to that peripheral region of politics where voices do not carry long or far enough. On this account alone the Congress facing the election was adrift and cast away by potential friends and allies. Additionally, the wide array of Congress rebels, standing as candidates as well as indulging in more quiet internal sabotage, possessed the means, as well as the will, to do serious damage to Narasimha Rao's campaign. These included senior stalwarts like N.D. Tiwari in Uttar Pradesh, Arjun Singh and Madhavrao

Scindia in Madhya Pradesh and a number of lesser known but locally influential leaders.

Organisational atrophy accelerated towards a deepening torpor in the corporate mindset of the Congress Party. The election itself was fought on clearer grounds than anyone could have expected. Corruption was an issue and gave the BJP line that it was 'a party with a difference' some strength. The inability to showcase its radical and far reaching economic policies in a popular light allowed the more anarchic elements of Indian politics, particularly the federalist, 'one issue – one region parties' to term them and the Congress as anti-poor. To its minority voters and a substantial number of secular Hindus, the Congress was more than ever the willing hand which guided the BJP to fulfil its rendezvous with its promised strife. For good or for worse, Rao was perceived as the man who forfeited his Nehruvian legacy and indulged in communal accommodation to prolong his spell in power.

The campaign itself was fast paced but for Congress candidates the haste of events led to a speedier deterioration. Along with elections to the Lok Sabha, elections also took place in six states, including Tamil Nadu where the Congress had seen vertical and horizontal splits in its organisation. Narasimha Rao campaigned tirelessly for a man who had been written off five years earlier on grounds of ill health. Nonetheless, neither his visage on Congress posters and billboards nor his election rallies and speeches were well received, in some cases not even by the Congress candidates themselves.

Prime Minister Rao had a considerable amount of state machinery at his disposal. An aircraft of the Indian Air Force ferried him across the length and breadth of the country. Upon arrival and departure, he was assured of a fleet of bullet-proof cars which conveyed him to and from the local rally grounds. Alternatively, helicopters were also available for inter-state use. His speeches were balanced and non-controversial, what he lacked in personal charisma he tried to make up through rational arguments in presenting his government's case to the people. The furthest he got to a violent speech was in Bellary in Southern Karnataka where he stated:

> The BJP is bent upon fomenting tensions between Hindus and Muslims and between Hindus and Christians, this has created a feeling of uncertainty among the minority communities.

Naturally he was more comfortable among the more familiar surroundings of his home state Andhra Pradesh where the regional opposition, the Telugu Desam Party or TDP, had recently undergone a vertical split. Any advances in Andhra, therefore, would have redeemed the Congress wipeout in the state in the elections of 1994. In the northeast, matters were slipping for the wily and experienced Hiteshwar Saikia and his government in Assam. Accusations of human rights abuse and state tyranny, while often unfounded, compelled the Congress to placate the public. In such trouble ridden parts of India, Rao would urge the public to continue with his government, calling on them to give him more time:

> Most development programmes need a 10-year period for implementation, a change of government now would only throw the programmes into disarray.[4]

This was the line to take in most economically backward states where the NEP had not permeated down to the low-income groups. The public, having already made up their minds, precluded the possibility of Rao's words sinking in on his mass audiences. At the same time, new and more rigorously enforced guidelines of the Election Commission of India prevented, at one level, the various political parties, particularly the incumbent Congress, from swaying that crucial bolus of fence sitters to their own cause. Expenditure was monitored, police forces became more vigilant, canvassing after hours was prevented. The usual colour and glamour of an Indian general election was missing. In the midst of this sobriety, opinion polls and media pundits in turn passed more sobre analysis about the likely outcome. A hung Parliament with the BJP

---

4. Prime Minister Narasimha Rao during the election campaign. Guwahati, Assam.

benefiting from a Congress loss was widely and consistently predicted. At the state level, assessments were less certain. Foreign news agencies noted:

> Recent opinion polls all predict that no single party will get a clear majority. But they all have the BJP securing a significantly higher number of seats, anything from 165 to 185. One survey by *The Week*, an authoritative local news magazine, gives the BJP the single largest bloc of seats, up to 215 of the 543 seats up for grabs. Congress rates only second with 145 to 170.[5]

Atal Behari Vajpayee, the BJP's face of the campaign, appeared jocular, even ecstatic when he noted that his party had become a national alternative to the Congress. This was a new development.

And so, as the 2,525,595 ballot boxes with 8000 metric tonnes of paper in them were slowly and laboriously stored and counted by the 4 million Election Commission officials, the fate of 16,000 candidates in the fray was to be revealed. The elections had cost the exchequer over Rs 500 crore (approximately $150 million). Of the nearly 600 million people eligible to vote, only 58 per cent had bothered to exercise their franchise. Democracy on this scale is not witnessed anywhere else in the world and as the verdict of the world's largest democracy was awaited, those standing trial, among them Narasimha Rao, waited with bated breath.

The ballot boxes discharged a barrage of bad results upon a half-suspecting Congress. As the 'walking wounded' of the party recovered from the shock of their individual defeats they were faced with a comprehensive desolation of national proportions. Across the Gangetic Plains of Uttar Pradesh and Bihar, the Congress was all but wiped out. It won only seven of the hundred and thirty-nine parliamentary seats in this region. At the other end of India, in Tamil Nadu, the party fared even worse and for the first time in its history, Tamil Nadu did not return a single Congress candidate to Parliament. These events readily granted prescience to the words of G.K. Moopanar who had been saying all along

---

5. *Asiaweek.* April 1996.

that the friendship with the AIADMK would be devastating for the Congress. The 'South' which had buoyed Rao and provided him with support within the Parliamentary Party for the length of his term now withdrew that succour from him. Of the 132 seats from the four states of Andhra Pradesh, Karnataka, Kerala and Tamil Nadu the Congress won 32. It was some consolation for him, as a leader of his state to see Andhra Pradesh provide the single largest contingent of returning Congress candidates. However, for a Prime Minister of a national party, even this could not have been more than a superficial reward. In the very heart of India things were no different. In Madhya Pradesh the illusion of a revival and consolidation generated by Assembly victories in 1993 lay broken and scatterred. The western length of India, once a seamless Congress fabric now reflected only a tattered vestige of former glories. In Maharashtra, facing isolation from the minorities as well as the sugarcane lobby, the tally of party seats plunged to 15. Overall the party accomplished a series of 'firsts' for itself, the most notable of these novel developments was the Congress national vote share which fell below 30 per cent for the first time. Its total number of seats also fell to a rather poor 138, its lowest aggregate ever. The development which competed with the magnitude of the Congress fall was the sudden emergence of regional parties. In all, 28 regional parties were now represented in Parliament, regionalism had never acquired such representation before.[6]

Narasimha Rao Comes to Grief

'Despite his stoic and calm exterior, Anand was inwardly demoralised by his defeat. Where had he gone wrong? Was this the future pattern of the democratic process in the country? At best a wave; at worst a gamble. How could he fit into this?... Anand decided to plough a lonely furrow.'[7]

---

6. However, an unsplit Congress (I), without the TMC, Tiwari Congress and Madhavrao Scindia's MVC going away would have gained more seats than the BJP. The TMC got 20 seats, Tiwari's party 4 and Scindia's 2, this would mean 164 seats for a combined Congress, four more than the BJP.
7. Narasimha Rao. *The Insider.*

Narasimha Rao wrote this in his semi-autobiographical work *The Insider*, portraying his own predicament, albeit in a fictionalised fashion, after he left office. It is doubtful that he could have felt any different as he surveyed the results of the 1996 election and his departure from the office of Prime Minister. Few thought that Narasimha Rao, nearly an octogenarian, heart patient and a man who weeks before he became Prime Minister had retired from public life, would have completed his full term in office. Not only did he complete it but did so despite numerous odds and challenges. No matter what crisis or storm was thrown at Rao, from within his party or from the outside, he displayed a propensity to carry on ruling which few in contemporary politics can claim to possess. Towards the end of his term, he was so entrenched in his position that he inevitably presided over the mass destruction of his own political party as well as an individual loss of grace. Yet, it is difficult for commentators in the present to offer views on P.V. Narasimha Rao with a sufficient degree of detachment. Future perspectives may provide a more balanced study, judging him less for his actions and more in accordance with the times which demanded such undertakings.

Rao was criticised from the outset about his handling of the politics of Punjab. When Beant Singh took office in 1992 as the Chief Minister of Punjab's Congress government, Rao had no alternative but to support him with whatever means at his disposal. The administration of a state like Punjab which had faced violence and terrorism for the best part of a decade required constant encouragement and consistent support from the central government. The assassination of Beant Singh on August 31, 1995 coincided with the twilight of terrorism in the state. It was the last act of desperation delivered by terrorism in Punjab. It hurt the polity hard, it even damaged the claims that Rao and his government had been making about peace and normalcy in Punjab, yet if the objective of the car bomb which killed Beant Singh that autumn afternoon was to revive terrorism, it failed. In subsequent months peace and normalcy were restored and Punjab did go to a peaceful election in 1996. The policy of coercion and cooperation practised by Rao did in the end restore peace to the troubled 'wheat-bowl' of India.

All historians of this period would benefit to remember that Rao did not choose the moment of his premiership. It came upon him when he, or anyone else for that matter, least expected it, quite literally by accident. To accept the office of Prime Minister implies confidence more than covetousness because he used it to bring change. It is not improbable that the cumulative pressures of leading the Congress Party, heading a minority government, presiding over a radical economic transition and attending to the momentous social tensions of the period may have been bypassed by another in his position. Rao's fortunes were inextricably bound to the circumstances that his premiership inhabited. Servility to these compulsions, of ever rising contingencies, rather than a forward propulsion of his own accord, became the defining 'method' of his period in office.

Not only did Rao have to preside over domestic transitions, which influenced the political, economic and social life of India but he had to renegotiate India's position in a 'New World Order' in the post-Cold War world. With the collapse of the Soviet Union, India's traditional diplomatic bearing required change and Rao's attempts in this regard were both bellicose and rational. On his state visit to the United States in 1994 he had an opportunity to present a new Indian economy to the only remaining super power. Addressing Congress, Rao fused philosophy and politics. He chose how he wished to present India and wisely switched the objectives to trade promotion:

> Mr. Speaker, I shall now skip the cold war. Not being a historian, I am under no obligation to recount it. Being transient, term-bound representatives of our peoples, you and I have neither the time nor the need to review what we do not wish to repeat. It is the future we have to think about, in fact worry about.[8]

---

8.   Narasimha Rao's address to a joint session of Congress. Washington DC. May 18, 1994.

And developed his theme along the following lines:

> The impact of the changes in India has had a profound effect on Indo-United States economic relations and has benefited both countries. American firms have been in the forefront of forging a new economic relationship. India's vast domestic market, huge educated, skilled and semi-skilled workforce, sound financial institutions and time-tested and democratic system offer tremendous investment opportunities for forward-looking companies.[9]

Other diplomatic victories were scored against Pakistan in Geneva but the systems and policies of international relations pursued by Narasimha Rao cannot be deliberated upon in the pages of this particular book. They require an alternative and more specific work. However, judging by the level of confidence that he acquired from overseas investors, despite his precarious political position, it is safe to record that Rao deployed his experience as Foreign Minister objectively. He managed above all else to divert the focus of Indian foreign policy from diplomay to trade promotion.

International objectives alone nor their successful deployment can be the yardstick by which historians come to judge Narasimha Rao. It was around this time that the columnist and writer Vir Sanghvi famously remarked, "the thing to remember about Narasimha Rao is that he is essentially a short-term manipulator who poses as a statesman." That was the kind of epithet journalism regularly applied to Rao, it sounded credible, even desirable, because his political conduct always left him vulnerable to criticism. His lack of confidence in his own party and colleagues was on show at the Tirupati session of the Congress in 1992 when he asked the newly elected members of the CWC including Arjun Singh and Sharad Pawar to resign and be nominated by him. His prolonged indecision over matters, most crucially during the long Ayodhya crisis ensured the demolition of the Babri mosque and lost him and his party the trust and support of a substantial number of their traditional voters. On this issue

---

9.   Ibid.

he was portrayed a collaborater, a quisling to his own cause, yet, ungratifying though it may be to his critics, containment of the communal threat was in his eyes impossible without some fraternising with the chief perpetrators of communal politics. Rather than perceive communalism in its menacing entirety, Rao's handling of the Ayodhya crisis as a whole suggests that he regarded it as a nuisance, a mere distraction from the singularly important economic objectives of his government.

Rao's impetus and initiative in implementing economic reforms – not merely supporting them – remains the most far-reaching and notable achievment of any government in the last decade. This cannot be precluded by the success or failure of economic liberalisation, for the implementation of the NEP itself suggests a sophisticated political will and resolve. Rao, and the Congress as a whole, was brought up on the sustenance of socialism. His ability to recognise the need for change, and, more importantly, to convince a large section of the Congress to do so suggests a proficiency in political management lacking in subsequent governments. He adapted his own ideas and those of 'the establishment' on the government's role in economic policy to the demands of the times, registering the sharpest transformation from an interventionist economic system to a more *laissez faire* approach.

Most controversial, however, and the final arbiter of whether he could, despite its occurrence, remain the President of the Indian National Congress, was the issue of corruption. The charges of individual corruption notwithstanding, it was the issue of buying MPs from the JMM in 1993 to secure a majority in the vote of confidence which rendered his reputation and regard for office asunder. The other charges, allegations and judgements caught up with this episode that middle class India viewed as the defining charactersitic of his government. The practice of politics became a coping strategy to safeguard the economic objectives of his government. To accomplish this agenda he required a stable government. Since the aim of securing stability required manipulation of the political machinery with the mechanics of the unconstitutional, perhaps even illegitimate, he did so too because the times and circumstances demanded that he remain in office for his full term.

Like all leaders of stature who sense their end in the declining deference of their supporters and the encroaching and emboldened hostility of former colleagues turned enemies, Rao too succumbed to shadows. In his final days in office, perceptions and images in his mind, not content to remain hallucinations, became realities. Figures on the peripheries of his imagination came to dominate his mind until he began to haunt himself but feared others were doing so. This discordance turned to near paranoia as he viewed the carefully constructed edifice of personal ambitions and administrative achievements coming to an end. Friends grew fewer and the list of enemies increased. To his credit, Rao did not intend to, nor did he, go down in a blazing *gotterdammerung*. No matter how closeted and inaccessible his mind became, Rao adroitly realised that his achievements were far more important than any individual ambition. He did not demand a price from the Congress Party for treating him as it did except by taxing its patience by his continuation in the office of Congress President and as the leader of the Congress Parliamentary Party. Instead, he chose the moment of his leaving. Unlike his arrival, Rao himself decided the moment of his departure. While it is true that external factors dictated the urgency for this departure, Rao nevertheless did not succumb to the pressures that peers put upon him. In the end he proved his detractors wrong, his achievements in office outlived their dissidence and their opposition, his aims were more far-reaching than their criticisms of those aims. Yet, his was the politics of a function. Rao could never have competed with the monumental statures of his predecessors, nor can he be judged in comparison with their traits. Nehru's vision was beyond him, Shastri's likeability too difficult for Rao to cultivate. Nor could he claim to have inspired the appeal of Indira Gandhi who had first brought him to political prominence and Rajiv Gandhi's charisma was impossible to emulate. Observing the end of Rao's political innings, Sanghvi, one of his bitterest critics during Rao's tenure in office, concluded:

In a political scene that is so dismally bereft of any talent, Rao still towers over most of his contemporaries. A man of stature and one of the best prime ministers in recent memory now finds that India has no use for him. Alas, he has only himself to blame.[10]

Ultimately Rao's departure affected a dual disassociation. The first was his own break from the Nehruvian consensus and all its elements. The second was the rejection of his politics and experience by the Congress Party. While the former suggested a permanence, the latter was never complete.

---

10.   Vir Sanghvi.

Two

The Rise and Stumble of Sonia Gandhi

In March 1998 Sitaram Kesri reluctantly relinquished power as President of the Indian National Congress. Narasimha Rao had been relegated to the hems of the party fabric and no longer remained a challenger. By popular choice Sonia Gandhi was installed as President of the Congress following another failed bid by the party to come to power in the mid-term general election of 1998.

This part of the book commences with a narration of that 'sterile interlude' which saw the rise and removal of Sitaram Kesri as Congress President, the months in power of the United Front governments of H.D. Deve Gowda and I.K. Gujral and the 1998 mid-term general election.

By the summer of 1998, Sonia Gandhi had entrenched herself as the unchallengeable leader of the Congress Party. The following chapters trace that 'honeymoon' of promised reforms, new programmes, and general bonhomie. Her crown encrusted with the gems of fresh election victories in a string of states dazzled the Indian media. For a moment, however brief, it appeared that she had given a new lease of life to her hitherto moribund party. There was the Panchmari conclave and opinion polls showing her as the most popular leader in the country. While that episode forms the core of the forthcoming pages, it is the events of 1999 which dominate. The workings of the Vajpayee-led NDA government and the fall of that government in March 1999 are illustrated vividly here. The events that followed, including the loss of face for Sonia Gandhi personally when she could not produce the required numbers, take the book along to the hard fought election that year. Intervening milestones, most notably the challenge to her leadership within her own party are covered at length. This may appear to have been given too much weightage but it was the first confrontation she had to face as leader of the Congress Party and thus deserveds and requireds detailed narration and analysis.

This section concludes, as does the last one, with a defeat at the General Election. There are questions raised and answered. It is a very dynamic component of the book since it relives the processes of becoming Sonia Gandhi, of transforming, first, her own persona and then the aura around and within her party. It portrays also the discrepancies and shortcomings, personally and in a corporate sense, which led to the failure to win the 1999 General Election, and pre-sets the stage for later recovery.

The future of the Congress Party hangs in the balance as Sonia Gandhi tries to recover from her stumble to regenerate the confidence which the party had lost.

A Sterile Interlude and a Change of Leadership

In Bed with the United Front - The Avuncular Mr. Kesri –
'Only Madam Can Keep the Party Together' –The Panchmari Conclave–Uttar
Pradesh Changes Tracks – The Emergence of
Digvijay Singh – A Winter of Content

In Bed with the United Front

There was nothing exceptional about the Indian Airlines flight arriving from Bangalore to New Delhi on a scorching day on May 13, in 1996. Along with a handful of newly elected MPs, alighting from the airplane was the 64-year-old Chief Minister of Karnataka, Hardanahalli Doddegowda Deve Gowda. His brief, to bring together the various regional and non-Congress, non-BJP political forces and cobble together a coalition government under the leadership of former Prime Minister V.P. Singh. H.D. Deve Gowda was a regional chieftain with a large enough chunk of newly elected parliamentarians under his control. Others like him, including the formidable Jyoti Basu from West Bengal, the charismatic N.T. Rama Rao from Andhra and the mysterious Dr. Karunanidhi of Tamil Nadu all carried influence and clout and had already pre-arranged their manouevres in the capital. All Deve Gowda was supposed to accomplish was to assist in the selection of a consensus candidate to lead this national coalition. The unanimous choice was V.P. Singh. Discouraged, restrained, suffering from ill health and already the victim of wrath and ridicule in equal measure, V.P. Singh was determined not to accept. He escaped, quite literally going round and round the Outer Ring Road encircling Delhi so his pursuers would not persuade him further. The next most acceptable choice was Jyoti Basu, but the iron reserve and a shrewd understanding of the compulsions of the time provoked disinclination here too. This apparent lack of interest by big-wigs in acquiring the throne of Delhi ought to have been enough of an indication to anyone concerned that perhaps Parliament was so exceedingly hung that the prospect of any individual successfully straddling the seat of power was impossible beyond a limited time. One man didn't think so. Arriving at Karnataka Bhavan after the last meeting of that day, at well past midnight, amidst the boom and jubilation of his supporters, H.D. Deve Gowda went straight to bed. It was 3 am, it was also his first night as Prime Minister. The 'Manninna Maga', or son of the soil from Karnataka, Deve Gowda had been persuaded by colleagues to accept what others had declined or could not muster.

The results of the 1996 General Elections had thrown up a more fractured and more diverse body of parliamentary representatives than ever before. Congress supremacy had been smashed, it was not even the single largest party in Parliament any more. The BJP, as trends had predicted, had taken that position but was in no strength to sustain a government, as events had proved. The alternative to the national parties; the United Front comprising elements of the erstwhile Janata Dal, a grouping of-left-of centre parties and disparate regional groups, required Congress support to stake their claim. Rao, still hanging on in the fray, and perhaps even keen to lead another government, no longer remained in a position to reconcile his ambitions with any possibility of achievement.

Barely two weeks before, the BJP, the largest single group in Parliament, had tried but failed, their government lasting a mere 13 days. Gowda was traversing territory that Vajpayee had covered, but could not keep. With the Congress promising outside support the new United Front government had the support of over 300 MPs.

In his first major interview after becoming Prime Minister, Gowda asserted, 'there is no question of the Congress or anyone else driving us...' a far from comforting statement for the recently removed party of power.

Such minor indiscretions aside, Deve Gowda and Narasimha Rao possessed or created a personal rapport that radiated comfort. As individuals it was important for them to get along and so they did, like two provincial aides holding each other up in the fracas which is a permanent condition of national politics at the centre. The affinity may well have been the result of both being southerners, surrounded by and hostile to their northern counterparts and determined to galvanise this regional identity which Rao, in his years as Prime Minister, had tried so hard to impress upon the polity. If Gowda was pleased with the situation he did not attribute it to Rao, plainly stating, "the Congress had made it clear that it would support the formation of a secular government. It had nothing to do with my relationship with Mr. Rao."

On his own turf, Rao was far from well entrenched. Dissidence within the Congress had a one point agenda, anti-Raoism. Rajesh Pilot, Ahmad Patel, K. Karunakaran, Ghulam Nabi Azad and a whole host of others may have disguised their complaints and sense of injury under the useful garb of declining public support, anti-communalism, probity in public life and other such noble and high minded issues, but their voices seldom, if ever meant to adopt recourse for these perceived conditions. As within any political party, so too in the Congress, the tumult and blips on the monitor were registering, not grievous public concern but the positions and prerogatives of the individual party leaders jockeying for power and influence. The only group with an unadulterated and genuine concern in the state of the nation and their position within it were the party workers, that dedicated and much neglected body of guardians who have proved more useful and helpful to the survival and success of the Congress than its own policy initiatives. For Rao personally it was now all about surviving, mauled but still there as the leader of the Congress, as its President and as Chairperson in Parliament. Repeatedly the dissidents demanded the convening of an AICC session to ratify the election of a new Congress President. Consistently Narasimha Rao and his camp denied them this. Party unity and the need to keep the leadership secure was the need of the hour. R.K. Dhawan, an accomplished man Friday, sometime typist, frequently trouble-shooter, one time Indira Gandhi confidante, now Rao rescuer, recorded his views on inner-party democracy in the following way, "Those who talk about saving the party should not raise such demands (of Rao's resignation) at this stage. The party should be united behind the leader now." Others like Devendra Dwivedi sounded out Sharad Pawar and his group on the need to formulate a dignified and grateful exit for the former Prime Minister. The CWC, the AICC, and the discussions about the function of these bodies now became limited to constructing exit options for the leader. This unfortunately became the truest regression, the avalanche that overtook the slide of the Congress into the declining abyss of political insignificance, which leaves its traces only in history.

Meanwhile, the United Front government under Deve Gowda must have been praying for this crisis within Congress to prolong itself. While Congress leaders fiddled, Gowda could at least get on with his job. Yes he would oblige Rao when possible. He was pressed to grant an extension to the CBI Director K. Vijay Rama Rao whose tenure was due to expire shortly. An appointee of Narasimha Rao, the CBI chief would be the man investigating the glut of accusations now accosting the former Prime Minister. At the same time, Deve Gowda would call Rao regularly, ostensibly to keep his largest ally informed of the progress of government. In order to maintain this deference it was Rao who required his clout to remain undiminished. His leadership of the party, within Parliament and outside, allowed him this privilege to parley.

Late afternoon on September 23, 1996 Narasimha Rao drafted his letter of resignation from the office of Congress President. The Additional Sessions Judge, Ajit Bharihoke had just framed charges against him in the Lakubhai Pathak cheating case. Other more damaging and more serious charges against Rao, like the St Kitts forgery and Jharkhand bribery cases were being investigated by the CBI. The ruling that, 'Prima facie case for offences punishable under Section 120 (B) read with Section 420 of the Indian Penal Code is made out against the accused.' In this event Rao could not continue a moment longer as President of the Indian National Congress. His letter of resignation sought to elicit a sympathetic appraisal of his character and his tenure in office. He claimed to have resigned, 'in the interest of the Congress and to avoid tension and confusion in the ranks.' That at least was the usual explanation given by whoever did resign and Rao had accepted the resignations of most of his colleagues at one time or another during those long five years as Prime Minister. What prompted him to resign when he did, however, was elaborated later in the letter which turned more confessional as it went on:

> I am totally innocent and the allegations levelled against me are false, frivolous and baseless, and are intended to cause harm to my reputation. During the period I was in positions of power, including that of Prime Minister, I have not done anything violative of the law, nor have I done anything which might bring discredit to my party or my government.

Finally came a more revealing line intended to sound out the Deve Gowda government whose longevity had rested in his hands right until that moment. It warned:

> I have full faith in the rule of law and I am confident the allegations against me will be proven false.

Within a week Sitaram Kesri was nominated provisional President of the Congress Party, the position being open to an electoral contest the following year. Sinisterly, for many of his remaining colleagues, Rao continued as the Chairperson of the Congress Parliamentary Party.

Relations between the United Front Government and the Congress Party, for all the apparent comfort on the outside, were never far from the probabilities of a premature end. While there were endless photo calls which showed Deve Gowda, the new Prime Minister smiling and reconciled to his much troubled but happy looking predecessor Narasimha Rao, personal relations between government MPs and those in the Congress were far from cosy. Rao's successor as Congress President, despite his exterior, was not a man to be taken lightly.

The Avuncular Mr. Kesri

Across party offices in India visitors can see certain characters who share a common appearance, a stereotypical 'neta'. Their gait and manner of movement is similar, their thought patterns nearly identical, their gestures, expressions, dress sense and humour are all true to a predetermined type, they nearly always seem to belong to a generation that appears to have been everlastingly old and timeworn. The stark uniformity of these sometimes venerable elders, in thought, appearance and utterance suggests they can be nothing but party apparatchiks. They look like figures whose entire life cycle must have revolved around paying homage to the prevailing culture of their political offices, politics having been their singular and lifelong pursuit, their refinements and debasements both stemming from political intrigue, its manipulations and its rewards. Outwardly incapable of a brisk walk, they reflect an inner state of a deep meditation that bears itself upon their exercise of power, in whatever capacity or at whatever level they choose to wield it.

Sitaram Kesri, venerable octogenarian and inscrutable treasurer of the Indian National Congress was just one of these. Warm, even effusive and 'down-to-earth', soft spoken, mild mannered and forever ready to bestow deference towards his chosen deity, Kesri was at once an avuncular figure. He began his career in the Congress as a cheerleader in the 1940s, even contested an election once, in 1967, from Katihar in his native Bihar and rose through the ranks to assume control of the party's purse strings in the wake of the defeat of 1977. A 'loyalist' to both Indira Gandhi and Rajiv, Kesri never once left the Congress Party, an uncommon feat among his generation of Congressmen. Known to party-men and the press as 'Chacha (uncle) Kesri' his elevation to the cabinet in Rao's government, as Minister for Welfare, complemented his character and temperament comfortably. Yet, was this image genuine? Or was it so genuinely cultivated to disarm that Kesri's image was taken for reality?

When Kesri was appointed Congress President on September 23, 1996, barely two days after his predecessor had been chargesheeted in cases of corruption, it was as a 'provisional President' that he assumed office. It was A.K. Anthony, himself a contender for the post who proposed

Kesri's name to the CWC, yet the decision to foist him as the leader of the Congress Party was not as unanimous nor as undisputed as some commentators have suggested. Sharad Pawar lurked uneasily in the background, plotting his own scheme for supremacy, a younger and more dynamic Rajesh Pilot was even more brusque and made no secret of his desire to contest a Presidential election.

It was only eight months later, on May 28, 1997 that Kesri filed his papers for an electoral contest to become the first elected President of the Indian National Congress since the 1950s and the President of the party who was not simultaneously the leader of the Congress Parliamentary Party, an unbroken tradition in itself since 1969. Furthermore, it was now that the overwhelming support for his name, some of it genuine, most of it contrived, was in evidence. Five of the seven Congress Chief Ministers filed nominations seconding his candidature. Of the 7460 votes polled by the AICC electoral college Sitaram Kesri received 6227. His nearest rival, Sharad Pawar managed only 882 and Pilot, the resident 'Young Turk' of the Congress Party could only get 354 supporters to endorse his claim. Pranab Mukherjee, apparatchik in chief and possibly the seniormost Congressman involved in the process described the results as indicative of 'a consensus at the top'. So why, when it had the opportunity to enforce change and reform in such a great degree did the Congress Party replace a discredited septuagenarian with a servile octogenarian? Why did the selection of its leader not symbolise progress for the party? Why, it must be asked, did the 'top' agree on a consensus to prolong the life of the very culture that had consumed it? As with many answers to the seemingly endless problems that beset political formulations in India, the answer lies in the questions themselves. The consensus that Mukherjee spoke of, the great register of votes that Kesri polled and his subsequent installation itself, should not have raised questions, they should have answered them. This is the *maya*, or illusion, of Indian politics. The consensus was not formed in support of Sitaram Kesri the individual, it was agreed upon because the majority of Congressmen weighed the consequences of Sitaram Kesri as leader and concluded that it meant greater leverage and influence for themselves. The register of votes did not sound the death knell for any generational change of guard. It was arranged by members of that very generation, so each of those younger leaders could have more time to posture themselves as future replacements, over and above their peers. Senior members like Mukherjee himself did not resign their chances for a leadership role, they deliberated and surmised that Kesri spelled a less hazardous survival for their various and diverse political positions. The Congress did not reinvent itself because it could not have survived the pangs and pressures which any rebuilding exercise would inevitably involve. Besides, with Kesri in place the most important member of the Congress Party, still silent but no longer averse or isolated, would find it easier to finally step in and alleviate the party as a whole. Sitaram Kesri belonged to a caste classified as Backward. In a political bazaar where factors such as reservations, caste backwardness, regionalism and social empowerment were valued as high-currency denominations, his identity made a difference to some. In a political arena where the super-gladiators were either Yadav, Kurmi, Vokkaligga and Pasi it payed to be on cordial terms with the leaders of these groups, as Kesri undoubtedly was, given his own identity and background. While this mattered publicly, the only and singularly important factor that won over the vast body of Congressmen in his support was the widely held perception that Sitaram Kesri was a candidate favoured by Sonia Gandhi. In this perception was hidden a hope, that in time Sonia Gandhi would enter active politics and soon progress to becoming the party leader herself. The party had been long accustomed to silences and a withdrawn presence from No. 10 Janpath, her residence. Kesri meanwhile enjoyed the protective cover radiated by her indifference and proceeded to exert his authority by dismissing those seen as 'Rao's men'. The strongest indication of this came even before he had been officially elected as Congress President. On November 23, exactly two months after being declared provisional President, he abruptly and summararily dismissed three AICC General Secretaries and replaced them with his own men. It was acceptable in the eyes of many because he appeared to enjoy Sonia Gandhi's backing.

Similarly, the three-day AICC session held after his election, in Calcutta onAugust 8th, endorsed his leadership further because Sonia Gandhi attended it as a member of the Congress Party. She had assumed primary membership in March of that year. She must have been conscious that Kesri was using her presence at the session to solidify his own position and prove to any existing or potential threat that his moves for party unity as well personal authority were constructed in collaboration with Sonia Gandhi. His accolades were addressed not to her but to the dissidence within when in his Presidential address he stated, "I have become old and I want you to be there. You are away from the party for the last five years. Now you should associate yourself with the party in a big way. You cannot deviate from the family tradition of being in the forefront of the party which has to be made strong and vibrant."

In characteristic fashion, he kept alluding to his age, but inserted a hint of his own seniority and position when he finally said: "You have come as a symbol representing the family. I am ageing and if the Congress collapses, the responsibility will be yours." The stress on the possibility of a Congress collapse also stressed a pre-condition to Sonia Gandhi as well as the assembled delegates. It was only in the event of a Congress collapse, due to either his failure or death that Sonia Gandhi could hope to become leader. In any case her leadership role and its capacities were his prerogative. As for the rest of the Congress leadership the choice of leader lay between him and Sonia Gandhi. Since he was certain that she would or could not make a bid for leadership he was in effect telling the party that he remained the undisputed and elected leader of the party, one who clearly enjoyed the support of the only likely alternative. The first dissident to shatter this illusion for him was the fiery West Bengal Congress leader, Mamata Banerjee, who decided to hold her own parallel show on the streets of Calcutta and declared that her only 'High Command' was Sonia Gandhi. Subsequently, in her first move to play the role of a party manager, Sonia Gandhi stepped in to effect a rapprochement between a dissatisfied Mamta and an offended Congress leadership.

Meanwhile, the Jain Commission's interim report on Rajiv Gandhi's assassination had been completed. Its release had been anxiously awaited. Many believed that the slow pace of the investigation had itself propelled Sonia Gandhi into active politics but that argument belongs to the realm of conjecture. In her own written deposition to the Jain Commission she held the 'conviction that V.P. Singh and his political advisers...could not possibly have been oblivious of the serious nature of the threat to his (Rajiv Gandhi's) life and the implications of withdrawing proper security cover...virtually providing an open invitation to liquidate him.' She further believed that the 'gross inadequacy (of Rajiv Gandhi's security cover) was a politically motivated act, carried out with the intention of increasing my husband's threat perception and reducing his level of mass contact.' While the matter of Rajiv Gandhi's assassination was primarily a political issue as far as political establishments, including Congress ones, were concerned, it was naturally a deeply and singularly personal affair for Sonia Gandhi and her family. Her children, Rahul and Priyanka, had attended the hearings of the Commission day after day for the best part of five years. It was a Congress government that had prolonged their unhappy vigil. The fact that the Rao government had dragged its feet over the probe must have been especially distressing and distasteful. Now with the UF government in power under its second Prime Minister, Congressmen had no qualms about turning the family's personal anxieties into political vendetta. In various degrees the Interim Report of the Commission of Inquiry implicated three DMK ministers in the conspiracy to assassinate the former Prime Minister. The DMK was at the time an important partner in the UF coalition of Prime Minister I.K. Gujral. The Prime Minister sensing a grave threat to his government invited a seven-member Congress delegation, led by Kesri, to his residence on of November 9th. Over soup and salads he assured his visitors that the report and the accompanying Action Taken Report (ATR) would be tabled in Parliament on November 9th. Just the previous day the CWC had resolved to back Gujral and his government, the Jain Commission's document therefore came as an unmitigated explosion for Gujral. Soon the response

118

of the Congress turned into a competitive chorus against the UF government as Congressmen outdid each other to decry it and its leaders. From Party Vice-President Jitendra Prasad's albeit diplomatic assertion that, 'a harsh decision against the government can only be averted if the UF takes action on the report', to more strident and vocal demands by senior leaders such as Karunakaran who fulminated saying, 'no Congressman can allow those responsible for our beloved leader's murder to go scot-free. There is no question of supporting any government that harbours such guilty men.' Kesri sensed that he was being overtaken by events and thereafter promptly·turned hawkish. Within the UF there were boisterous noises of defence too, and he hurtled the entire issue towards an impasse and ultimately towards a confrontation. Any such confrontation could only end with the fall of the UF government. The November 24th issue of *India Today* captured the mood of the Congress Party unusually well. It reported:

> Not that the Congress rank and file are worried by a threat of dissolution. Regardless of Kesri's apparent feelings to the contrary, they are convinced that the Rajiv murder issue provides the party with a simple and emotive theme to fight an election, particularly if Sonia agrees to campaign…Even BJP leaders concede Sonia's presence will make a "big difference" to Congress prospects. The Congress internal assessment is that it will increase its tally from 138 to at least 205 seats in case of a mid-term poll. Along with pre-poll alliances this will ensure a Congress-led Government at the Centre.

The following passage in the same report was more revealing and an apt guide to the motivations of those involved:

> If there are 138 sitting MPs who feel it is best to have a go at government formation in this Lok Sabha, there are at least double that number of ex-MPs who want to take another shy at the hustings.

Parliament was dissolved on December 4th. India prepared to face its second general election in two years. Kesri had prepared the path he was certain Sonia Gandhi would not traverse. Instead, she took it by storm.

When Zafar Agha, a senior political correspondent, had asked him about what role Sonia Gandhi would play in the party, Kesri had replied, 'I think she doesn't want to get into active politics. She is interested in unity.' That was in December 1996. The following year, Sonia Gandhi had not only united the party around her, she became the lead campaigner in the elections that followed the fall of the Gujral government in December 1997.

'Only Madam Can Keep the Party Together'

"She is the real leader of the party. Only she can lead the country......Each time the Congress has delinked itself from the family, the party has been weak. Now with Sonia coming in there is a new wave in the country."

Periodic thunderings of this kind had become habitual for Sitaram Kesri during the General Election of 1998. Credit for electoral victory was preordained for Sonia Gandhi, not only by Kesri but by other senior members of the party as well. "If we do well the credit is all Soniaji's" was an all too familiar chant of leading members of the Congress Party at the time. What Kesri and the other party grandees making such assertions did not realise was that the mass of Congress activists and grassroot workers saw them as the prime obstacle in the ascent of Sonia Gandhi. So while the elders held court, gave interviews and bestowed patronage upon favoured acolytes, they began to face a corresponding decline in their own popularity among the mass of the party cadre. More and more party activists, legislators and other dignitaries preferred to wait out this sterile interlude in their own constituencies rather than lining up, as they had done previously to pay salutations to party bosses in New Delhi. Even while the queues outside their residences grew shorter and the telephone calls for appointments steadily rang themselves out the party officials at the top of the Congress pyramid continued to take private counsel, very privately indeed. Most of them were concerned with how to ingratiate themselves with and within a new regime, once it did assume power. Others, more vain and detached from the actual pace of events decided to hatch grandiose schemes to establish control over any newly emerging leadership.

This period, which lies between Sonia Gandhi's decision to become a primary member of the Indian National Congress in March 1997 and her subsequent appointment as AICC President in March 1998, witnessed a sharp and steady eclipse of the rest of the Congress leadership.

However, this was a more prolonged pause of nearly comical proportions. While the rest of the Congress demanded Sonia Gandhi's installation as its head, the temporal heads of the Congress Party, while resonating the same demand could not forsee that occurrence until after the general election was over, a year later. Presently they were too concerned with forging the blue-prints of their own survival strategies to worry about the details of any new enthronement if it did actually occur. Sonia Gandhi became a primary member of India's oldest political party the Indian National Congress in March 1997. The reactions to her entry into party politics ranged from Jyoti Basu's characteristic remark: "I did not know that she was not in the party" to more jubilant if over dramatic scenes and serenades which pronounced that the Congress had been delivered. At the time there were as many opinions as the people making them on the subject of Sonia Gandhi's leadership and the potential fallouts which that would entail. However, the predominant view did consider her entry as something of a prerequisite for the alleviation of the party, if not immediately in electoral terms then at least in matters of party organisation. In his *Hindustan Times* editorial, Vir Sanghvi commented:

> It will not be an exaggeration to say that Mrs. Gandhi's entry into the Congress is an event of enormous significance for the party. After the tragic assassination of her husband, there has not been any comparable occasion with the potential of making such an impact on the organisation. Considering that the Congress remains even in its present not very robust state a crucial player on the political scene, there is little doubt that the fallout from Mrs. Sonia Gandhi's formal, political debut will be widely felt at the national level as well.........It is too early to say how successfully

Mrs. Sonia Gandhi will be able to fulfil this role, but there is little doubt that her presence in the organisation will make much more of a positive impact than that of almost any other leader at present.

Meanwhile the personality at the vortex of the entire matter, Sonia Gandhi herself assumed a strange silence on the question of party leadership. Apart from a single or signal speech (depending from which side of the party spectrum one looked) during the campaign, Sonia Gandhi said little and did even less to display any haste or urgency to assume the leadership role she was confident would be served to her on a platter. Her sole indiscretion, if one terms it that, was when she declared:

> *With the right and able leadership, it* (Congress) *is the only party which has the experience and capability to give India what it needs most, a stable government.*

Such references may seem subliminal and subtle to casual listeners, but to the trained ears of politicians and analysts, this was a resonant demand and a declaration at the same time. A few carefully placed words had again said more than loud banter or demagoguery would have achieved. Sonia Gandhi had said what she meant: that the present leadership of the Congress Party was unable to reconcile itself to the country and to success. Hers alone was the right and able leadership and she alone possessed what it would take to get the Congress and the country back on track. Arguably, this was a justifiable line to take as the events that followed illustrated.

Until and during the General Election her role had been to market the Congress Party to a disgruntled electorate. Technically she remained only a primary member of the Congress throughout the 138 public meetings and rallies she held covering a distance of 25,000 kilometres. However, in reality her face was the recognised one at every public meeting in that election. Candidates had sought her attendance at their respective functions and she alone represented the party on the election banners and posters throughout the country. When Kesri had commented that her coming had brought a "new wave" in the country he may have been right, though the makings of that wave may not have been what he meant them to be. The line she took throughout the campaign is suitably articulated in her speech at Hyderabad in mid-January, as the campaign was gaining momentum. It was a culmination or sum-total of all that she had been saying throughout the campaign. It was a four-pronged emphasis; emotional references to the Nehru-Gandhi family were enunciated between blows struck for secularism and scathing attacks on the BJP combine and its agenda. What was remarkable was the understanding she displayed about the position of Congress politics and the tenor in which she expressed this understanding. There was an accountability which the Congress under Rao had virtually dismissed during its period in office: 'In 1992 when the Babri Masjid was demolished by religious fundamentalists, all right thinking Indians were outraged. I too was devastated.' There was an appeal to the ideals of her late husband Rajiv Gandhi which the unemotive blanket of the New Economic Policy had all but subdued in previous years: 'Just about a month before he was assassinated, my husband had said to me that if ever an attempt was made to touch the Babri Masjid, he would stand in front of it and they would have to kill him first. Such was the power of his dedication to a secular India.' Most importantly, there was an unmitigated, unapologetic attack upon the fundamentals of the right-wing which the Congress had been nervous to undertake, given the perceived mood of the country at large. Without mincing words, Sonia Gandhi decided to choose her battle-ground by taking the communal bull by its horns. 'These elections represent a clash of some fundamental values, ideas and ideals', she thundered, 'The choice is between the forces of harmony and progress and those which seek to exploit our differences in order to win power.' In the same vein, she stirred the crowd before her with the very secularism which her party had come to fear speaking about: 'Secularism means equal respect for all religions. This is the only basis for India's unity and integrity...It is a complete negation of our values and heritage to convert religion into an instrument to divide', she stated. It was this approach of direct statements, strong on ideological preserves, untouched by uncertainty that set her apart from the rest of the Congress leadership.

While the number of seats the Congress attained was almost the same as in 1996, there was a notable increase in the turnout of voters in the states where Sonia Gandhi campaigned. Similarly, the turnout of female voters was up at 55 per cent from the 37 per cent in 1996, a margin of 18 per cent. In the first phase of the polling the turnout of Muslim voters touched 85 per cent in many places and never fell below 60 per cent. These are interesting statistics if one realises that the chances of the Congress at the hustings in 1998 had been very bleak indeed. The party was solely blamed for the fall of the United Front government and this had created a bitter divide between them and the usually sympathetic and secular Left. When the Congress had withdrawn support to Deve Gowda earlier in 1997, Indrajit Gupta then Home Minister had warned the Congress: "If you withdraw your support to this government the people will do something to you." In the circumstances a general election had been avoided as Gujral succeeded Gowda as Prime Minister. However, that statement by Gupta had gone to the heart of the matter then and it rang equally true in 1998. Many Congressmen, especially in marginal seats, feared that the people would indeed "do something to them". Simultaneously the prospect of having the octogenarian and uncharismatic Sitaram Kesri as the chief salesman of the party in the general election did not appeal to many Congressmen either. Particularly when one considers that for any legislator, all else is relegated to secondary importance when the matter of their election comes up for a periodic review by their electorate. For Congress legislators this is singularly true, the most important factor in their allegiances and reversals of these loyalties is the possibility of a loss or gain in their personal balance of power. The former condition being unacceptable in almost every degree, the latter being welcome whenever the possibility arises. Therefore from their point of interest Sonia Gandhi simply appeared a better personality in a more viable leadership role to market their careers to a largely disenchanted electorate. Consequently, in their eyes, she succeeded as well. None can say what the ultimate tally of the Indian National Congress would have been had she not joined the party and campaigned as she did for its repair. General opinion largely suggested a rout and the word in the political bazaar was that the party would be lucky if it crossed double figures. However, once the results had trickled in and the numbers had become known, it fell to Sharad Pawar to articulate what most of the party candidates had known throughout: "Had Soniaji not campaigned for the party our tally would have been less than a hundred seats." In the event, the Congress stood at 142, merely one more than what it had got in 1996. Nevertheless, nothing summed up the situation better than a byline in *India Today*, it simply read:

The gloves are off. The Gandhis is are back in business.

All Sonia Gandhi now had to do was to wait for the party to request her to sign on. She had established herself as its saviour, it would now anoint her as its undisputed leader as well, otherwise it would fall apart.

As the final results from the Jammu and Kashmir election arrived on the evening of March 10, Sitaram Kesri dramatically but stumblingly spoke of a 'decision to resign' from the office of Congress President. There was much more in this statement than a simple will for renunciation. It was the Congress Party's way of adjusting itself internally to make way for the inevitable. It did not signify a transition but a circumventive tact to soften any consequences which a transition might entail. Kesri did release a sting at the tail of his statement, he stated that he wished to place the reasons for his decision at a convention of the AICC. The *Frontline* Magazine, a good gauge of behind the scenes meanderings, quoted a Congress leader saying, 'Kesri is trying to play a new game to retain some position of power within the party...If Kesri wanted to accept Soniaji's leadership, he would have merely announced his resignation or placed it before the CWC without making a call to convene a special session of the AICC.'

In her private discussions with Congress leaders, Sonia Gandhi had been assured that her passage to the leadership would be smooth and unchallenged, a fair enough presumption, but a presumption nonetheless.

A belligerent Sitaram Kesri and a revived and ebullient Sharad Pawar now appeared to be obstacles, no opposition being stated, but implied from their respective camps. Pawar had been the leader of the Congress in the Lok Sabha with Kesri retaining the post of leader of the Congress Parliamentary Party (CPP) as well as that of Congress President. With his strength now buffered by a substantial number of MPs from his home state of Maharashtra, Pawar hoped to extend his control to the leadership of the CPP at the very least, some felt he wished to negotiate terms with Third Front leaders about joining the government. Sonia Gandhi's proposed entry brought in an unchallengeable contender into the domain of top party posts. Between Sitaram Kesri and Sharad Pawar there had to be a sacrifice. Sonia Gandhi's managers operated deftly and created a situation where neither Kesri nor Pawar received any new *accoutrements*. Going by the resolution of the CWC of March 5th which had asked for Sonia Gandhi to play a larger role in the party organisation and his own 'decision to resign' they circulated the idea of installing Sonia Gandhi as the head of both the AICC and the CPP. On the morning of the 14th a CWC meeting, reluctantly presided over by Sitaram Kesri, moved a resolution asking Sonia Gandhi to take over the party. Kesri was non-committal and wound up the meeting abruptly and walked over to his office unhappily and radiating hurt. At 5.30 the same evening, Sonia Gandhi became the fifth member of the house of Motilal Nehru to become Congress President. The occasion was marred only by Kesri's display of grief. She overcame this by calling on him before anything else. He climbed down but speaking to the media, his voice choked with emotion he stated that it would have been much better had she taken over after he had actually resigned. Technically therefore, Sonia Gandhi became Congress President through a coup mounted from within. Within days, this was forgotten and Kesri reconciled himself to circumstances. Sharad Pawar meanwhile continued as leader of the party in the Lok Sabha but nothing more. Sonia Gandhi was elected CPP leader herself, within days of taking over the party. His grievances, unvoiced, were left to fester. Injured, he bided his time.

The Panchmari Conclave

In September 1998 the Congress Party retreated to the pleasant surroundings of Panchmari, a hill station in Madhya Pradesh. The objective was to hold a "Vichar Manthan Shivir" or brainstorming session and debate the "vital issues concerning the Congress Party". The choice of location, Madhya Pradesh, was appropriate, as the state was only two months away from an Assembly Election which many predicted would bring down the Digvijay Singh government. The attention and publicity generated by holding the meeting there would, it was hoped, provide aid to the government. Nevertheless, the Panchmari conclave was Sonia Gandhi's first attempt at party-building and re-vitalisation and it is for this that it will be remembered. A lot of symbolism has been attached to this conclave. It has been represented variously, but largely the relevance of Panchmari is its appearance as the official endorsement to the programme of change, both structural and ideological, begun by Sonia Gandhi. In scale and importance only the Narora session of 1974 and the Bombay AICC session in 1986 stand up to Panchmari as a point in the post-Independent Congress Party's life when an endeavour was made to reconsider and accommodate new ideas. The importance of Panchmari lies in this latter observation. It was indeed a genuine attempt by the party to restore its bearings. The Nehruvian Consensus which dominated the party's thinking upto the late 1980s was in tatters. Not much thinking had been devoted to any alternative concepts, the breakdown had merely been accepted, not improved upon. Within its own party forums too the consequences of economic liberalisation and coalition politics had not been discussed adequately leading to a confusion in the ranks. The urgency was compounded by the emerging notion that the BJP-led coalition government appeared to be losing its control over key allies in its government, thus making it all the more necessary for the Congress to assert itself. While the BJP-led alliance weakened, eager topplers, in the form of the Left Front and other constituents of the erstwhile United Front, began to look Congresswards to take the lead.

A lot of homework had been processed before the conclave effectively

127

began. The Sangma Task Force had handed in its suggestions and views on the state of politics in the party and the country. It had made recommendations and established the causes for the party's electoral defeat in 1998. This too was on the agenda under discussion. Dialogue and interaction had been established with all Presidents of election going states and the views of various party leaders had been sought before the party arrived in Panchmari. Sonia Gandhi's words of welcome to the Congress delegates were realistic and missing the rhetorical overload which politicians are prone to making:

> Some of us often see only the dark side. I have neither the 'all is well' and so 'sit back hand in hand' attitude nor do I see despair and defeat all around. We must harbour neither of these in our minds. Neither complacence nor pessimism will behove us. We have to look forward to the future. We have to learn from the past, not remain stuck with it."

It was a rational beginning, significant because it accepted the importance of modification, crucial because it was under observation by potential allies in opposition. The media reserved their judgement. The sources of inspiration remained familiar with pictures and paintings of Nehru, Indira and Rajiv among other familiar faces appropriately draped over the meeting venue. The principal issues to be dicussed were only two. More than issues, it is this double-barrelled dilemma over which bewilderment continues to blight Congress decision-making in opposition. First of the two is, of course, the matter of how far and how much the party is willing to go along with Dr. Manmohan Singh's New Economic Policy. Second is the political question of whether like its national competitor the BJP, the Congress should also collaborate with regional and other opposition parties to go in for coalition governments.

The first matter is difficult to address. Within the party there was and continues to be a divergence of views. The pro-liberalisation group is unequivocal that economic reforms are a must and that there can be no turning back, no halfway measures, that they must be implemented in full. A second group is more antidiluvian but equally adamant and for them the new thinking (and practice) of "Manmohaneconomics" is not pro-poor, anti-socialist and a break from the Nehruvian tradition. Unable to appreciate some of the benefits which the new order has to offer, they are concerned solely with the negative fallouts, more particularly the political fallouts of this economic practice. The subject of a cut in subsidies is closest to the heart of this group, followed by cuts in public spending which may follow. The dilemma for the pro-reformists has always been the need for a balancing act between support for policies which were initiated by a Congress government and an equal opposition to the manner in which these policies are implemented by a BJP-led government. Subsidies are naturally popular and their advantage is maximised. However it is difficult to make a case out for non-merit subsidies in a liberalised society with a level playing field for all sectors of the economy. So while in government policies were formulated and implemented and sometimes showed quick results it was and continues to be necessary to define a clear difference between the Congress way and that of successive governments. In fairness the differences are there, both in terms of indicators and in policy making. Subsequently, the results are disparate too. Nonetheless, leaders arrived in Panchmari to debate this very issue and in her words of welcome the Congress President evidently endeavoured to build a bridge between the two sides:

> We must constantly reinterpret our economic philosophy in the light of changing circumstances, emerging challenges and the experience we gain while implementing policies. Our economic policy will have to be multi-dimensional to meet the needs of our people at various levels. No one dogma, no one formula will cater to the diverse needs of the economy and of our society.

A similar articulation about future economic policy was made in May 1985 by Rajiv Gandhi. In an economic resolution circulated within the CWC at the time he stated:

> In the process of development, the policy instruments relevant to one stage cannot be treated as permanently sacrosanct. Nor are they ends in themselves.

At the time, this was considered too radical and too quick a shift from the socialist pattern of economic planning, with all the doctrines of state control, power of patronage and monopoly which that entailed. However, Sonia Gandhi's speech at Panchmari espoused exactly that line. Clearly "multi-dimensional" was the operative word. This is the "third-view". The mixed economy with a commitment towards affirmative action as well as public (meaning private sector) participation in order to cater to the "various levels" of Indian society. Where the onus lies on the creation of a stakeholder society, within which social development and responsibility are not the exclusive prerogative of the state but of society as a whole. However, this view does not give a free run to either the "complete liberalisation and nothing else" group, nor does it offer its patronage to the "only socialism should prevail" lobby. It is the political answer to economic practice. As such there is often a danger of falling between two stools for neither side is aware of how far it can go, either in terms of extending cooperation or in terms of opposing non-Congress government policy and thus the confusion is prolonged. The declaration on economic affairs itself is at least equally addled. It states that the Congress:

> Reassert its commitment to socialism and the socialistic pattern of society as spelled out at Avadi in 1955 and in subsequent resolutions of the Party; Appreciates the remarkable recovery and impressive economic achievements secured through the reforms of the period 1991-96; Deplores the squandering of that legacy by successive governments since the Congress demitted office in May 1996; Reaffirms that the removal of poverty and the empowerment of the poor as effective partners in the growth process is the essence of the Party's economic policy...

Further to this, the resolution added that it sought to maintain economic growth rates of 7 per cent and over annually, perhaps impossible under the old regime of quotas, licenses and a plethora of regulations. So what does this mean? Fundamentally it seeks to create a "clear blue water" line of difference between the Congress way of doing things and the pursuit of economic policy as practised by the BJP-led government. So while the 1991 NEP is conductive to the "socialistic pattern of society" the BJP economic policy "squanders" that commitment by promoting (among other things) jobless growth, privatisation of state-owned profit making enterprises, financial instability and generally an interventionist rather than market-driven policy in the private sector. Simultaneously, the BJP, with its image of a party of banias and the shopkeeper culture of their milieu is loath to approach economic policy making with a socialistic perspective. That is the theme of the Congress attack.

The second and purely political question which demanded an answer was the subject of coalition government. As such, the political trend of the time continues to be favourable towards coalition government. The model of a central party around which ideologically sympathetic groups gather is certainly one which appears to have suited the BJP, even if that has meant a complete negation of their own more right-wing party commitments. It makes perfect sense for the BJP to hover around political groups like the TDP even though the two may not share any ideological similarities. Nationally the BJP is still relatively less deeply and widely entrenched than the Congress. Wherever the BJP has opted for regional alliances they have gained (sometimes merely inches) political ground where previously they had none. For the Congress to submit to an alliance translates into ceding political territory previously under its exclusive control. Naturally, therefore, the political balance of interests, the prospects, pitfalls and opportunities of coalition politics are all considered within the original and guiding principle that coalition politics translates into the voluntary sacrifice of political monopoly for the Congress Party. In the words used by Sir Roy Jenkins elsewhere and for different circumstances one can conclude that Congressmen believe they "must keep themselves from being defiled by overt collaboration", with other political groups. What in such a defiant temperament of political protectionism can the political resolution of Panchmari mean as it:

> Affirms that the party considers the present difficulties in forming one-party governments a transient phase in the evolution of our polity: Pledges

to restore the party to its primacy in national affairs; Decides that coalitions will be considered only when absolutely necessary and that too on the basis of agreed programmes which will not weaken the Party or compromise its basic ideology.

These particular affirmations, pledges and decisions accept that coalition politics is a compulsion of politics, but only in the form of a "transient phase". This implies a belief that voter choice will revert to a preference for single party government at a later stage. Therefore, the commitment to coalition governments cannot be binding upon the Congress Party for any indefinite period. Yet the motivation behind the stated intention lies elsewhere, perhaps it was said with a view to assembly elections where coalitions and seat adjustments may have been required. A more pragmatic reasoning suggests that rather than a charter of their beliefs, the message on coalitions was a message the Congress was sending to other parties in opposition, particularly the Left Front. Certainly that is a possibility given the strong doses of socialism which dominated the party's thinking on economic policy at Panchmari.

Panchmari was the creation of parameters; political, economic and strangely, moral ones as well. The success or failure of an adopted strategy can only be gauged once its implementation begins. While the declarations of Panchmari have found expression in the Congress Party's actions, these actions have been selective. The larger process of party reform and revival and thus political progress which such revitalisation aids has not evidently benefited. At the same time the "mapping out" does provide a compass which is useful to any organisation. The difficulty in identifying success and failure is due to the fact that in opposition very little counts. The promising indication of Panchmari was that no unilateral radical agenda was created which is the cause of many an opposition party not making its transition to power. Unless there is something evidently and fundamentally wrong there is usually no need for a political party to form a drastic disassociation with its political or ideological roots. The decision to view coalitions more favourably when they became necessary was both a pragmatic and confident outlook. Certainly the message of Panchmari within the party was a positive one because it signified at the very least, an illusion of progress and a revival of thinking. As for communications with the outside world, a strategy was formed which would be relayed through the forthcoming assembly elections. The new dualism of Congress political thinking, mixed economy and mixed government, would be put to the test in all subsequent elections from now on.

Uttar Pradesh Changes Tracks

Uttar Pradesh has come to represent, for the Congress Party, what a troublesome overseas colony may once have been like for a global imperial power. Its organisational network is plagued in equal measure by stagnation and intense factional feuding. Leaders are everywhere, the statisticians are not far wrong when they say that there are 3.5 leaders to every party worker in the state. Circulars are despatched with unfailing enthusiasm. Committees assemble regularly to chalk out grand campaigns and programmes of action. The outcome is the launch of something which falls between Mao's Long March and Napoleon's retreat from Moscow. All discussions, and activities are performed for a limited audience of former MPs, ex-MLAs, motley collections of have-beens and sometimes a handful of new recruits. A press note is issued as routine to a band of correspondents who decide for themselves whether it makes good copy.

A visit to the UPCC headquarters on Mall Avenue in Lucknow will reveal a downtrodden resemblance to the grand Awadhi building that Nehru Bhavan once was. This imposing structure was once the repository of political power in the state, and a source of considerable political strength to the Congress in the rest of the country. Now, the compound is nearly deserted except for the clerks and infrequent visitors who lend the façade a pretension of activity. The crowds have moved next door to the residence of Mayawati, the Dalit leader who receives them like a feudal matriach in her fortress like home.

This was 2003, let us visit the past.

When Sonia Gandhi became Congress President in March 1998, one of the first briefs she found waiting on her table contained references to the situation of her party in UP Even her intense campaigning in the recently concluded General Elections had yielded not a single seat to parliament of the 85 which UP held. She knew all too well what the situation was. Over the next few weeks she would be inundated with visitors and "experts" from the state each of them professing a deep knowledge of the existing situation. Evidently the numbers didn't add up, without UP electoral victory was not possible. The problems were speedily identified: no bloc support from any community, organisational weaknesses, excessive central control and factionalism, among other factors. The Sangma Task Force, constituted after the election defeat, recommended giving "special attention to major states like UP." It also suggested that:

> In addition, there should also be Divisional Congress Committees for these states. The tenure of the committees should be for four years instead of two years as at present.

The panacea for all political problems in the Congress, it would appear, is a change of leadership. N.D. Tiwari, the incumbent UPCC President and veteran Congress leader was recalled. The party had tried various combinations. Upper caste leadership had been unable to prevent the slide of upper caste voters away from the Congress. The installation of Mahavir Prasad, a senior Dalit leader, had coincided with the largest erosion of Dalits, who opted instead for the BSP. No backward leader in the state Congress had been groomed to challenge Mulayam Singh Yadav and his SP, who also held the Muslims in their grip, post-Babri. Jitendra Prasad, recently removed Congress Vice-President too had been given a chance in 1996 but was unable to advance the party's course. In such a situation, when no obvious candidate is apparent, the Congress goes into a mode of politicking which negates its long experience of Indian politics and its traditions. Almost anyone associated with the party, some with very weak links indeed, present themselves as prospective candidates. In this particular situation, leaders not even hailing from UP preened themselves as the apparent heirs to its faltering leadership. Lobbying was intense. Anyone hopeful of securing a selection arrived in New Delhi and immediately headed for the home of the nearest dominant leader from whom they expected some sympathy. These leaders in turn expostulated and held forth their own assessments and strategies to restless groups. Meanwhile, Sonia Gandhi had already made up her mind. Her choice, had they known it immediately, would have surprised her most prodigious talent scouts. Salman Khurshid was a former Minister of State for External Affairs in Narasimha Rao's government. He had represented the constituency of Farrukhabad in UP between 1991-1996 and had thereafter lost two successive elections. At the time, few expected his elevation to the post of UPCC President, an office as perilous as it is prestigious, wrought with chronic factionalism, impossible procedures and a multitude of problems whose cure had not been attempted since 1989. In early June he was summoned to 10 Janpath where Mrs. Gandhi informed him that he was to go to Uttar Pradesh, there was little else said except that he was not to tell anyone until the announcement was made by her formally a few days later. Khurshid may have suspected the decision to alter since no announcement was being made immediately, nonetheless he stayed silent. That evening Rajesh Pilot who was himself a leading contender for the office invited Khurshid home in the evening to discuss the emerging scenario. Pilot was confident of his own chances and began by telling Khurshid that he (Khurshid) was out of the race. He sounded him out instead on the only apparently pragmatic course of action now. "You support me," said Pilot, unaware of the proceedings of the day. He set out his wares and narrated at length his plans for the UPCC and for the renewal of the Congress in the state. To his credit, Khurshid kept a straight face. Here was Rajesh Pilot, a senior leader of the party, popular, with a strong base and network of contacts, a friend in fact, as far as political relationships can be classified under that term. However, Pilot had missed out, yet again. He was working on assumptions, from his own incubated position, through the favourable responses of those around him and from a natural inclination to believe that he was indispensable to the cause of a Congress renewal. Pilot faltered for the second time in two years. The leadership election had snatched away the chance in 1996 and Kesri had emerged the winner. This time, although there was no competition involved, Pilot was to discover that his scansion had gripped the wrong resonance emanating from the leadership. By the time Khurshid's selection was announced on June 6th Pilot would have forgotten whatever he had said. It was not in his nature to show embarrassment. He would endorse Khurshid's candidature and like Jitendra Prasad would lie low for a time.

In the scorching heat of the summer, Salman Khurshid's arrival in Lucknow and at the UPCC headquarters itself trumpeted, at least on the face of it, a change in the state of the UP Congress. Khurshid was shrewd enough to realise that the enthusiasm which greeted him did not necessarily translate into support. His own brief outlined the enormity of the task ahead and he was acutely aware of the challenges. He still had a lot to prove and, most importantly, to fulfill in substance the aims with which Sonia Gandhi had sent him to UP. It was a confident move, for the first time in twenty years a Muslim had been put in charge of affairs in UP by the Congress leadership. It was apparent to everyone that Khurshid's image did not conform to the Congress culture in UP. He, as a lecturer from Oxford and Supreme Court lawyer, had floated comfortably among the *corps diplomatique* in Geneva and New York as External Affairs Minister. The milieu he now found himself in demanded almost a reversal of roles. The Congress in UP in turn had got a leader it had not bargained for. To the leaders and power brokers of Lucknow and the rest of the state, a man who at first seemed a pushover would eventually pose the greatest obstacle to their ambitions.

The Emergence of Digvijay Singh

Very few people are aware that when Digvijay Singh was sworn in as the Chief Minister of Madhya Pradesh in 1993 he had already completed 25 years in public life. Digvijay Singh began his political career as the Chairman of the Raghogarh Municipal Corporation at the age of 22 in 1969. Despite the anti-Congress wave of 1977, this scion of the Raghogarh royal family won his election to the Madhya Pradesh assembly from the Raghogarh seat and in 1980 was elevated to the Arjun Singh Ministry. In contemporary politics and particularly within the Congress Party Diggy Raja, as he is popularly known, has come to represent the epitome of a regional chieftain, with experience of government and a solid regional support of his own. More importantly he enjoys the confidence of both his peers within the Congress as well as the admiration of his opposition rivals[1]. It is difficult to ascertain what goes on in his mind, behind the charming demeanour, the affable and jocular style and the cheerfulness which appear to be permanent features of his character.

Singh became the President of the Madhya Pradesh Congress Committee in 1991 and Chief Minister of the state after victory in the elections which followed the dismissal of the BJP government in 1993. Five years of his government produced the all too familiar chant for his removal as the Congress faced up to its prospects in 1998. His political assailants were many at this time as rivals and mentors alike figured that they had a chance to engineer his removal before these crucial elections, the first since Sonia Gandhi's ascent to leadership. If Uttar Pradesh is considered to be the most fractious and politically volatile of all states then Madhya Pradesh must come a close second. Ranged against Digvijay Singh was a host of party heavyweights. Among them the Shukla brothers, infamous but toothless, though still capable of stinging him, his former mentor and the paterfamilias (almost) of the Congress Party, Arjun Singh himself. A more docile but tremendously powerful adversary was of course Madhavrao Scindia, the eight-time MP and former Maharaja of Gwalior. Their reasons given were fewer but familiar. He was held responsible for the party's far from satisfactory showing in the 1998 general elections when the Congress won only 10 of the 40 Lok Sabha seats in MP, this in Assembly terms translated into a paltry 89 seats in a house of 320. Equally importantly, party grandees like Arjun Singh had suffered their second election defeat in a row. The Committee, headed by AICC General

---

1.   This condition has remained largely unmitigated despite the defeat of the Congress Party in Madhya Pradesh in the 2003 Assembly elections.

Secretary Rajesh Pilot, which was looking into the causes of the debacle suggested a "revamp of the state unit at both the organisational and legislative levels." Not much could have changed, they argued, since March and November. Digvijay Singh was portrayed as "unfeasible" for leading the party in another election. Nonetheless no other name even gained circulation. Not even when speculations about his removal were at their pinnacle and the suspense was slowly turning into disillusionment among the party ranks back in MP did anyone venture to suggest an alternative. With the pressure slowly mounting against him and the enormity of the task ahead of him, Digvijay Singh flew into New Delhi to resolve the uncertainties himself in May. Six months still remained until the elections, enough time for a suitable successor to carve out support among the electorate and goodwill within the state unit. One can imagine the normally cheerful and genial Diggy Raja plunged in melancholic gloom as his aircraft descended into Delhi. If that was the case, he didn't let it show. Rather, in accordance with his regular style, the Chief Minister incumbent arranged appointments for dinners with his friends as well as a meeting with the Congress President herself.

Sonia Gandhi's attitude to decision-making is a mild departure from the practice of her mother-in-law which generally produced purely instinctive and relatively quick decisions and responses. However, Indira Gandhi had the advantage of a political career which spanned four decades, and the experience of governance.

The present Congress chief, on the other hand, is perhaps more decisive, in that her decisions are ones in which consensus and a plurality of opinion are the operative themes. A judgement may take long in coming, nonetheless it is the result of careful consultations, widely taken soundings and often, for those whose fate is being decided upon, a browbeating patience is required. Once taken it is irrevocable. And so it proved to be for Digvijay Singh in this period too. At a dinner hosted by Ahmad Patel, at the time Political Secretary to the Congress President, the Chief Minister was unnerved enough to insist that the decision on who was to lead the party in the polls be taken immediately either way. Later at his meeting with Sonia Gandhi, he was frank and confident enough to declare with equipoise that if the polls did not go satisfactorily for the party he would not hold any office for the next ten years. His arguments were based on statistics and a personal instinct which must have prompted him to plead his case with such overwhelming certainty.

Whether it was the absence of an alternative or his solid demeanour and record or Sonia Gandhi's instincts which told her that Digvijay Singh was the man to lead the party in MP is arguable. The last case is possibly the most convincing for there were almost as many voices ranged against Singh as there were friends willing to defend him. Sonia Gandhi reached her decision at the end of the week. Despite the long consultations with senior party functionaries and leaders the conclusion was purely her individual choice. On May 7, Kamal Nath, the MP from Chindwara was summoned by her to inform Digvijay Singh that he would indeed be leading the party at the polls. Kamal Nath did so the very next day. Singh had returned to Bhopal and was due back in Delhi on May 8th to consult with the Congress President on his plans for a pre-election cabinet reshuffle. Naturally his supporters were delighted but the Chief Minister will have known all too well that to win a second term was an unenviable and, to many, an insurmountable task. He could not afford to lose. If his interviews of the time are anything to go by it is clear that he was aware of this. To N.K. Singh of *India Today* he said: "The high command has put the ball in my court now. That means the buck stops here." For Sonia Gandhi personally the decision to retain Singh as the party leader in MP against every conceivable opinion displays a keen understanding of personalities in her party. Singh owed his regeneration to her.

On November 29 the results of the elections began trickling in. Of the three states in the Hindi heartland, a victory was widely expected in Delhi and Rajasthan. The prospects for Madhya Pradesh seemed irreversibly dismal and exit polls pontificated a return of the BJP to power. The final results overturned this depressed chorus of gloom into a crescendo of jubilation as seat after seat, widely predicted to be marginal and, therefore, lost, fell into Congress hands or was retained. By early morning the following day it was clear that the party had crossed the required majority winning 172 of the 320 seats. For the Congress, Madhya Pradesh had been saved from the "fascist" threat. For Digvijay Singh, however, the victory was even more profound. If one wishes to understand the meaning of the word "resurrection" it could be found in Digvijay Singh's situation at that moment. Henceforth his would be the example which would be cited to demonstrate political success. Long emerging trends of study on anti-incumbency models, opinion polls and exit polls, and the vanity of various think-tanks were demolished overnight by this victory.

For Sonia Gandhi it immediately established a control and legitimacy which was urgently required. Moreover, the spirit of Panchmari had been delivered credence. Two months ago, Sonia Gandhi had declared from this very soil:

> I can now see a new discipline and goal in our method of working. A beginning has been made to induct a new work-culture in the AICC and the Pradesh Congress Committees. This will go on.

The example of Madhya Pradesh and its leader proved this commitment to be true. The party had much to be thankful for. A man had emerged when the situation required him. Much maligned at first, then suspected, and finally, in the last degree against which all else is judged, he came to be revered by delivering success when it was least expected and most required.

A Winter of Content

The role of the opposition never suited the Congress Party. To begin with, the first prolonged spell away from the Treasury Benches, which began in 1996, seemed to have left the Congress Party both surprised and unrepentant. The surprise stemmed from an inability to reengineer a way back to power. For party leaders it became difficult to believe that they were no longer in power. The vagaries of opposition politics which require conciliation with figureheads of the rest of the opposition forces and an ability to coordinate strategies against the government in collusion with them, was not a state of affairs Congressmen were used to. The surprise was almost superficial because at first many Congressmen believed themselves to be umbilical to the Deve Gowda government. It was, after all, on the basis of the outside support extended to him by the Congress that Gowda had formed his government. However, as it became increasingly apparent to them that outside support did not mean partnership in government, Congressmen were displeased and the role of auxiliary turned to that of an *enfant terrible*. Proselytes to the cause of opposition that they were, the Congress proved even more incapable of reconciling that to their role as "supporters" to Gowda's minority government. There seemed only one way out of this impasse. Unable to make friends, after all the principal oppostion was the BJP, and incapable of providing sustenance to the United Front, many of whose constituents were old "socialist" foes, the Congress decided that an aggressive approach to politics was required. While they supported the government in Parliament Congress MPs were viewed as poseurs, when they were garrulous towards government policy, they were called puerile. In time, Gowda was deposed, a more acceptable, former Congressman, Gujral was appointed Prime Minister. Soon the pretended *bonhomie* with him was exposed too and, finally, the Congress settled for another election in early 1998 after the party withdrew support to the United Front. Their maudlin justifications notwithstanding, this flatulent behaviour appeared to invite a condign punishment as Congressmen traipsed towards another general election. Defeat also seemed inevitable but for the intervention of Sonia Gandhi. For the Congress a terrible situation was salvaged. It was defeated again but returned with a respectable 142 members to parliament. Having led its campaign, Sonia Gandhi became the party's leader and this change at the top appeared to be a satisfactory conclusion to the party's travails which began even while it was in government in the early 1990s.

By the winter of 1998, Sonia Gandhi had settled in well as the leader of the Congress Party. The year began on a note of defeat in January and Atal Behari Vajpayee assumed power as the leader of the BJP-led coalition. Sonia Gandhi became Congress President in March and immediately began a tenacious campaign to show the Congress as a party which was reforming under her leadership. The Panchmari conclave supported this transformation and the election victories in Delhi, Rajasthan and Madhya Pradesh defined it. The constituion of high powered committees like the Sangma Task Force provided for a visible reformation. Throughout the rest of the country, party workers and leaders were comforted by the new leadership, in itself a symbol for change and ultimately a ticket to power at the centre. Factionalism and the politics of factional intrigues seemed to have slowed down though not completely melted away. Most importantly the BJP-led government at the centre appeared unable to manage itself and everyday issues. A fractious coalition, spiralling prices of basic commodities, a general feeling of anti-incumbency, successive defeats in assembly and sultry by-elections all contributed to this growing disenchantment for Vajpayee. The nuclear tests in June, far from mushrooming into a cloud of popularity for Vajpayee, vapourised quickly and variously, with slight suggestions of bolstering his party's reputation. In an opinion poll conducted by ORG-MARG for *India Today* which was released in December, it appeared that the Congress had ended the year on an optimistic note. Of the respondents, 31 per cent preferred Sonia Gandhi as Prime Minster to Atal Behari's 27 per cent. Projections for electoral competition suggested the Congress and its allies would win between 295 and 305 seats, while the BJP and its wagon would be left at a maximum of 135. While most politicians and observers take opinion polls with several pinches of salt and discount their measures, the effect of a favourable opinion poll is instantly energetic. Low morale is transformed into buoyancy, pessimism is offended against and facts and figures are quoted and summarised at length to further justify optimism. This is what occurred in the winter of that year. While Delhi draped itself in the warmth of shawls, the home fires burned in the villages and around them party workers recalled the memories of halcyon days. The high-command, that repository of uncertainty and friction, appeared satisfied and settled with its new leader. Party workers in the districts, right down to the block-level, were no longer feverish with anxiety but aggressive in posture and speech. The last issue of *India Today* that year concluded:

> For the dejected band of Congressmen who saw in the Nehru-Gandhi name the only hope of restoring its status as an umbrella national party, the installation of Rajiv Gandhi's widow as the undisputed leader is a gamble that seems to have paid off. The opinion poll indicates there could be a staggering 15 per cent national swing to the Congress and against the BJP-led coalition in the event of a snap poll.

While the enthusiasm was justified, the mood upbeat and capability enhanced, the party over-developed its political testosterone. Sonia Gandhi was determined to finish the tasks of organisational reform before any attempt was made at government formation. Slowly it became apparent that the mood of the party invited immediate, not patient, movement towards installing a Congress government. The arrogance of elation persevered into the new year and party leaders began talking of a comeback. Sonia Gandhi was not so sure.

Circling the funeral pyre of her husband. May 1991. For the next five years she would withdraw into her self while the Congress party played politics over her silence. (Photo: T. Narayan / Outlook)

Alone in a crowd. Facing an uncertain future in her early days as Congress President. Surrounded by a dour Sitaram Kesri, a pensive Ghulam Nabi Azad and an impenetrable Narasimha Rao. (Photo: T. Narayan/Outlook)

'Baptism with Fire'. In her first days as Congress President Sonia Gandhi was ranged against the veteran line up of the NDA leadership. (Photo : Sunil Malhotra)

At her first CPP meeting in 1998 with Sharad Pawar. A year later he would desert her and vertically split the Congress party. (Photo : T. Narayan / Outlook)

Filing her nomination for the Lok Sabha from Amethi in 1999.
(Photo: Gauri Gill / Outlook).

The Home Minister and Deputy Prime Minister L K Advani stated that "Sonia Gandhi went by the book" to attain citizenship of India. At a Rashtrapati Bhawan function 2001. (Photo : Sunil Malhotra).

In an uncharacteristic exchange with former Prime Minister Atal Behari Vajpayee. The Prime Minister and his Leader of Opposition shared a strained relationship. (Photo : Jitendra Gupta / Outlook).

Sonia Gandhi took to the streets protesting against the Gujarat riots. Seen here sitting on *Dharna* outside Parliament House 2002. (Photo : Sunil Malhotra).

"Stooping to conquer" explaining tactics to a   political   activist as former Prime Minister V P Singh looks on. (Photo : Sunil Malhotra)

Taking Congress to India. Sonia Gandhi almost single handedly galvanized public support for her party during the Lok Sabha election of 2004. (Photo : Sunil Malhotra).

Election night May 2004. Sonia Gandhi had already made up her mind about staying away from the Premiership. Seen here in deliberations with Pranab Mukherjee and Dr. Manmohan Singh. (Photo: Sunil Malhotra).

With the Prime Minister elect Dr. Manmohan Singh at Rashtrapati Bhawan May 2004. (Photo : Sunil Malhotra).

When the world comes calling with US Secretary of State
Colin Powell at her 10 Janpath. residence. (Photo : Sunil
Malhotra).

In respect and gratitude. Members of the Union Cabinet line up. The Congress Party returned
to power at the Centre after an eight year interlude. (Photo : Sunil Malhotra).

Keeping her smile in the midst of the strain. A relaxing moment as Chairperson of the UPA Co-ordination Committee. (Photo : T Narayan / Outlook).

A Crisis of Leadership

For Want of a Vote the Government is Lost - The Case of Mr. Pawar –

Engineering a Coup – Resignation – The Rebels are Tarred – Restoration

For Want of a Vote the Government is Lost

While the Congress Party found recourse in affecting its own revival, Atal Behari Vajpayee's NDA government found itself in a sombre session of trying to simply survive successfully. Even before the November elections which had snatched away Rajasthan, Mizoram, Delhi and Madhya Pradesh from its rule, the NDA had been feeling hemmed in and heckled from all sides, even from within.

In the late autumn, friendly scribes, such as that arch-beacon of all things saffron, Swapan Dasgupta called the government a 'flop show' and wrote in his column:

> Atal Behari Vajpayee shouldn't suffer from delusions of grandeur. Behind the genuine respect he commands for his long years of public service lurks an intense disappointment. Today that disappointment is fast turning into disgust, anger and antipathy. The real tragedy is not that hope has turned into despondency, but that a cocooned prime minister and cocooned government are not even aware of it.[1]

With the nuclear tests in the summer of 1998, Vajpayee had fired off a big gambit, involving the subcontinent in tension and complicating India's responsibilities within the theatres of international diplomacy. Early into 1999, the Defence Minister George Fernandes sacked the Naval Chief of Staff, Admiral Vishnu Bhagwat. This created considerable controversy, as the opposition parties readily embraced him as a fallen

---

1. *India Today*, October 19, 1998.

hero. The situation was not dissimilar in the Finance Ministry where the sacked adviser Mohan Guruswamy made some strong allegations against the government. With two of its principal ministries embroiled in internal haemorrhages and an arraigning opposition that repeatedly stalled proceedings within Parliament, Atal Behari Vajpayee himself appeared addled and intemperate. It came as no surprise that he found comfort in the company and dialogue of his neighbouring and much troubled counterpart Nawaz Sharif, the Prime Minister of Pakistan. The success, as it appeared at the time, of the Lahore visit, the confidence-building measures between the two countries and the frequent interaction of people across the border acted as an anti-depressant to combat the pains of running what was turning out to be an impossible government.

The Opposition, meanwhile, was coming together, albeit with some difficulty. In the Lok Sabha election of 1998 Saifuddin Chowdhary a Communist leader and a candidate of the CPI (M), urged the voters of his West Bengal constituency to vote for Congress if they were unsupportive of his party, advising them in turn not to waste their vote on the BJP. At the same time it was the cadre of the CPI (M) who filled up the grounds for Sonia Gandhi's Calcutta rally in late February. This was reciprocated by Sonia Gandhi herself. Notice the welcome she extended to Jyoti Basu, the invincible West Bengal Chief Minister, to speak at the 30th Jawaharlal Nehru Memorial lecture:

> It is our privilege today to have one of our country's senior most public figures, one who had personally known Jawaharlal Nehru, as our honoured speaker. Chief Minister of West Bengal for a record of 21 years, he has through his dedication and drive, won the esteem of his people and of the whole country......Whatever our political differences with Shri Basu, we are sure that the good of India is his foremost concern.[2]

The tone was unmistakably conciliatory, ingratiating. As the Left parties and Congress moved closer, aided by Sonia Gandhi's objectivity,

---

2.   Welcome address at the 30th Jawaharlal Nehru Memorial Lecture. October 13, 1998.

others began to be drawn in. The most serious threat to this still nascent exercise appeared in the form of the Bihar crisis, in February 1999. The Central Government had dismissed Laloo Prasad Yadav's RJD regime in Bihar led by his wife, Chief Minister Rabri Devi. The dismissal had come in the wake of the massacre of 12 Dalits in Jehanabad District. Before touring the affected area on February 13th, Sonia Gandhi had demanded the dismissal of the government stating that 'a government that cannot prevent the massacre of Dalits forfeits its moral authority to govern.' This was modulated two days later after taking soundings into an observation that, 'Central rule is no substitute for good governance.' It was the CWC meeting of February 22nd, which finally called for support to Laloo Prasad Yadav. The political thinking behind this support was three fold; first, Sonia Gandhi knew she had to keep as wide a base of national allies as possible, second, the Congress Party needed Laloo in Bihar and finally, against which all else was to be judged, the Congress Party desired to test the waters on the floor of the Lok Sabha by pushing the NDA government into a corner. The Lok Sabha ratified the imposition of President's Rule in Bihar on February 26th. What was important, however, was the size of the majority. The government managed to win a whipped vote by no more than 29 votes, a far from comfortable majority. The Upper House was sure to block it and all that Laloo had to do was wait for his reinstatement.

The entire Bihar calculus tested Sonia Gandhi. She had had to rely on advice and consensus to a very large degree. Delegation and external inputs were the *modus operandi* of the entire operation. While Sushil Kumar Shinde and Arjun Singh represented the view and meditations of the Congress Party, Harkishan Singh Surjeet, the ailing Communist leader directed movements from his hospital bed at the Institute of Medical Sciences. Laloo himself consulted variously with Congress leaders. There was little to suggest instinctive *realpolitik* on her part. A 'bunker syndrome' had engulfed the Congress leadership which remained oblivous to movements outside itself. There was a perception, in the eyes of party-men themselves of a leadership that could only function by guidance.

While Sonia Gandhi had so far proved useful and efficient in matters of party organisation, she appeared too fastidious even incapable of handling inter-party relationships. It was at this stage that some of her own colleagues decided to judge her capabilities based upon these initial observations. In effect, she was 'under watch' from some within her own party.

Subsequently, Atal Behari Vajpayee began to breathe more easily. Pakistan and the promises of peace were still on track. Pushed to the corner, he had managed to survive over the Bihar ratification. His ministers finally appeared to be defending themselves robustly against a flagging opposition. All seemed to be going as well as an Indian government could expect until members of that very government erupted in revolt. This revolt was fatal because it came from within.

In the 1996 Assembly elections in Tamil Nadu, Chief Minister Dr. J Jayalalitha and her party the AIADMK lost power in a landslide verdict. Her *bete noire*, Dr. K Karunanidhi, the venerable, mysterious and dramatically attired leader of the DMK, assumed power and ordered a prompt and punishing inquiry against the former Chief Minister, in the course of which she had to endure a term in prison. It was around the time of Sonia Gandhi's decision to actively join Congress that Jayalalitha cast her fortunes with those of Vajpayee and his BJP coalition. Fortune proved favourable and with her 18 MPs she became a member of Vajpayee's second government. The *bonhomie* did not last long. Incessant clamouring which finally culminated in a written demand for more cabinet berths and portfolios, the placement of 25 bureaucratic appointees of her choice and the induction of Subramaniam Swamy as a cabinet minister, provoked misgivings, if not an outright rejection by other members of the coalition. Kumaramangalam, one of the BJP's 'bright boys' and trouble shooters could not be silent any more and declared that Jayalalitha lacked credibility. From then on, it was a downward spiral. By early April, she had withdrawn her two cabinet ministers from the Vajpayee government and opted out of its Coordination Committee. In such a vacuum she was isolated.

It was now that Subramaniam Swamy, a self-styled 'one man demolition squad', former minister and man of letters, took it upon himself to bring together an alternative government. Contemporary accounts have attributed far too much credibility and credit to this rather eccentric and insubstantial figure, who subsequently became little more than a bumptious political chiropractor. Circumstances were already fast moving towards a realignment of forces without his intervention though he did provoke their speed. In Tamil Nadu itself, Jayalalitha was isolated. She had self-indulgently broken her alliance with Vaiko's MDMK. The two other regional outfits, the PMK and Vazhapadi Ramamurthy's TRC were already beyond her. The traditional and grievously personal enmity between her and the DMK meant that she needed a bridge to the Congress Party. Swamy provided that bridge. Happily for Jayalalitha the mood within certain ranks of the Congress leadership was in favour of a bid for power. It was this substantial caucus, which Swamy set to work upon. He persuaded Jyoti Basu to in turn sound out Sonia Gandhi about coming together against the BJP. His 'tea-party' in Delhi, where Jayalalitha met Sonia Gandhi, proved to be the match that finally set alight the bonfire of the Vajpayee-led government. From then on messages travelled fast between Congress and their potential allies. Harkishen Singh Surjeet became so excited with the idea that he cautioned inquisitive Congressmen wondering about an alternative government saying, 'the question of government formation will unnecessarily bog us down. First let us ensure their defeat.' Unfortunately for the Congress, not only did the Party take him at his word, but Surjeet assumed the mantle of the Congress Party representative to other opposition leaders and their supporters. The idea to topple Vajpayee may have been a good one but its method was fundamentally flawed. At first Sonia Gandhi maintained, 'we are not going to jump to anything, we are watching the situation and will act when necessary.' In this case the Party would have been better advised to follow P. Chidambaram who coolly observed, 'One can only dine with the devil with a long spoon, but there is no spoon long enough to dine with Jayalalitha.'[3] Sonia Gandhi continued to take soundings and circulated ideas variously and perhaps far too credulously. On April 14, 1999, Jayalalitha withdrew her support to the Vajpayee led government. A few days earlier, L.K. Advani had himself stated that though he was optimistic about survival, he could not be entirely confident. By the time the President had asked Vajpayee to call a vote of confidence, what had begun as an adventitious tantrum of a regional party chieftain appeared to be a full-scale national crisis. For all its resources, its assignations and promises, its back-breaking complaisance and at times fantastic mechanisms to 'adjust' individual MPs and smaller regional parties, the Vajpayee-led government lost the vote of confidence, by a single vote.

Contrary to Harkishen Singh Surjeet's acclamations, it was now that politics as a whole got bogged down. It was not until the 21st, a full four days after the defeat of the Vajpayee government in the Lok Sabha that Sonia Gandhi met the President of India to stake a claim on the formation of a government. Looking confident and radiating strength she declared the support of 272 MPs to her Party. Parliament passed the Budget the next day without a discussion, and the CPI, CPI (M), RJD and the AIADMK sent the President their letters of support for a Congress-led government. There was little to worry about. Harkishen Singh Surjeet was left to negotiate and tie up loose ends with the disparate regional outfits who had voted against the government and it was expected were therefore automatically in support of Congress. Meanwhile, Arjun Singh and M.L. Fotedar became the eyes and ears of the Congress leadership, certainly the only individuals with power to negotiate on behalf of Sonia Gandhi. She busied herself in interactions with political elders such as Chandra Shekhar, I.K. Gujral and Jyoti Basu. Among the entire opposition turned government hopefuls, only Mulayam Singh Yadav, sometime wrestler and, at the time, a former Chief Minister of Uttar Pradesh remained uncommitted. With 20 MPs he held a crucial bolus of support. Sonia Gandhi realised this early on and he was the first leader she conferred with after the Lok Sabha vote. On the 20th, she had spent no less than 45 minutes with Mulayam Singh Yadav at 10 Janpath.

Competing with her attention were the pleas of the UP Congress which spoke of strong but valid reservations about accommodating Mulayam. Nonetheless, Mulayam returned from the meeting with dramatic overtones saying, 'we have never shied away from sacrificing in the battle against communalism.' It was mystifying, for barely 24 hours later, he had denounced her, 'foreigner' and the very next day wrote to the President saying he would not support any Congress-led formation. Not unknown to Sonia Gandhi, Mulayam had his own supporters within the Congress Party. On April 23, Sonia Gandhi had still only mustered the support of 233 MPs, 39 short of the required 272. Mulayam Singh's 20 MPs mattered gravely; he knew that only too well. A new possibility now emerged; the installation of Jyoti Basu as the Prime Minister. This aberrant suggestion, the brainchild of Mulayam Singh and other 'socialist' groups, was designed to force the Congress hand to support a new formation from the outside. Jyoti Basu himself did not publicly circulate the idea, however, and it was left to the General Secretary of the Samajwadi Party, Amar Singh, to crow this around, which he did most visibly, though unconvincingly. He took the line that his party's decision not to support a Congress-led government was 'not irrevocable'. It was the selection of the leader which apparently proved the stumbling block for the crude and fluctuating mindset of the Samajwadi leadership. Much to the chagrin of the 'Third Front', an informal meeting of the CWC unanimously rejected the idea. Sonia Gandhi met the President for the last time in this matter and conveyed her party's inability to support the CPI (M) offer. The next day, having exhausted all options, President Narayanan asked the 'interim cabinet' to draft a resolution recommending the dissolution of the Lok Sabha. A third election in three years is what India got because its politics lay crushed between the adventurous aggro of an impatient leader who was not satisfied with what she had and the personal pique of an ambitious regionalist who could not wait to get more.

Addressing a meeting of her PCC and CLP leaders, she did little to hide her own anger:

> If an alternative minority Congress government did not come about, much to the disappointment of the Left and the Third Front, as also the country at large, the blame lies squarely at the door of a small, regional party, which placed its narrow interests above the larger interest of the secular future of the country.

Until that time, her strongest vocabulary had always been directed at the BJP and its right-wing brotherhood. The tenor of her utterance, the language and the intention of her speech as a whole revealed what she felt. Sonia Gandhi is not a demagogue and her speeches are remembered more for their measured and nurtured ideas, this one was quite different. Linking the BJP with Mulayam Singh Yadav, she declared:

> We were not prepared to succumb to political blackmail. Bending at the knee is a BJP habit. It is entirely appropriate that the Samajwadi Party has found its destiny in the arms of the communal forces of this country. The clandestine contacts between leaders of the Samajwadi Party and the BJP have ruthlessly revealed the nexus between them, a nexus which has led to the present situation. These nefarious links, now exposed, must be rejected through the ballot box.

Having relied so overwhelmingly on ultra-party individuals and having delegated leadership roles with such alacrity to those around her, Sonia Gandhi had intended to run politics as she was running her organisation. This reliance on a motley collection of "hollow" men had been the causative factor in the failure to achieve power. Not once had she declared her own intentions about leadership, though the Congress Party had clearly said she would be the leader of any formation, yet these were not her words. Her words, resonant of rationality, were lost in those heady and unreal days. 'It is not the business of the Opposition', she said, 'to ensure the survival of a government that has lost its majority.'[4]

---

4.   Meeting of the PCC Presidents and CLP Leaders. May 6, 1999.

April 1999 had perhaps been the toughest month yet of her year-long stint in politics. It set the tone for the difficulties that lay just round the corner.

The Case of Mr. Pawar

What symbolises strength in politics and how does this benefit the power of an individual within a larger political group and within the polity itself? Perhaps charisma constitutes inherent confidence which in turn supplies the political spirit with the extension of support and admiration of peers and contemporaries. Rajesh Pilot possessed this in abundance. The success of a leader is certainly dependent on electoral victory, not merely his own but that of the group he is leading, especially at a juncture where his prerogative is challenged. Digvijay Singh exemplified this in 1998. And finally, for a leader in the Indian political environment, national recognition, not merely the physical recognition of what he looks like but an empathy for his ideas and a level of mass appeal is necessary for even an illusion of success. This was made available to Madhavrao Scindia through his long innings at the political wicket.

The case of Mr. Sharad Pawar is a complete contrast to the three examples above. His power defines some other aspects which are evidently required to radiate strength. For Sharad Pawar has always exuded this while he was on the political stage performing different acts at different intervals of his dramatic career. That he commanded a strong regional base is an unchallengeable fact. At any given time since he rose to prominence, Pawar was able to galvanise a chunk of the legislators of the Maharashtra assembly around himself. However, here the illusion of his power ends. It is another matter that a favourable press added weight to his force and portrayed a perception of unassailability. A chronological reading of his career highlights certain shortcomings of judgement at moments of crucial importance. Such a reading also calls the bluff of pretences to unchallenged power and its exercise. It is important therefore, to study the biographical detail of Sharad Pawar's record at length.

This story began on a promising note in 1978 when as a young man of thirty-three, Sharad Pawar weaned away legislators of the Vasantdada Patil-led Congress government to form his own Progressive Democratic Front (PDF). While this made him the youngest Chief Minister of Maharashtra, it is important to note that this was a government made up of defectors, not one whose credibility had been guaranteed through elections. Barely in his second year and things didn't look quite so smooth for Pawar. In 1980 the Congress (I) swept the country and Maharashtra was no exception. In an assembly of 288 members the Congress won 186 seats with Pawar's PDF managing barely 90. While that was the result of the assembly elections the PDF fared worse in the 1980 Lok Sabha polls winning only 1 of the 48 seats, the sole survivor being Y.B. Chavan himself. Pawar sufferred a personal blow losing his Baramati bastion. Five years of Congress rule was bound to generate some element of an anti-incumbency factor. Perhaps sensing this disquiet and disillusionment with the Congress among people and politicians alike, Pawar courted the rest of the opposition in Maharashtra and soon succeeded in projecting himself as the fount of the anti-Congress front in the state. For the Congress Party, the elections appeared to be a test of sorts. In its five years of power between 1980 and 1985 the party had appointed and replaced five Chief Ministers and the state of its organisation resembled a parody. Babasaheb Bhosale followed the removal of A.R. Antulay in 1982 and in turn was succeeded by Vasantdada Patil who in turn was replaced by Shivajirao Patil, the party finally settled on S.B. Chavan to lead it in the election. Despite the consequent confusion and chaos, Pawar in his avatar as the leader of the opposition was unsuccessful again, the combined opposition barely managing to cross 50 seats while the Congress (I) won 160 of the 288. More was expected when the opportunity for success was available to him. This then remains the electoral record of the Maratha strongman who was now forced to open parlays with the Congress leadership to engineer a return, which he negotiated in 1986. However, while that is a record of his politics outside the Congress, his period within it does not signify any change to this now familiar litany of defeat. He was twice

Chief Minister of Maharashtra after his return to the Congress fold. In 1990 the party lost its long held majority in the elections and had to split the Shiv Sena to be able to form the government. Sudhakar Rao Naik took over as Chief Minister while Pawar returned to New Delhi to bide his time. In 1992 he returned to Bombay after the infamous post-Babri riots, as insufficient energy on the governmentt's behalf to contain them prompted Naik's removal. Then, in 1993, an unprecedented event occurred; the Congress under Pawar, blundered to its biggest electoral defeat and was reduced to 80 seats. It was the first time that a non-Congress government took power in Maharashtra as the Shiv-Sena BJP alliance, riding the crescendo of the 1992 riots and gaining from the subsequent polarisation of votes, emerged victorious.

It was at this stage, after the Sena-BJP alliance had staked its claim over Maharashtra, that Pawar decided to focus solely on his role at the centre, devoting more time in New Delhi than in Bombay. The reputation he cultivated in New Delhi, however, was one of a man of power, without whom the politics of Maharashtra did not function. Even rivals were mildly apprehensive of challenging him since he was able to portray a hold over both events and people, failure being dubbed as the result of his own deliberate creations. Evidently, this was not ill founded in every respect, after all his contribution to the Congress war chests, his rapport with the press, contacts in industry and his influence in vast tracts of the Marathwada region, particularly the sugarcane belt of the west, won him considerable influence. Every friction that occurred in the high command prompted observer and commentator alike to interpret its consequences through what it meant for Sharad Pawar politically. Rao managed him particularly well, placing under him the large and important Ministry of Defence. In return, Rao bargained for his support within the CWC and the AICC whenever trouble arose from the "northern crowd" of Messrs Arjun Singh, N.D. Tiwari, Rajesh Pilot and others. Similarly, other possible challengers to Rao who wielded some influence in Maharashtra, like Madhavrao Scindia, were balanced by the image of Pawar's own towering stature in the state. As the Minister of the Union for Defence, one of his most important achievements was the negotiations with Russia for the sale of military hardware, including the purchase of the fleet of Sukhoi SU-30 fighter jets. Alternatively, his first speech for the Defence Ministry in parliament is best left forgotten. In party political terms there was plenty of superficial activity for him but it was only after Rao had been effectively cornered by Sitaram Kesri and his acolytes that Pawar came to be viewed as a possible contender for the post of party President. While the tussle was simmering, Pawar would run with the hares and hunt with the hounds and effectively camouflage this with a neutrality that appeared to bear no grudges. His own eyes were firmly focused on the 1997 leadership election when he threw his hat into the ring along with Rajesh Pilot and A.R. Antulay, another former Maharashtra Chief Minister, against Kesri. Of the twenty CWC members, Pawar could gather only three to support his candidature. On the eve of the election, he briefed a journalist saying, "If the elections are held in a free and fair atmosphere, I am sure to win the election with a huge margin as the Pradesh Congress Committee delegates want change in the party leadership." However, he was careful to feather his fall too and to make preparations in case, as was becoming fast apparent, he didn't win. He added, "Gone are the days, when the party was controlled by towering personalities like Jawaharlal Nehru, Indira Gandhi and Rajiv Gandhi, who were in a position to influence the rank and file of the party. Today in the absence of such leaders in the party, the only alternative is to develop collective leadership." The results of the leadership election were more one sided than anyone expected. Kesri was widely believed to have won long before the results were announced. The enormity of his victory only strengthened him. Pawar had only managed 882 of the 7557 votes polled. A far from satisfactory figure for the strongman. Thereafter, Kesri assumed charge of the Congress Parliamentary Party (CPP) as well, while Sharad Pawar had to content himself with the post of leader of the Congress in the Lok Sabha.

Engineering a Coup

Sonia Gandhi's arrival as leader of the Congress signalled the beginning of an unsettled period for Sharad Pawar. He may have delivered the bulk of Maharashtra to the Congress in the 1998 general election but whether that was due to his personal efforts or the emergence of Sonia Gandhi as Congress leader has not been decided. After all, Maharashtra did reject the Congress in 1996. Nevertheless in view of this it was widely expected that he would be made leader of the CPP too. The post of CPP leader is a vital one in opposition. While in government the Prime Minister would assume this charge, in opposition the CPP leader is a counterweight to the Congress President. Rao had very shrewdly kept both, in contemplation of being outnumbered in the AICC. Kesri too took over to extend his control over the Congress legislators, not being one himself. For Pawar it always remained elusive and with Sonia Gandhi's unanimous nomination to the post he would naturally have been disappointed. Nonetheless, he continued to be the leader of the Congress on the floor of the Lok Sabha. Perhaps this is the genesis of his conflict with Sonia Gandhi and the majority of the Congress as a result. On the other hand, some trace it to an even earlier period, immediately after the 1998 general election when he believed the Congress was capable of forming a coalition government and held consultations with various Left Front and Third Front party leaders. Sonia Gandhi, on the contrary, abhorred the idea of a khichri coalition and informed the President that the party did not possess the requisite numbers. She had desired change and reform and sought to spend time reconstructing the party. Presciently she did not view the results of the 1998 elections as a mandate for the Congress to govern. It was almost exactly a year between Sonia Gandhi's formal nomination as Party President in March 1998 and the fall of the Vajpayee government in 1999. In between, elections to state assemblies had been won, organisational changes were both being contemplated and implemented, the Congress had almost rediscovered itself at Panchmari. In this period, Pawar had not posed as a challenger to Sonia Gandhi. His grievances were aired in private circles and sometimes perhaps the press caught a whiff of what might have been termed mild dissidence. It was immediately after Vajpayee's fall and during the frantic attempts to cobble together an alternative that Pawar began to reveal a discordant disposition. There were several reasons for this. First, it was Arjun Singh and not himself who was presented as the engineer of an alternative government. Second, Pawar felt humiliated that the Congress Parliamentary Party issued a resolution authorising Sonia Gandhi to take steps to form the government. According to him this prevented the President from directly dealing with him, as the Leader of the Opposition. Finally his estrangement would appear complete when he was "relegated" to dealing with the smaller regional parties like the Indian Union Muslim League and the RPI of Maharashtra. Certainly, while these may have been valid points for him to feel isolated, they cannot be construed as important enough to explain what occurred next.

On May 15, less than two months after the fall of the Vajpayee government and the Congress Party's failure to muster up an alternative, a CWC meeting was called at the AICC. The aim of the meeting was to formalise strategy, to discuss ways of countering the noises emanating from the BJP and some of its allies about Sonia Gandhi's citizenship and general discussions on the party's election plans. Sonia Gandhi's response, and what she is believed to have said to the members was that she would not be intimidated by the BJP. At this point P.A. Sangma, the former speaker and Congress leader from the northeast intervened and suggested that there was nothing wrong with the BJP offensive since it was a genuine issue of concern. Rajesh Pilot hurriedly advised that the matter should be left till after the election and to the prerogative of the Congress MPs. Meanwhile the matter was quickly absorbed in the wider discussion about the elections but Sonia Gandhi sat silently observing the manner of the other CWC members who had not ventured to counter Sangma. After the meeting was over, Sharad Pawar, Tariq Anwar and Sangma met at the latter's residence to draft a letter to the Congress President. Certainly the motivations expressed within it, the temperament of the draft, and the suggestive possibilities of a rapprochement make an interesting study. A careful reading would suggest that the trio (the rebels were from now on addressed plurally) were engaging in some form of brinkmanship.

Perhaps the objections at the CWC meeting earlier had been a case of testing the waters, for there had been no tide against them. Simultaneously they may actually have believed that their point of view would find favour with a substantial section of the Congress Party. Much of the letter is actually a narrative of their world view, on the history of the Congress, on the role of its past leaders and on the relative usefulness of Sonia Gandhi herself. As far as the troika was concerned Sonia Gandhi had an ascribed role to play and nothing more:

> Soniaji, you have lived as a daughter-in-law to India for the past 30 years. You have in your own way, absorbed much of this country's spirit. You are in the line of many non-Indians who have loved and adopted this country and worked for its benefit. The Congress Party which you now lead was the brainchild of a Scotsman, Sir A.O. Hume. The seat you occupy was once adorned by Annie Besant. It is in this selfless tradition that we see your services to the party and the nation.

The letter went on to address this theme:

> At the risk of repetition we would like to emphasise that, as Congressmen, we look up to you as a leader who kept the party together and is a source of strength to all of us. We hope that you will continue in this role for many years. But as a responsible political party, we also have to understand the genuine concern of the average Indian who may or may not be a Congressman.

At one stage, it would appear that the bestial saffron nonsense of an RSS ideologue had found utterance through this letter. This was emphasised in the ominous line that:

> We accept with interest and humility the best which we can gather from the North, South, East or West and we absorb them into our soil. But our inspiration, our soul, our honour, our pride, our dignity, is rooted in our soil. It has to be of this earth.

These were profound references to honour, to the soul and to inspiration. However they couldn't exactly be described as flavours of the month. Their lament that an "Indian" must lead the country is one more addition to the enduring argument about who is an Indian? India has historically never had a definitive concept of citizenship. Indian culture is remarkable in its capacity to absorb and integrate foreign concepts and cultures and thus broaden its own cultural and social experience. Rajiv Gandhi once likened India to a "test piece for future society". His vision of an increasingly internationalist society, multi-culturalism, and a true unity in diversity, whereby maximum integration is achieved is not a utopian ideal. It is the cumulative experience of India over centuries of human history which pre-dates the creation of the Indian Republic in 1952.

More importantly, while the three urged Sonia Gandhi to "consider the issues" they had raised, they carried out an adequate pre-emptive strike against any positive response from her by asserting that:

> The average Indian is not unreasonable in demanding that his Prime Minister have some track record in public life. The Congress Party needs to respect this very justifiable expectation. We need to understand that, during an election campaign, every Congress worker has to be able to be aggressive about his party's line. Our workers cannot afford to be either defensive or apologetic. This will negatively affect the party's performance.

Having chosen to decide for themselves that Sonia Gandhi was not an Indian citizen, having adhered to the Golwalkar like philosophy that nothing of substance exists outside the soil of one's own "motherland" and having concluded that Sonia Gandhi had decided to become Prime Minister the three rebels rounded off with a particularly curious theme:

> We have discussed this matter today in the CWC at great length. We stand by the views we have expressed there. There can be no two opinions that this personalised campaign started by the BJP against you is reprehensible and needs to be opposed strongly. At the same, time, we would again state that the issue raised by us at today's meeting is real as far as this country is concerned and cannot be wished away.

This final section does produce queries. Was this an extension for a compromise? For how else could the triad mean to blunt the BJP offensive? Their proposed course was that the Congress manifesto ought to suggest an amendment to the Constitution which would hold that only natural born Indians could succeed to the office of President, Vice-President and Prime Minister. This, in effect, defeated the very purpose of combating the BJP line but, happily for them, opened up the possibility of an alternative Congress Prime Minister taking over. They must have gambled on some success and without doubt relied on patronage from influential people within the party and outside it to carry out the scheme. As for the entire nationality issue, it is almost sinister that this hadn't arisen earlier. It did not surface in 1998 when Sonia Gandhi assumed the mantle of Congress President and leader of its parliamentary party. Again it did not surface once efforts to bring down the Vajpayee government were underway. Nor do we see even a hint of either Pawar or Sangma debating this matter within any party forum while Sonia Gandhi to'd and fro'd between her offices and Rashtrapati Bhavan with letters of support for an alternative government. Barely four days before the CWC meeting, Pawar had in fact been despatched to Madras to hold talks with Jayalalitha, a crucial ally in the state. What made his statements even more bizarre now was the fact that only a month ago he had declared, at a public meeting in Benaras, (even though she herself never did) that Sonia Gandhi was the Congress candidate for Prime Minister. Whatever else there may be behind the conspiracy of the attempted coup, the expression of the Congress over the next few days revealed only how irrelevant and secondary the issue of Sonia Gandhi's nationality was, but how angrily the party as a whole responded to the manner in which the triad had expressed their feelings. Naturally it had been raised by the BJP and some of its allies and as far as the Congress was concerned the 'three wise men' could take the issue there and 'debate it with the likes of George Fernandes'.

Resignation

Sonia Gandhi's response to these events were revealed in her letter to the CWC which said:

...certain of my colleagues expressed views to the effect that my having been born elsewhere is a liability to the Congress Party. I am pained by their lack of confidence in my ability to act in the best interests of the party and the country. In these circumstances, my sense of loyalty to the party and duty to my country compel me to tender my resignation from the post of the Party President. Though born in a foreign land, I chose India as my country. I am Indian, and I will remain so till my last breath. India is my motherland, dearer to me than my own life. I came into the service of the Congress Party knowing that it is the only party capable of providing India with a stable, secular, progressive and independent government. That belief remains unshakeable...

The letter immediately isolated the trio from the rest of her Congress colleagues. It duly turned the attack that Sangma, Pawar and Anwar had made on her origins into a question of leadership and opened a debate about who was more fit to lead the Congress. For party members the answer could not have been more obvious. The most crucial passage of the letter, however, came at the end:

I came into the service of the party not for a position of power but because the party faced a challenge to its very existence, and I could not stand idly by. I do not intend to do so now. I have been privileged to receive the love and affection of ordinary Congress men and women from all over the country, and I will continue to serve the party as a loyal and active member to the best of my ability.

It is almost an echo of a challenge, shades of Indira Gandhi before the Congress split in 1969. Her intention to remain active coerced Congressmen to choose for themselves which way they wished to turn. It drew the line between two alternative concepts of Congress politics and two separate models of leadership. If it was an ultimatum it certainly worked.

Having delivered this note, she returned to 10 Janpath. It sent a shockwave through the rest of the party, the majority of whom were unaware of what had transpired over the last few days. As the news broke, the crowds trickled into Delhi and onto Akbar Road. Meanwhile, the motivations that prompted Sonia Gandhi to deliver her resignation were conveniently forgotten by leaders who had sat mutely in the CWC meeting itself. Now, in a knee jerk, reactionary fit of damage control they issued statement after statement to demonstrate their loyalites.

The Rebels are Tarred

It was the timing more than any other factor of the revolt which prompted such an outburst against the rebels. Sharad Pawar was never comfortable in politics unless he was in the driving seat. His methods of power-play were consistent half-measures which partially succeeded in their conception but died because he could not sustain a drive or offensive. Hence Pawar always travelled but never really arrived, his engines burning out each time that he was almost there. After Rajiv Gandhi's assassination he almost became Prime Minister before Narasimha Rao gained the crown. Similarly, he almost succeeded in gaining acceptance as Rao's successor for the office of Congress President but Kesri ruined his chances. Sonia Gandhi's entry and her larger role in reforming the party finally placed him aside. While she adorned the canvas of the Congress organisation with restorative measures, Pawar only felt slighted further. His concept of politics and his exercise of power did not correspond to the methods and ethics pursued by Sonia Gandhi in her plans for renewal of the Congress Party. Therefore, press speculation and gossip always guessed about the chances of his peaceful cohabitation alongside the new establishment. His final attempt to regain pre-eminence forever diminished his chances of success.

Alternatively, P.A. Sangma had cultivated himself as both a confidante as well as a key adviser to the Congress President. He was also the Speaker of the Lok Sabha and headed the committee responsible for reform measures within the party which led to the once famous Sangma Report. None expected him to demand more to fill his political platter. Sangma represented the northeast region of India, bordering the far reaches of Bhutan, Burma and Bangladesh. He was by no means the sole leader of the 15 Congress MPs elected from the region but occupied the most senior position among them in Parliament.

Tariq Anwar, like his mentor Sitaram Kesri, lost control over vast swathes of the party with the arrival of Sonia Gandhi. As Kesri's trouble-shooter, Anwar possessed the means of access to the then Congress President. Consequently his role as General Secretary was minimised, he complained that he hadn't even been consulted over the appointment of the new UPCC President, Salman Khurshid, the state of which he was in charge. Nonetheless, all three men were leaders of an unequally divided recognition and stature. Even while personal power and prestige may have declined, at least for Sangma and Pawar, they were popular and considered senior members. Immediately after they unfurled the banner of revolt, the combined political prestige and possessions of this triad were summarily dismissed by thousands of Congress workers who saw in their actions a betrayal of the party cause.

The drama which erupted on the scenes of Delhi and across the rest of the country has been portrayed as an attempt by the high-command orchestrated to belittle criticism within the party. This form of outlook to dismiss all political action as a pretentious *tamasha* which is activated and sustained by careful design is unhealthy. It mistakes fervour for flattery, it cannot distinguish between reverence and rhetoric and dismisses what is essentially a political expression for the pretence of sycophants and reactionaries. The burning of effigies, the sloganeering, the fasts and demonstrations may have been tinged with elements of the ridiculous. Sometimes individual leaders too may have overplayed their hand and indeed indulged in polishing their own presentations for personal advantage. However, that was merely a side show to the larger demonstration of loyalty and longing by the party workers. These faceless millions have no voice or recognition apart from the assurance that they belong to a political party they believe in and are led by a leader they hold in the highest veneration.

When Sangma had originally raised the issue *en comité* with the seniormost members of the Congress Party present no one had challenged him and Sonia Gandhi sat through the rest of the meeting in silence. After her resignation, the offensive against the trio was launched by the party workers before any leader got into the act. This was not an arbitrary engineering of some senior leaders to outdo each other in sycophancy. It was instead a genuine and overwhelming show of strength by grassroot party workers who instinctively challenged the issues raised by Sangma, Pawar and Anwar on their own initiative and eventually succeeded in gaining the high ground on an intellectual plane. The leaders of the Congress Party joined this exhibition of contempt only after it had already begun and shuffled alongside each other competing in their bombastic speeches and grandiloquent gestures.

Thus, while the challenge to Sonia Gandhi's leadership had emanated from the top, her succour arrived in the form of sentiment and support from below. It signalled the existence of political thinking, expressed in action, sometimes hyperbolic, by grassroot activists. To dismiss this support as a charade is a faulty assumption. For the much snubbed worker of the Congress, the triad rebellion and the immediate apathy of the senior leadership was an infringement of his and her political space, a zealously guarded though often suppressed domain. No other leader in the Congress since Rajiv Gandhi could have possibly attracted this massive and tumultuous support from the far reaches of the party. The rebels were duly tarred, not by their peers but by those whose support they had always taken for granted. The workers of any political party are often used as nothing more than 'gigantic walk-on crowds' by their leaders, in the Congress they now demonstrated against these very machinations.

Restoration

"Unity cannot be brought about by enacting a law that all shall be one."

Rabindranath Tagore, 1902

A cabal had tried to draw Sonia Gandhi into a realm of definite disengagement from the prospects of Prime Ministership. If the triad had hoped to produce some conclusion to their personal problem of who would be the Congress Party's Prime Minister, they were unsuccessful. Sonia Gandhi did not say yes, the Congress did not say no. As far as she, and to an extent the party, was concerned, the issue had been conveniently drawn to a close.

The "foreigner issue" in itself is a very simple one. Its complexities are made difficult because the attack upon Sonia Gandhi's nationality was and continues to be based on rhetoric and abstractions rather than matters of constitutional law. Given the cultural context within which this debate has raged, that is understandable. Nonetheless, this makes it impossible to counter these objections from the basis of technicalities and laws. Thus abstraction has been combated with further abstractions. The facts of the matter remain the same.

Sonia Gandhi was born in Orbassano, near Turin in Northern Italy. In 1965, aged eighteen, she enrolled at the Lennox School for Languages in Cambridge where she met Rajiv Gandhi. In 1968, Rajiv and Sonia were married in New Delhi and she became an intimate and close confidante of her mother-in-law Indira Gandhi. Since then, she has remained a resident in India and a citizen of the Republic since 1983. Her detractors question why she took so long to acquire Indian citizenship. After all she was eligible for it in 1973. The answer to technical queries regarding the acquisition of citizenship, its timing and manner, are laid to rest from an unexpected quarter. L.K. Advani, the factotum of the Indian right-wing and recently re-appointed President of the BJP, has stated that "Sonia went by the book" regarding the acquisition of her citizenship.

Meanwhile, her supporters argue that with Rajiv Gandhi's death in 1991, she could have returned to Italy if she wanted to. They contend that unlike many Indians who are willing to give up their nationality and Indian citizenship for comfortable jobs abroad, Sonia Gandhi remains an Indian through her own choosing. Her "Indianness" is not the result of an accident of birth, it is the result of a deliberate and conscious selection to remain Indian. A conversion no less profound than a religious transformation whereby the past is delinked and a new faith and culture embraced. The argument itself is typically Indian. India is perhaps the most socially and culturally diverse state in the world. Its present political position is merely 55 years old, its civilisation overlaps several millenia. It is not possible to apply the experiences of other nations and states in a country like India where matters of national identity must be more sophisticated because they are more ancient, and are tempered with experiences unknown to many modern societies. India's uniqueness is its diversity and rich multi-culturalism, these have survived invasions and bigotry, political turmoil as well as the numerous tests of modern political societies. Cultural and social integration is incomplete and is by no means likely to be complete in the near future. However much Indian leaders have tried to achieve tolerance between communities in the past, they have not wholly succeeded because an equal and opposite force does not desire levels of tolerance which would lead to cultural and social exchange. It is forces working on these principles which find favour and voice through forums like the RSS, the VHP and often the BJP too. It was these forces which now found representation through Pawar, Anwar and Sangma. Before Sonia Gandhi had stepped into politics the trend and political fashion had claimed the Muslims of India as the outcasts, or as the BJP called them, "Babur ki aulad". The progeny of Muslim invaders who had arrived in India in as early as the 8th century AD were described as foreigners and as fit to live only in Pakistan. The arguments being used against Sonia Gandhi now were merely extensions of those same expostulations. The question now was not merely who is an Indian but who defines who is an Indian? Thus to be an Indian is much more than to simply profess to the technical and constitutional issues of citizenship within the dry and staid frames of laws and rules, which incidentally, Sonia Gandhi has completed. For her supporters, Sonia Gandhi's position in power will decide once and for all whether India will accept this past of synthesis and whether, after all, it will be able to generate itself as a "test piece" for future society where citizenship is more than merely about an "accident of birth". For someone who has lived in India for three decades, who is more well-travelled in the country, more well-versed in its customs and traditions than many who happened to have been born here it is a torture to have to give oaths of allegiance every time the issue is kindled and rekindled to assuage the motivations of myriad political causes.

As for questions over the degree of her patriotism or level of national feeling, which proponents of the anti-Sonia line argue are matters of not only cultural but security concerns too, none can answer it better than perhaps Sonia Gandhi herself. In her comeback speech at the Talkatora Stadium she thundered:

> What is the meaning of their questioning my patriotism? Mother India took me to her bosom thirty-one years ago, the very day I came here as Indiraji's daughter-in-law. Not only has this land borne witness to my life, every second of my life has mingled with this land. It was here that I married, here that I became a mother, here before your eyes that I was widowed. The greatest daughter of this country, Indiraji, breathed her last in my arms. Each drop of blood in my being cries out that this is my land. This is where I belong, this is my country. It is not I who will answer those who question my nationality, it is the people of this country who will give them a befitting reply. As regards the post of Prime Minister, as is customary when the occasion arises, this will be decided by the Congress Parliamentary Party. Remember, friends, in the days to come, it will be the unending endeavour of our opponents to raise false issues.

This particular passage of her twenty-five-minute-long but forceful speech brought tears to the eyes of many in the Congress. The willingness to use emotion and evoke nostalgic evocations is not new to political oratory in the Congress leadership. Nor was it the first time that Sonia Gandhi cast emotion as a weapon against her detractors. Rather than simplistically dismiss it as cynical, one would do well to acknowledge it as a method of unity, in a political world where divisions often exceed the limits of rationality and go deeper than the norms of social exchange will permit. For some leaders it is convenient to use religion as a method of bringing about political unity, others harp on the less refined aspects of patriotic fervour to achieve this. Sonia Gandhi merely used Congress history and her place in it as a 'uniting factor'. Her references to the question of the party's Prime Ministerial candidate however required elaboration. Why did she not reveal her cards? In the internal politics of the Congress the issue had been brought to its furthest point of argument. After the tribulations of the past weeks the one outcome was that once and for all the issue of her origins had been settled forever. No one would raise it again since the time for that had passed. In such a situation, Sonia Gandhi could have seized her chance and declared herself as the Congress Party's candidate for Prime Minister, indeed many urged her to do so, certainly no one would have challenged her. The alternative course which she adopted was to procrastinate under the shade of traditions of the party. Does this indicate an unwillingness to accept the office or as her critics have commented, did she perceive that there was indeed a public posture which opposed such an aspiration? Remaining at the helm of the party while 'allowing' a 'personal candidate' to take over the reins would certainly give her far more control and power, that ultimate power which wields itself without the attachments of accountability or the compulsions of responsibility. However, Sonia Gandhi did not escape to this position either. Nevertheless, the strategy to remain non-committal on this very crucial question reduced the options open to her and the party in contesting the issue on an electoral field. By deliberately deciding to fight on an uneven battlefield, the Congress and its leader entered the election through the most difficult terrain available. However, as a long-term strategy, it was the most viable one. Having presented herself as the unchallenged leader of the party with the residual opposition to her now dissipated, Sonia Gandhi had the confidence of the assembled faithful to fall back on. Most importantly, it would remain to succour her irrespective of her success or failure in the forthcoming election. She had assured that the endorsement of her leadership was the most collective and the most plural possible.

Most of those who came to hear her speak were ordinary party workers, dedicated to the Nehruvian ideals and ideas of secularism, plurality and equality. They did not enjoy the benefits of Pawar's high office, nor did they possess the shrewd and calculating mind of a Sangma. For them it was sufficient to be in the presence of their chosen leader and to be part of an organisation whose membership they have held onto since Independence. They had come from the far flung corners of India. From districts in Tamil Nadu where Rajiv Gandhi was assassinated and from the far corners of Uttar Pradesh where the Nehru family came from. There were others for whom her ascendancy and leadership of the Congress had ignited a new spark of political action and vitality. It was at their insistence that Sonia Gandhi had joined the Congress Party. The cynicism of today may well jeer at the thought of an individual as an icon of public and political admiration, but for many Congress workers, who have spent their lives in a singular dedication towards their party organisation, Sonia Gandhi symbolises an ideal. For this very "walk on crowd", who are more informed of the realities of their own lives and better educated in the culture and tradition of Indian deference than many opinion-makers, Sonia Gandhi is a link with a past too glorious and golden in their eyes to be emulated by lesser individuals. Their adulation is not the result of a motivation to acquire power, the majority of them do not even bear office and the privileges which go with them. They seldom get a chance to display their political feelings or even acquire a hearing in the very competitive political space of India. Nonetheless, the Talkatora speech united these very different and often disparate individuals into a massive caucus who suddenly found themselves sharing not only their emotions but a purpose as well. She reminded them:

> It was in 1998 that I entered the political arena, having consistently refused over the previous seven years to do so. You are well aware of the circumstances which compelled me to take this step. The Congress was in grave difficulty, it was imperative to meet the challenge of the communal forces. The great achievements of the great Congress leaders of the past were in jeopardy, there was the danger of the sacrifices of Indiraji and Rajivji going in vain. I could not bear to see this happen. A year-and-a-half later, this is where I am. The very people who had come to me with folded hands to plead that I emerge from my seclusion to save the Congress began questioning my patriotism. They sought to sow seeds

of suspicion about me in the minds of my fellow-countrymen and women. And they did this in concert with those very forces whom I had entered the political arena to combat."

The Congress President extended the arguments she had made in her resignation letter. Then there had been no justifications to remain, simply a resolve to do so. Sensing the overwhelming support for her position in the party the attack was now carried into the camp of the 'renegades'. She need not have alleged a 'concert' between the rebels and the anti-Congress political parties, as far as the Congress Party was concerned that was plain from the first instance of the rebellion.

Among the deluge of applause and sloganeering, Sonia Gandhi thanked the party faithful and despite the overwhelming emotional support that was extended to her she now chose to justify her return to the leadership:

If today I stand before you, there is only one reason for this. Over the last nine days, I have thought a great deal, reflected a great deal. From every corner of the country, our workers have come to me. I was able to see who my true companions were. You rekindled hope once again in my aching heart, you gave me the reassurance without which my assuming the post of President would have been without purpose. You gave me your dedication, your affection, your support. I could not let you down. The testing times we have been through these last few days - me, you, our party - all this is a call for renewal, a call to build anew.

The Talkatora speech was a rallying cry to unite the Congress behind her leadership. The party had been reconciled after the jolt from Sangma and Pawar, still wounded but nonetheless prepared and unified again the Congress awaited the election. However while its internal pressures had been effectively curbed not even Sonia Gandhi could control what was brewing on the external front. This new threat would cost the Congress the General Election.

The Thirteenth General Election

The Kargil Crisis and the Brink of War – Malice in Wonderland – The Varied Roles of
Sushma Swaraj – The Middle Class Jumps Ship – The Management of Defeat

The Kargil Crisis and the Brink of War

"After each war there is a little less democracy to save."

Brooks Atkinson

For India and its citizens the situation of war has happily existed as a
far away notion; of battles fought out on the frontiers of the nation and of
firepower exchanged between unseen troops along its national edges. The
prospects of aerial bombings, fleeing refugees, penetrating armour tearing
down the Punjab in the west or infantry divisions rushing down the
Himalayas in the East is, fortunately, not an experience the vast population
of India has had to face. Perhaps the closest India came to look at such an
occurrence was the 1962 war with China, but the important consequences
of that campaign were more political than militaristic. The 1962 war
demolished the Indo-Sino amity but subsequently the breakdown was
repaired. The Bangladesh war of 1971 sustained and won by Indira Gandhi
was removed from Indian terrain and the closest Indians came to facing
up to it was through the experiences of the millions of refugees who
flooded into India at the time. The last war India fought was in the 1980s
in the distant terrain of Sri Lanka where the IPKF was sent in to "help
out" the Sri Lankan forces in their offensive against the LTTE. That, it
may be argued, was not a conventional war as such but a limited operation
with specifically designed objectives to secure peace. It was, nonetheless,
a conflict in which Indian troops were heavily engaged.

The situation which developed in 1999 was unprecedented. Reports
that infiltration from Pakistan had been going on for months into the
remote Kashmir sector of Kargil, deep inside Indian sovereign territory,

had been coming to the government's notice since 1998. Therefore, this must have been going on even while the BJP was staking its reputation by carrying out confidence building measures with the Pakistan government. So while the Prime Minister made diplomatic forays into Pakistan, infiltrators arrived from the other side, bypassing the efforts of both the Pakistan and Indian governments. In a remarkable coincidence, the concrete bunkers, enemy entrenchments and weapons stores were identified just after the Lok Sabha had been dissolved and India was preparing for the general election.

In the normal sequence of manouvres, frontier posts manned for most of the year by fortified garrisons are abandoned in winter, passes and supply lines being unnegotiable, and troops move down to a second line of defence where the climate is (only slightly) warmer but supplies are available. As winter recedes these forward lines retrench themselves in their mountain outposts. In 1999, Indian troops returning to their command posts after the Himalayan thaw had set in found their positions to be in enemy control. The BJP called it an outrage, which it was. The media set about presenting this "war-like situation" as a substitute for all other news. For the government (now of a caretaker status) the entire crisis never at any time amounted to a full scale war, it was always described as a "war like situation". The accompanying propaganda, the creation and recreation of patriotic symbols and their televisation and the subsequent presentation of hysteria as national feeling could have fooled anyone. The ensuing conflict was certainly intensive in the pockets where it was fought out. The Bofor howitzers and rocket launchers pounded the intruders on the hilltops as helicopters flew sorties in fairly dubious weather conditions in what turned out to be an engagement on the highest battlefield on earth. The bunkers were gradually taken, the infiltrators driven out. It was all over in four months which coincided with the duration of the election campaign.

This Kargil conflict was the first instance of a war taking place during a General Election in India. For any political party, to conduct an election campaign when the nation is at war is an ordeal. Criticism of the government has to be curtailed while it is engaged in the defence of the country. At the same time politics of the opposition has to bring to light the bungles and mistakes of a government, not only the failures of the incumbent years but of its immediate conduct. The only other comparable episode to the prevailing situation in India in that summer of 1999 can be found in the past, in the politics of another nation in another era. It was in 1942, the Second World War was at its peak. The Germans had just opened up their Russian Front and had taken Tobruk from the British in North Africa. Yet the House of Commons felt responsible enough to place a motion on June 25 expressing "no confidence in the central direction of the war." There was no such understanding or trust available in New Delhi, even during a conflict which the government refused to term as a war. Instead, any demand or justification was hysterically termed as "unpatriotic" or equally inappropriately as "unfortunate". Ridiculous suggestions and expectations that politics ought to cease during a crisis, especially one of war, were in circulation. Of course, while a military response must be allowed to continue unhindered by the political establishment, within the political world, however, a firm and united facing up to the enemy has to be balanced by a check on the policy of the government conducting a war. The guidance of war strategy becomes the responsibility of not just the government but the political establishment as a whole. Slaughter, strikes and sorties cannot be conducted in an arbitrary fashion in a democracy by the government. Particularly by a party which does not enjoy a majority on its own but is supported by a coalition which in turn can be easily appeased through policy decisions in their favour. At the same time credit for disengagement from a war cannot be allowed to be passed off as a victory as a result of which a government wallows in glory and expectant gratitude. The politics of war have never been and can never be an arbitrary practice, in which the government of the day unabashedly parades itself as the saviour of a country while the opposition must sit quietly as the causes and outcomes of the war itself are brushed over and the prospects of a future peace are thus mitigated.

The entire conduct of the Kargil campaign was a military success. However, the military option had to be applied only because of a preceding political failure; first in the capacity to understand Pakistani ambitions and second through the complacency towards the reports which identified an infiltration. Consequently, over four hundred Indian soldiers lost their lives in ejecting infiltrators from a handful of snow peaks. It is pretentious to say that anyone knew what the political implications of the Kargil war would be. There were numerous speculations. Naturally, many expected that the war would shore up patriotic goodwill for the BJP all over the country. Others argued that the body bags coming home to villages all over the country would indicate a Pyrrhic Victory, after all had not these soldiers laid down their lives throwing out militants who had occupied Indian territory? What then was the point of proclaiming a victory when one was merely ejecting an enemy who had been allowed to take over a national territory in the first place? Neither impact was wholly sustained. While the conflict drew patriotic fervour in many places, in others it was criticised as reactionary and a matter of concern for security. In some places it was even too distant an issue to make much of a dent as a valid election issue and voters questioned what the palaver was about. As is often the outcome of such episodes, only the military deserved accolades. The government stood guilty of negligence, the opposition lacked a cohesive strategy to enforce accountability and concentrated instead on attacking the government. The much vaunted and valid calls for calling an emergency session of Parliament were dismissed by the government and, therefore, the criticisms had to be aired in the public realm. The Prime Minister had the option of calling secret sessions or, at the least, a joint parliamentary meeting of some kind. This trenchant attitude which negated the possibility of creating consensus within politics also prevented discussions within the various political parties whether in government or the opposition. The press replaced parliament as the arena for debate, argument and counter argument. The requirement was dialogue between parties, the outcome degenerated into trading charges. The CWC resolution which supported every move to dispel the invaders also called the government policy "coordinationless, cohesiveless and careless." L.K. Advani, the BJP Home Minister, described the Congress stand as a "conduct against national morale and pride." Individual meetings between leaders were insufficient to forge the necessary unanimity. Instead, the lack of a composite approach of the kind former Prime Minister I.K. Gujral argued for, made the debate a grievously public affair.

Malice in Wonderland

"A week is a long time in politics," observed Harold Wilson, the famour Labour Prime Minister of Great Britain. His comment has become part of a historical political lexicon because it is acknowledged to be universally true, wherever politics is pursued and practised. So it proved to be the case in India as well. Everything had changed between early 1999 and the period immediately after the dissolution of Parliament in April. As late as March 1999, the Congress had been consolidating its gains made in the assembly elections in November 1998. Confidence and inspiration were high. It appeared, not only to Congressmen but to the public at large, that, given time, the party could make a suitable comeback under the popular and fresh leadership of Sonia Gandhi. This heady euphoria was strengthened by the disarray in the ranks of the BJP-led coalition government. Jayalalitha's constant tantrums and the threat of the withdrawal of support were gaining momentum daily under the buoyant juggernaut of the Congress. Then two things went wrong, both were troubles from within the ranks of the party itself. The first was the manner and the motives, apparent or real it is unclear, of the Congress decision to deliberately and systematically topple the BJP-led government. The Congress Party had always insisted that the government would crumble "under its own weight". Sonia Gandhi had herself stated at Panchmari:

> I once again wish to make it clear that as and when the need arises our party will fulfil its constitutional obligations without hesitation and provide stability and purpose. We have never opposed for the sake of opposition. We have highlighted the failures and follies of the government. We will continue to do so.

The party had always maintained that it would not itself first move to bring down the government until and unless it cracked itself. In fairness, this stand was a valid one, borne out by subsequent events. The BJP-led government did fall only after Jayalalitha and her AIADMK withdrew support from the coalition and the President asked Vajpayee to prove his strength in the Lok Sabha. However, public perception, always of a brittle and selective measure in India, proved to be insensitive to this fact. In the public mind the Congress Party had once again over-played its hand. By bringing down Vajpayee's government, and then by not providing an alternative and, finally, by "foisting" another general election on the country, the Congress had displayed a very primordial instinct to desire power. Alternatively, the Prime Minister and his party successfully portrayed Sonia Gandhi as both the inspiration and the force of provocation which led to the fall of his government. Thus Sonia Gandhi had once more followed Sitaram Kesri down the alley of power politics. Nothing seemed to have changed in the Congress, it was business as usual. This was the prevailing mindset among the electorate as well, certainly a handicap for the Congress of no small measure.

The second, and perhaps the more damaging of the two developments was the internal rebellion by the Pawar, Sangma and Anwar trio. More so perhaps because the voices of discontent came from the central citadels of the Congress Working Committee. It is important to reiterate how this open defiance against the Congress President and the nature of the oppostion to her emanating from within provided the BJP and the rest of her opposition with a cutting edge to their rhetoric. Simultaneously, it deprived the Congress of a show of unity before the election. In Maharashtra where Pawar undoubtedly wielded considerable clout, even if that did not translate itself into electoral victory in the past, the Congress organisation was vertically split. In the last election Maharashtra had contributed a significant thirty-six MPs to the party kitty, admittedly that was not wholly due to the efforts of Pawar, but perceptions held otherwise. The resulting sabotage and consequent damage done to the Congress Party and to Sonia Gandhi herself was not insignificant.

The Kargil "war" of that summer had made the election a "khaki-election". War, patriotism and nationality, tempered with a generous amount of sentimental and romantic nationalism was bound to give the ruling coalition an edge. Tied to the question of Sonia Gandhi's foreign origins the entire temperament of the election campaign was against the Congress leadership. This in turn was a reading the electorate could not ignore.

With so many factors in play, Sonia Gandhi's entry into the arena of electoral politics was therefore set with complexities which had been completely absent when she first arrived into national politics in 1998. It would not be incorrect to suggest that Sonia Gandhi's initiation into electoral politics, as an individual and as the leader of her party, was a baptism of fire.

The Varied Roles of Sushma Swaraj

This is what the official BJP website had to say on Sushma Swaraj:

> Ms. Sushma Swaraj was active in Haryana State politics from 1977 to 1990 and held the post of a Cabinet Minister in the State. Elected to the Rajya Sabha in 1990, this former socialist made her maiden entry into the Lok Sabha in 1996 from South Delhi and retained the seat in the recent poll. Articulate both in Hindi and English, Ms. Sushma Swaraj is one of the leading BJP speakers in Parliament. Endowed with the face of the quintessential housewife, Ms. Sushma is a great hit with the common people of the Capital.

This brief sketch does not do justice to the versatility of a woman who in a single year moved from the Vajpayee cabinet to become Delhi's first woman Chief Minister in 1998 to help salvage whatever could be recovered in the assembly election. Once the Congress tsunami had blown away the BJP, the lady with the "face of the quintessential housewife" was replaced by Sheila Dixit, a lady suitable enough to play the benevolent mother-in-law to Swaraj's housewife. Nonetheless, Swaraj was once more, and not for the first time in her career without a high profile job. This was rather a brief interregnum.

By mid-July the monsoon was in its element. Campaigning was already becoming difficult in some areas of the country. While the rains lashed the subcontinent the media dryly speculated on the choice of seats of various leaders. Needless to say, something resembling suspense had been created about where Sonia Gandhi would stand from. The names being circulated were shortlisted to three: Amethi, Bellary or Cuddapah. It was a foregone conclusion that Amethi would certainly be the seat of her choice. Earlier in August, while visiting her ancestral Anand Bhavan home in Allahabad, she had remarked that she would not disappoint the party workers in Uttar Pradesh. With only days to go before the nominations closed for the seats in the first round of elections, Sonia Gandhi arrived in Hyderabad on the late evening flight from New Delhi. She was received by the General Secretary in-charge of the state, Ghulam Nabi Azad. The next day a small entourage drove to the rural district of Bellary in Karnataka. The scenery of this rural district can be rather misleading, for while Bellary offers views of vast lush acres and well watered paddy fields the truth is that it is one of the most impoverished regions of India. The population reel under the twin blows of unemployment and a lack of education and resources. Women are therefore, even worse off and the rate of infant mortality is high. As most of Karnataka today registers progress in the various indicators of regional development, Bellary is not part of that success story, the people are forgotten.

While Sonia Gandhi filed her nomination papers the District Congress Committee hoped that her candidature would generate both awareness and much needed aid once she represented their constituency. Meanwhile cameras and the press had followed her every move from the moment her aircraft had touched down in Hyderabad the night before. The BJP managers, on the other hand, had been observing the movements of the Congress President for weeks with all the sinister dexterity of a dictatorial mole machine. Within hours of Sonia Gandhi's departure from Bellary, the BJP hoisted Sushma Swaraj as their own candidate against her. This decision assured Swaraj of limitless publicity and media coverage, perhaps more than any other NDA candidate including the Prime Minister Atal Behari Vajpayee himself. In a quick interview after her nomination the media began feeding lines to Swaraj. It was, in fact, the Star TV team who first used the reference of Mrs. Swaraj's *swadeshi beti* (Indian daughter) against Sonia Gandhi's *videshi bahu* (foreign daughter-in-law) taking a cue no doubt from the BJP's much vaunted hype over the issue. The expected injection of a xenophobic election campaign against Sonia Gandhi was thus inserted into events by people from a private news network eager to sell their bytes. Naturally Swaraj grabbed the opportunity and set herself to work. A contest against Sonia Gandhi provided Swaraj with much needed, and a much desired, puffery to boost her stature. Naturally, a high profile campaign was expected. For Sonia Gandhi, who soon filed her second nomination from Rajiv Gandhi's former constituency Amethi in Uttar Pradesh, time was stretched, the capacity to campaign in Bellary limited. Her time and efforts were needed all over the rest of the country too. Bellary was left to be managed by her daughter Priyanka with help from the state unit of the Karnataka Congress Committee and district party workers. The styles of the two campaigns were rather different. While Priyanka Gandhi availed herself of small and low profile gatherings, Sushma Swaraj's meetings and rallies were readily available to the national media. More than anywhere else for the BJP, Bellary was not the archetypal election campaign. It was a media show, developed and launched with an enthusiasm nearing that of circus participants, and little else. The cameras filmed, the press rolled out their printings and the celebrities poured in, all colourful cheerleaders in this apparently patriotic bandwagon of the "Indian" Swaraj marching against the "foreign" Sonia Gandhi. RSS volunteers arrived into the district armed with pamphlets and a vocabulary which can only be described as racist invective. The Prime Minister and almost every other member of the cabinet made periodic visits. Film stars were bundled in by the dozen to protect what appeared to be a slipping national identity for them all. For an observer it was a one way show, the show presented Swaraj as a winner. Much was also made of Sushma Swaraj's ability to converse in the local dialect and her growing rapport with her constituency. Her meetings were large and well received and always with some "big-shot" in attendance.

Sonia Gandhi was neither visible nor available for comment. However, when she did arrive, for a short interval of two days to capitalise on the quiet and sedulous work being done by Priyanka, both mother and daughter appeared to have taken not only Bellary but the rest of Karnataka by storm. The press was not beckoned, but they naturally came. Crowds were not organised by any staunch cadre but they lined the roads in their thousands when the family pair drove across the town in an open jeep. While neither knew the local language, a few words in Kannada from the daughter charmed the crowds at a rally in Siruguppa, enough for them to break the cordons and rush towards the dais. However, the acknowledgement for this was limited and the BJP roadshow, being performed with the precision of a propaganda exercise, was visible everywhere across the country. Nothing typifies this more than a curious report in an online journal by M.V. Kamath in which he confidently asserted the following theme:

> Indeed it is now considered doubtful whether Sonia Gandhi will even win in the one constituency, Bellary in Karnataka, where the Congress had always been considered undefeatable, and which she had chosen as a safe one. But, according to an opinion poll conducted by TNS MODE, opinion seems to have swung decisively in favour of the BJP candidate Sushma Swaraj who pitched in with her candidature at the very last moment to challenge Sonia Gandhi. The poll shows that Sushma Swaraj would obtain about 61 per cent of the votes, while Sonia Gandhi would barely get 31 per cent. If this poll turns out to be correct it would mean a massive rejection of Sonia Gandhi by the Indian electorate. Sonia Gandhi, of course is also standing for elections from Amethi in Uttar Pradesh where the chances of her getting elected are considered slim. If Sonia Gandhi loses in Amethi as well, the chances are that her political future would have to be written off. It would herald the end of her leadership of the Congress Party which had elected her as its president in the hope of her alleged charisma and the fact of her being representative of the Nehru-Gandhi clan would yield results.

It was necessary to quote this at length because of the style of this particular opinion. It is more or less a summary of the kind of views being put into general circulation by the BJP's very well managed media machinery. Such instances of opinionating and reporting were widespread, through which Sonia Gandhi, her lineage, her character, the Congress Party and the entire future of its politics were written off. It is normal in the course of elections for opinions to border on the extremes of sane argument, this is true in any democracy in the world. There are as many opinions as there are issues at play. However, the gravity of personal abuse directed at Sonia Gandhi in the 1999 Lok Sabha election was unprecedented. Along with the xenophobia and a generous (though maliciously so) dose of wide ranging allegations of corruption, BJP minister Pramod Mahajan likened her to Monica Lewinsky. He then apologised and finally settled for the view that he had not made any such comment in the first place. On the other hand, George Fernandes summarised for himself that Sonia Gandhi's only contribution to the country was that she gave birth to two children. Presenting such a political offensive exhibited a terrible employment of vulgarity as political thought and revealed the mind set among ministers. It was against this mounting barrage of a deeply personal offensive against her that Sonia Gandhi won both her elections by comfortable margins. In Amethi she did so by the largest margin in north India of over 350,000 votes. However quick some political pundits may have been to write her off and analyse what her projected loss would mean, they were not equally gracious when her election victory completely overturned their previous judgements. Their yardstick seemed to apply only when ascribing defeat.

The Middle Class Jumps Ship

"Getting on is the opium of the middle classes."

Walter James

The Indian middle class is the creation of the Indian National Congress. The rise in the influence of the Indian middle class is a development which began in the late 19th century and spread to span the progress of politics throughout the last century, hence "we are all middle class now". The (largely) Hindu leadership of the Congress was drawn from the bourgeois elite of Indian society during the independence movement. (The Muslims being represented largely either by the clergy or the landed aristocracy.) This degenerated into a show of strength in terms of an espousal of "socialistic" policies of the 1950s and their implementation in the late 60s and early 70s, to "take apart" the old order of precedence, as it were. It is evident now that land reform and the abolition of a patrimonial order has helped the socio-economic situation perhaps just as much as nuclear tests have succeeded in eradicating illiteracy. There is little evidence of a co-relation. Estimates about how many of the rural, landless poor benefited from land reform are certainly sketchy, because there is nothing to be proud of there. What we do know is that less than 1 per cent of the total sixty million acres of arable land under ceiling has been redistributed. Simultaneously rural indebtedness to bankrupt state exchequers is still high and widespread. What has developed instead is a highly successful indigenous capitalism which benefits from an imbedded and prolonged political culture enjoying corrupt relations and collusion between the bureuacracy and the *nouveau riche*. Nevertheless, the representation provided to the middle classes in politics and, therefore, policymaking, followed by campaigns to eliminate the "old order", has created, much to the agony of the poor and the unlettered, a system of patronage far more deplorable than the worst feudal practices in memory. Similarly, the active participants of this corruption, the middle-class bureaucracy itself, is not the high minded and fine-tuned administrative body of any Weberian fantasy. Instead, it is a cabal within government which perpetuates its longevity through an esoteric red-tapism and profits by it. By taking the "patricians and the plebs" out of the system, India has assumed a pyramidical administration of an immovable, trenchant inequality run on the basis of corruption. David Selbourne writes:

> The political economy of India since independence has been a battleground; not only a battleground between the classes, but between

the shifting economic and political oppositions and compromises within the ruling classes. There has been vacillation and irresolution in reform (and the capacity to "plan" only a backward and dependet economy)......There has been alternation, in foreign and trading relations, between appeasement of India's paymasters and belligerent assertions of a largely illusory political and economic independence of them.

Budgets in India have become merely a "ratification of proposals" made by vested interests, mere statistics, from the theoretical to the rational with emphasis on growth and little emphasis on social responsibility, from those who misproportionally benefit from an increase in private income. These are the vested interests now, dictating the economic path to be followed, lauding economic initiatives when it serves the cause of self-aggrandisement, condemning it when policy shifts or intervention occurs which diverts economic attention away from them. This is the *nouveau riche*. Separated from the old world through now abstract concepts like *noblesse oblige* and patrimonial duty, disparaging about social responsibility, envious and therefore critical of the political empowerment of the former socially and economically backward masses. It does not stop here. A latent embarrassment and a shyness to relate to their own roots is another feature of this new, mobile elite. To admit to the transition from proletarian shores and the subsequent arrival on the beach-heads of social and political elitism in the ostentatious style of a parvenu is to confess that their economic upliftment is indeed the result of a helping hand and interventionist state generated neo-corporatism. This is difficult to admit, certainly incompatible with the image of the 'self-made man'. Conveniently it mitigates any demands of social duty made upon them. Meanwhile, the state of intellectual reasoning, value systems and such cerebral aspects of this class as a whole have been left behind on the shores they abandoned to quickly reach the higher grounds of economic prosperity. So what is wrong with the acquisition of riches? What is objectionable with pay packets rising higher and higher as performance in the market gets better and better, what indeed is the palaver about if more people can now afford to 'enjoy life' as it were?

Certainly no one can make a case for the defamation of social enrichment, that after all should be the ultimate intent of any economic measure. However, the new elite inhabits a strange realm of moral (perhaps even spiritual) twilight, where the desire for the accumulation of personal capital and economic goodies must necessarily confront what is generally good for social welfare (the Maheshwar Dam on the Narmada, for instance). Where political and bureaucratic patronage must be extended to those who can pay for services rendered, thus immediately diluting the larger public responsibility of government and administration to those who cannot afford to stuff bulky envelopes up their shirt sleeves (prevalent everywhere). In this realm, which survives because a sizeable section of the Indian "citizenry" (about 300 million at the last count) can and will pay to have their demands accommodated, to access the loopholes of money laws and escape the commitment to a socialist and welfarist pattern of growth, India dies. As for the direct impact of economic reforms:

> The hype surrounding this new elixir reached a peak in 1997, when the world joined India in celebrating her golden jubilee. According to the celebrants, India's prospects had never looked rosier...With the confining superstructure of state control and planning on the way out, India's boundless potential could come to fruition, said the celebrants...In India, it is certainly that the top one-tenth to one quarter of the population, huge numbers in themselves, will benefit enormously in the near future, as the bulk of them have already done from the faster growth of the past two decades.[1]

Indeed, with increase of average incomes poverty recedes, as India becomes the world's largest market for goods the exchange of goods and consumer levels increase and standards of life improve. However rather than eradicating poverty, the economic reforms have already indicated the development of a dualistic society, with an increasing entr'acte between rich and poor. How many lives are going to be transformed by the new economy? With stress on lower public spending and cuts in subsidies across the board the onus for bringing socio-economic change falls on the private sector as government resigns responsibility towards

---

1. "In the Land of Poverty" Dubey. 1997

labour and the working mass. While this promotion of a stakeholder society which is responsible for its own welfare is a noble one it is near-utopian to expect the private sector to invest in meaningful philanthropic exercises like the management of social diversity, in such an early stage of capitalistic growth. For India's new economic elite the problem is not about eradicating poverty, the problem is the existence of the poor. And yet, the Indian National Congress initiated economic reform through liberalisation without the "advantages" of any economic pressure group to reform. It was a development which is contrary to the established and accepted view that dynamic economic groups exert pressure on the state to evolve new policies. Furthermore, the genesis of this reform lies not with Manmohan Singh but with a predeccessor, V.P. Singh, who served as Finance Minister in the Rajiv Gandhi regime. The three-pronged approach to economic reform: export and import incentives, tax rationalisation and the liberalisation of economic regulation increased growth. Certainly it was Manmohan Singh in the Rao regime who intensified the process. Thus incurred a transfer of not only control but, more importantly, the transfer of social responsibility to the new emergent class, the new economic emigres. Naturally the Congress expected support for its economic policies through political ratification. Yet it was not forthcoming, certainly not from the urban rich, the upper-middle class or the middle class, or however one wishes to address this elite. When the Rao administration went to the country in 1996 it was, ironically, those who benefited most under this regime who "twisted the knife" into the Congress body. Comparatively, the BJP did exceptionally well. Of the "top half of society", an average 54 per cent voted for the BJP in 1996, this sunk to a slight 53.7 per cent in 1998. The Congress on the other hand got 38.3 per cent and 41.3 per cent from the upwardly mobile and the rich in the respective contests. Hardly a ringing vote of confidence from those whom its economic policy represented and favoured. After the 1998 General Election, Salman Khurshid commented:

> The 'failure' of our liberalisation strategy lies essentially in our inability to 'sell' the idea of economic reform. We left it to the few chosen civil

servants, operating in the cloisters of industrial and business associations. Political salesmanship, vividly associated with our earlier socialist programmes of nationalisation, etc. was conspicuously absent. We failed in PR, not in the substance of our reform package.

It was no wonder then that this rejection would be on display again in 1999. However, in the thirteenth general election it was so complete and so overwhelmingly represented that the party simply could not understand what went wrong. Manmohan Singh himself. a man of unassailable integrity, the savant of the modern Indian economy, of moral rectitude and a figure who epitomises probity in Indian public life, lost his election from the South Delhi seat. South Delhi is perhaps the most diverse constituency in India. It is certainly in the top bracket in terms of social composition. The fact that the vote went against him demonstrated conclusively to the world at large that progressive policies alone cannot enlist electoral support. Compulsions of voter behaviour demolish any attempt to rationalise them. As for the new elite, they had received what they wanted, for them the priority in terms of political action remained only to get on. The new rich jumped ship. Having received a system where the power of their economic activity was assured they embraced new concepts and themes to radiate a feeling that they had political ideas of their own as well. So while the repositories of neo-elitist intellectualism, the press and media, churned out high falutin thinking on nationalism, war and patriotism for their associations, the vast wallowing middle class, this latter day elite, excitedly swallowed these ideas and regurgitated them as their own.

For Dr. Manmohan Singh personally it must have been a blow. He had often struggled within the Congress Party itself to have his ideas accepted. Through purely personal intellectual stamina he had even converted a large section of the party towards reform. His rejection, ostensibly by 'his own kind', gave his detractors within the party an opportunity to be more condescending about economic reform and liberalisation and more focused on the other economic elements of the Nehruvian consensus. The 1999 General Election was the third time in a row when the New Economic Policy had been rejected by the Indian electorate. It was, after all, the singularly most important element of Congress policy making in the 1990s. Just as Mandal, once implemented could never again be rejected no matter what the platitudes of personal opinion against it may have been, similarly no government following Rao has rejected the NEP. It found favour with Gowda's UF and Vajpayee's NDA.

Those it benefited did not, however, reward those who initiated it.

The Management of Defeat

Immediately after the election a committee was formed to introspect and inform the Congress President about the causative factors of the party's defeat in the 1999 General Election. Led by A.K. Antony, the Kerala leader and a man with an enviable reputation for propriety, the eleven-member Introspection Committee presented its final report, on schedule. Covering two hundred pages, the spiral bound report was not for public consumption, a single copy being presented to Sonia Gandhi. Broadly, the report outlined five generic factors for the loss. Principally the defeat was attributed to poor management arising out of communication gaps. Secondary, causes were outlined as a series of bad alliances, Bihar in particular, and to a lesser extent, the Vajpayee factor too. We shall perhaps never know the contents of this weighty introspection but it is possible to analyse and calculate the adverse organisational aspects of the Congress Party with a general reference to the problems of party organisations.

Arguably, for a political party an election is the biggest test of its organisational preparedness and strength. Between 1996, when it lost power and 1999, when it last fought an election after an apparent exercise of re-organisation had been carried out, the state of the party machinery hadn't improved. Even if we take into account factors like voter turnout and social issues which are external, the party lacked certain key organisational strengths. Factors which determine the success and failure of a policy and its exercise are multiple and include: leadership, decision-making and the procedures which determine whether it is defective or effective, levels of communication, policy formalisation and implementation and finally recruitment. Out of this collection, we can even pick a few. Here our discussion will have to be confined to certain qualitative factors like leadership and communication gaps, procedures of decision-making and the problems of role conflict which are chronic institutional problems, particularly of the AICC.

Let us consider the first one; leadership and communcation gap. In structure the Congress Party organisation is based on a hierarchical model with a highly centralised unit of leadership. Thus it is possible that the central leadership is too far removed from its workers in terms of decision-making, as Antony observed. There is evidence that the relations between members of the CWC and their district party workers are governed by a "high power distance" which is the result of the Congress culture of past practice. This culture has ensured stability in a large measure in the past . In the present this traditional system is construed as the basis of the organisational weaknesses of the Congress. Naturally the leadership is used to an autocratic and paternalistic style of control which places strong dependence needs on the rest of the organisation. What then in terms of setting goals is the impact of this on subordinate Congress committees and other units at the lower end of the Congress pyramid? Since they do not have any constitutional participation in the process when and whereby the party goals and aims are set in the first place, it is difficult for them to meet the objectives as there is little choice in the selection of resources. At the same time, it is difficult for the leadership to conduct a performance appraisal exercise as there is no basis upon which to do so. As this is an aspect of procedure, we shall examine it in more detail later. However, procedural effeciency and leadership control are in this case interdependable. Since there is no system for quantifying or measuring the success or failure of a task the leadership can only appoint a panel to look into these and submit its findings consequently. A more detrimental aspect to the absence of a performance appraisal system is that the leadership cannot purge the party of "dead-wood". While this has been declared from lofty podiums, in Panchmari and on numerous occassions afterwards, it has never been implemented. The classic source of leadership failure is seen to be the actions of leaders themselves which impose detrimental constraints on the rest of the organisation. That failure is accentuated if the leader does not have in place measures or systems through which a crisis can be controlled or alternative coping strategies and strategies for change can be put into play. This is borne out whenever there is an absence of a carefully thought out strategy for change as well as a lack of communication between those who set these strategies and those who implement them. A goal setting theory would suggest that this betrays a confused thinking on the ends and means of organisation and administration while general organisation theory would raise the question of whether this depends on organisational structure and the high power distance evident in the Congress Party. This leads us on to a study of procedures which govern the organisation.

It is generally accepted that there are esentially five causes which contribute to defective decision-making. These are; oversimplified beliefs, faulty assumptions regarding good solutions or the consequences of choice, evidence of reports which are taken into consideration being too ambiguous, the information being erroneous or inconsistent and, finally, one must allow for the inclusion of bad luck; this last can be discounted from the analysis here for obvious reasons. Evidently (and this view is supported by the findings of the Introspection Committee as well), the factors listed here were causative to the failures of the 1999 campaign. Faulty and simplified assumptions underlined the thinking in the Congress that Mulayam Singh would support the Congress to form a government. Similarly, favourable reports emanating from parts of the country, particularly Andhra Pradesh, were considered reliable while the level of damage suffered in Maharashtra was only slightly acknowledged. Therefore, not only are these factors crucial in determining the outcome of a policy or a programme but they play a part in the everyday life of the organisation which includes recruitment, communication, assessment, information retrieval among a number of other things. In the Congress the leadership and others with whom responsibility for a particular objective resides have to conceptualise and define a policy, initiate a series of decisions and actions implementing that policy and ultimately shape the future of a work system, of the organisation and in the case of the Congress in government, the future of the country. Above all, this implies a requirement for accountability from those "responsible few" exercising their authority over the un-empowered many. This is a subject which lies in the realm of role conflict. One of the principal problems in decision-making and the exercise of authority within the Congress emanates from the perennial bureaucratic nightmare of role conflict. This is because those responsible for the execution of a policy or decision sometimes do not have a role to play in the formulation of that particular order. If they do, then the resources and means which should be allocated to them are either not well-distributed or are inadequate. These problems arise because there are no clear divisions of responsibility. As a result, expectations about outcomes may differ between the "formulators" and the "implementors" of a strategy. For an alternative style or system of negotiations or policy evaluation to occur the culture of the Congress Party will have to adapt itself from being a rigid, hierarchical, authoritarian one to a more "flat" structure with much lower power distances between the various chains of command.

THREE

"In the Crucible of Leadership"

With the defeat of the Congress Party in 1999, Sonia Gandhi's political career appeared to many to have reached a premature end. She was now an elected member of Parliament and Leader of the Opposition. Within her own party, she faced a rising level of discontent which in 2000 led to a leadership contest. Having established herself once more as the leader of Congress through this internal election, she grappled with national issues. Within Parliament, she faced a hostile government but remained combative. Around the country, Congress registered victories in several Assembly Elections and defeats in some. These five years saw her profile grow, from silent spectator to a demonstrative leader. They were also years that saw the death of senior colleagues and peers such as Madhavrao Scindia and Rajesh Pilot. The biggest challenge came in the face of the genocide in Gujarat and the subsequent elections there. It was a seminal occurrence in her, so far, short political career. Gujarat changed something about Sonia Gandhi. Her political view hardened and she grew more focused. In the post-Shimla conclave in 2003, she had achieved the full potential of her office as Leader of the Opposition. It was then that she personally led the no confidence debate against the Vajpayee-led NDA government.

Soon after, General Elections were called and the BJP rise and shine seemed unstoppable. Sonia Gandhi seemed to have been caught unaware and out of her depth. The results to the elections of 2004 proved otherwise.

Of Coteries, Committees and Courtiers

Winning Small Change – Breeding Discontent – The Quiet Death of the Bengal
'Mahajot' – UP: Fear and Loathing in Lucknow – Death of an Airman –
The Leadership Election

Winning Small Change

Early in 2000 the government of the State of Gujarat passed an order allowing state civil servants to attend the functions and felicitations of the RSS, the right-wing Hindu nationalist organisation. The move drew strong criticism from all the opposition parties and from some constituents of the NDA itself. Constitutionally the right to association for civil personnel in the employment and services of the government comes under the purview of the Civil Service Rules. Traditionally the civil service is seen to be a non-partisan body whose principal purpose is to provide smooth and unhindered administration. By providing for a link between an apolitical civil arm of government and a highly controversial and right-wing political (not merely cultural) organisation like the RSS, the government of Gujarat had created an unneccesary controversy. Sonia Gandhi, in her capacity as the Leader of the Opposition, expected little response from the Prime Minister and wrote to the President on the matter. This letter illustrates her genuine contempt for all things communal or sectarian and needs to be cited in full length. It is also her personal reading and record of the deteriorating situation in Gujarat which by now had the notorious reputation of the BJP's laboratory, its citizens classified and discriminated against, depending on their political and religious hues. The emotions and concerns raised in the letter are uncanny for barely within two years Gujarat would find itself embroiled in the worst ever communal riots to occur there in over thirty years.

"Dear Rashtrapati ji,

It is my duty to draw your attention to a matter of grave concern to all those who draw inspiration from the struggle for India's freedom and whose hopes and aspirations are mirrored in our Constitution. The essence of our Constitution is the spirit of secularism, equality, fraternity and justice that it seeks to establish, which must also remain the guiding principles of governance and administration. The decision of the BJP Government of Gujarat to remove the ban imposed on State Government employees from participating in the activities of the RSS would seriously jeapordise these principles, especially the secular character of the government and the administration.

The administrative ethos established in this country does not permit permanent Civil Servants to be associated with any entity whether political, cultural or social, which militates against the letter and spirit of the Constitution. This decision becomes all the more objectionable when one looks at the real nature of the RSS, as reflected in the thoughts and words of its ideologue Shri M.S. Golwalkar.[1] Till date his words have not been repudiated by the RSS. He had the following to say on his Vision of India:

> The foreign races in Hindustan must either adopt Hindu culture and language, must learn to respect and hold in reverence the Hindu religion (sic) must entertain no idea but those of the glorification of the Hindu race and culture, i.e. of the Hindu nation and must lose their separate existence to merge in the Hindu race, or may stay in the country, wholly subordinated to the Hindu nation, claiming nothing, deserving no privileges, far less any preferential treatment – not even citizen's rights. There should be no other course for them to adopt. We are an old nation, let us deal as old nations ought to and do deal, with the foreign races, who have chosen to live in our country.

He added :

> To keep up the purity of the race and its culture, Germany shocked the world by her purging the country of the semitic races – the Jews. Race pride at its highest has been manifested here. Germany has also shown how well-nigh impossible it is for races and cultures, having differences going to the root, to be assimilated into one united whole a good lesson for us in Hindustan to learn and profit by.

---

1. Ideological 'father' of revivalist Hindu nationalism. One of the earliest and strongest influences on the RSS which he guided in the early days of its inception.

As the President of our Republic, we look upon you to protect the Constitution. Unless the RSS disowns the views of Shri Gowalkar, any association with this body by public servants would completely undermine their capacity to serve the country in accordance with their constitutional obligation. It is hardly necessary to state that Shri Golwalkar's views are antithetical to all that is held sacrosanct by the Constitution of India. It is thus no surprise that such a perverted ideology helped Nathuram Godse rationalise for himself the heinous act of assassinating the Father of the Nation, Mahatma Gandhi.

It is my earnest request to you to advise the Prime Minister to direct the Government of Gujarat to rescind the circular issued by them on January 3, 2000. The Congress Party and, I am sure for that matter, all secular democratic political parties and citizens would not accept such an obnoxious decision which must be reversed if we are to safeguard the principles enunciated by our founding fathers in our Constitution."

Further to this, Parliament was virtually boycotted by the entire opposition and the Congress took to launching sit-ins in front of Parliament and organising protests in New Delhi. Perhaps sensing that a strong case for the Gujarat Order was perhaps indefensible and facing disruption within its own NDA ranks, the BJP government wisely decided to rescind the circular. With the Vajpayee government cornered into a surrender, the Congress Party earned credit with its opposition partners, though not enough of it to balance the deficit which had been created by other issues. However, it was a welcome palliative and certainly bolstered her image of the anti-fascist crusader. The Gujarat issue established certain definitions about Sonia Gandhi's political strengths and provided a correct measure of how strongly she felt about the issues of communalism and sectarianism. This is a subject she is most comfortable fighting against. Meanwhile, her policy on the matter is a direct departure from that of her predecessor Narasimha Rao, who within the constraints of a minority government felt obliged to accommodate the right-wing. Sonia Gandhi, alternatively, has adopted a policy of direct confrontation on issues which challenge the secular order set by Pandit Nehru. Arguably, she does not suffer from the restraints of government, which exert pressures of their own and subjugate personal feelings to those of political and administrative concern. That restraint does, however, exist in Congress ruled states. Nevertheless, even in states where Congress governments are in power the preservation and restoration (in some cases) of a secular order are the priorities for Congress Chief Ministers. Critics have further argued that in Maharashtra the Democratic Front coalition government led by the Congress and its Chief Minister Vilasrao Deshmukh had failed to discharge its obligations towards the report of the Sri Krishna Commission of Inquiry which was constituted to investigate the Bombay riots of 1992-93. Implementations of many of its recommendations are still awaited.

Breeding Discontent

But for the brief and promising beginning regarding the Gujarat Order, the Millennium did not bring much to be festive about for the Congress Party. For Sonia Gandhi personally, it promised even less. Had she been keeping a book of accounts of how the Congress Party and, more importantly, her own control over it, was faring, the first three quarters would have posed a dismal outlook. The trouble came from three fronts.

Within Parliament, the Congress appeared unable to lead the opposition, giving rise to speculation, both within the Parliamentary Party and among allies in other parties in the Lok Sabha about whether they could effectively take on the government on the issues of the day. These ranged from the ongoing Review of the Constitution, and discussions on the Subramanyam Committee Report on Kargil, which held potentially embarrassing information for the NDA government, to thinking across the political spectrum on the New Economic Policy. On the latter issue, the Left parties were more vocal and strident than they had been for a long time before. With just over a year to go for the West Bengal elections, they naturally wished to cultivate the distance between themselves and the Congress. Other parties simply did not desire to work with the Congress. *The Asian Age* reported:

Mrs Sonia Gandhi has been unable to take the lead in working out a common Opposition strategy against the government in Parliament. The Congress has been virtually isolated under her leadership with the other Opposition parties refusing to accept her lead in matters of parliamentary import.

Meanwhile outside Parliament and in the election battlefields the party could not hold its ranks either. While opinion polls varied in their estimates on which other party stood where, they were almost uniform when it came to predicting the chances of the Congress in the election going states. Among the four election going states, the Congress was defending Orissa, where it was the incumbent. No one expected it do do well. The state had been ravaged by a cyclone recently and the state unit of the party had recently seen changes in its leadership, already suffering from chronic factionalism. Moreover, the Chief Minister Giridhar Gomang was neither charismatic nor able to gain the goodwill of his own party cadre, far be it of the electorate. Manipur was slated to witness a hung Assembly. In Haryana, it appeared to be a case of love's labour lost for the party, with the unending feud between Bhajan Lal and his adversaries taking a toll on the party's chances. The window of opportunity had opened and closed about 11 months ago, when the Congress had the chance of installing Bansi Lal as Chief Minister and supporting him from the outside, the situation appeared beyond salvage now. In Bihar, where the NDA was expected to make huge strides, Laloo Prasad Yadav, former friend and ally of the Congress was expected to lose badly. Yet it was Laloo Yadav who was portrayed as the champion of secular India, fighting against a resurgent BJP and its allies. Few expected him to survive. The Congress remained unsympathetic and attacked the Laloo-led RJD, pouring vitriol and vehemently criticising his "style of governance". Here too the state unit was divided, though unequally, over whether or not to extend support to the Rabri Devi[2] regime. The majority was against the idea, so the leadership decided to go with the majority. Minimal attention

---

2.   Rabri Devi regime - Facing allegations of corruption and a jail sentence in 1997. Laloo Prasad Yadav, until then Chief Minister of Bihar, resigned office and nominated his wife Rabri Devi as Chief Minister in his stead. She has since remained Chief Minister of the state.

was paid to the consequences of turning against Laloo, nor did the Congress leadership comprehend that accoutrements of office and promise of power is a strong currency in the market where political power is exchanged, often to purchase even loyalty. If it possessed pretences to "going it alone in order to strengthen the party", an oft heard phrase, the Congress would be at pains to explain what it did after the election results had come in for the four election going states.

With the exception of Manipur, the Congress lost everywhere. In Bihar, Laloo did what few, even his most ardent supporters could hardly have thought possible. He survived the NDA onslaught, though not getting a majority, but went on to form another government with Congress support. In Orissa, the Congress was wiped out while in Haryana it did not even get close to a majority. The paralysis over Bihar, however, acutely demonstrated the deep mental crisis which penetrated the Congress leadership. It may have appeared prudent to have abandoned Laloo and the Rabri government who appeared to be on the losing side and then taken on a new NDA government in Bihar. However, not only had the Congress ended up as a rump, outside the electoral divide (it won only 23 of the 324 seats in the Assembly), the Congress had misjudged the minds of its own state leaders. They were now teased and tempted by Laloo with offers of cabinet posts and ministerial rank and in turn put pressure on the central high-command to accede to his demands for support to his new regime. Simultaneously, he expressed his hope, all over the media that the "Congress would join hands with him against the fascist forces of the BJP". Either way, it seemed for the Congress to be the only prospect of claiming some kind of victory, by joining hands with the RJD in Bihar. During the course of the election campaign the tenor of her speeches had indicated that for Sonia Gandhi alliances and coalitions were of neither promise nor import. She had come down heavily on Laloo Yadav and his government, preferring to "go it alone". Her actions, therefore, to now extend him unqualified support would invite ridicule and criticism from not only the media but some unexpected quarters too. The decision to extend support was perhaps enough of a reprieve for her party. Anything else would have amounted to a collapse of opposition unity and a total isolation of the Congress from sympathetic friends. However, rumblings had already begun in the press as reports began to echo the view that:

> Dissident activities may surface in the party at the national level after the results of the Assembly polls in Bihar, Orissa and Haryana start coming in......as the party's prospects in these states appear bleak.

In a parliamentary democracy, for a party leader to stay on in their incumbent position requires multiple talents. It requires them to deliver and, above all, to satisfy the expectations of a victory in an electoral contest. For MPs and legislators of any other variety, the level of personal loyalty is directly proportional to the ability of those towards whom this loyalty is subject to win them their seats and consequently, grant rewards. The defeat, first in the general election of 1999, and then in the assembly elections of early 2000, signified to Congressmen that their situation had not improved since the last contest, if anything it had deteriorated. The first to publicly voice his resentment was senior Congress leader and former minister from Karnataka, Jaffer Sharief. He advised the Congress President to "change her style of functioning." It was not a scathing attack, it almost never is in the Congress where quiet asides such as, "we are sending the wrong message to the country" or equally that "the morale of the party is very low" are usually considered the heights of indiscretion and dissent. Such sentences issued either to journalists from the privacy of their government bungalows or the guarded secrecy of AICC offices are the ones usually attributed to that all too familiar, "senior party leader", "prominent MP" or less conspicuously to a "certain heavyweight" from particular states. However, in the crisis which began to engulf her now, Sonia Gandhi would not need to guess or suspect the dissidents at work. Barely had the dust on the Assembly elections settled when the elections to the Rajya Sabha for 58 seats came along. The Rajya Sabha election as an occasion does not evoke much enthusiasm or competition when a party is in government. Nevertheless, when a party is in opposition, and the fruits of reward are fewer to dispense, an election to the Rajya Sabha becomes both an object of desire and, if successfully contested, an indication of individual success and superiority. In 2000 therefore, it became all too important for the Congress leadership to define and carry out distribution carefully. There were a large number of prospective candidates, many of them could justify their desire for nomination through service and work for the party. Others, though no doubt senior in rank and profile, were people who had lost the last general elections and now sought to enter Parliament through this ladder. Still others expected it as a reward they had been long promised. Few could have been satisfied. Many of those who were selected to contest were confident of victory. While in a state like UP their defeat could have been a foregone conclusion, in West Bengal and Maharashtra where the Congress did indeed possess the numbers, it was just another blow. Throughout the country, however, the elections saw heavy cross voting and "horse trading", none more so than UP where Congress Party MLAs were both instructed and rewarded to vote against the official party candidate by their own party bosses in New Delhi. Whatever the outcome of the elections and whatever the methods employed to achieve them, the lines of dissent within the party were accentuated as a result.

Veterans and newcomers, trusted lieutenants and those with no voice previously, now began to form a trickle of dissidence. The existing caucus of disgruntled party leaders, men who had been denied Rajya Sabha tickets, office-bearers who had found themselves without prestige in the new regime and a few who genuinely felt that the "wrong sort of people" were being given undue leverage, suddenly accumulated new supporters in their ranks. Leaders in turn would often accost would be conspirators, often clumsily, on the lawns or among the colonnades of the AICC headquarters at Akbar Road and usher them into their offices. Even officially called meetings began to be viewed with suspicion by those who refused to be drawn into any controversy.

The number of episodes that could be construed as forms of dissidence, and which are in the normal course of events few and far between, now began to occur with conspicuous regularity as though the work of a larger design. Vasant Sathe, veteran leader from Maharashtra followed Jaffer Sharief's cue but went a step further, preferring to voice his views in the party news magazine *Sandesh* and highlighted the "confusion and mental depression" within the party. It was not only the senior leaders whose tone suggested unhappiness. Recognised figures like Jairam Ramesh and Kapil Sibal too voiced concern. Sibal, an urbane lawyer, Rajya Sabha MP and, for a time, a party-spokesperson was not too far off when he revealed to a daily:

> There is a definite hiatus between the aspirations of the people and the objectives being followed by the party...There is a lot of confusion within the party over basic issues such as its approach to the liberalisation policies, its stand on the nuclear issue...the party cannot afford to send contradictory signals on these crucial issues and must spell out its agenda clearly.

Some of these concerns, as articulated above, were indeed genuine reflections of a confusion over issues. The single most important one being the issue of economic liberalisation and the question whether the party ought to follow in opposition what it practised, indeed pioneered, in power. It did not make political sense to support the government on this matter while in opposition, the fact that it was the Congress that had initiated these reforms notwithstanding. That was the line taken by, among others, Arjun Singh. In any case, he had always maintained that the matter of economic liberalisation was, above all, a political issue. The confusion was once more highlighted when, much to the chagrin and discomfort of an already besieged leadership, Manmohan Singh, leader of the opposition in the Rajya Sabha, in all sincerity supported the governments move to cut the rate of subsidies:

> We need to evolve a national consensus. The problem is there and we cannot push this problem under the carpet... It cannot be anyone's argument that the magnitude of subsidies that prevail — at nearly 19 per cent of the GDP — is sustainable. It is obligatory for us, as a nation, to take measures to bring subsidies down within the limits of prudence. The non-merit subsidies alone accounts to about Rs 1,30,000 crore. If

the government can come up with a proposal to save the money spent on non-merit subsidies, we can finance the entire backlog of primary education.

He spoke convincingly on a sensitive subject, even if the response of the Treasury Benches was itself maladroit. Nonetheless, his speech could not have come at a worse time, as it did merely hours after Sonia Gandhi had concluded a protest outside the Prime Minister's residence against the move to slash subsidies on PDS grain and fertilisers. The reactions both in the party and in sections of the media depressed this as just another voice in the bandwagon of dissent. The BJP played it up as a confrontation between the highest echelons of the Congress on the all important issue of economic reforms. Sonia Gandhi understood that Manmohan Singh's utterances were not part of the general chorus of disenchantment against her. It was more difficult, however, to explain this to others in the party and outside. When the principal figure of economic reform and his own leader differed on the basic issues of economics what message was the party conveying to the country, was their reasoning.

Nonetheless, while some voices died down or were muzzled others joined the choir. "Loyalists" spent their energies extinguishing, the burning fires. The various Chief Ministers, and others like the habitual courtiers who owed their political existence to Sonia Gandhi, took it upon themselves to put out these bushfires. Digvijay Singh went on record saying, "Mrs. Gandhi, has the leadership qualities required to lead Congress. Those who are not happy with her leadership are welcome to leave the party. I would advise them to leave at the earliest, to make room for the elevation of other deserving leaders."

For the first half of that year the Congress grappled with itself. "Rebels" would fire a round to be met with volleys launched back by "loyalists". For the outside world, the Congress had degenerated into an entity of warring factions. The response of the leadership was a studied silence. In time the voices were silenced on most fronts, subdued by time.

Elsewhere they rose in unison threatening to split the party. In the State of West Bengal, a menacing problem began to brew.

The Quiet Death of the Bengal 'Mahajot'

For over a quarter of a century now the Left Front has had a free run over the governance of West Bengal. Under Jyoti Basu the Communists, Marxists, Leninists and other sundry socialists of various denominations under the aegis of the Left Front have been returned to power in every single assembly election since 1977. Their support is held and maintained both through a programme of popular policies like agrarian reform and the benefits which come from having a strong and well organised party cadre. It was this policy of land redistribution, under the name of Operation Barga, which led to 20 per cent of the all-India land redistribution taking place in West Bengal alone.

This legislative Communism of the contemporary politics of West Bengal is far removed from the radicalism of the 1950s. It is somewhat different from the appreciation of sections of the CPI for the socialistic policies and programmes of the Congress in the 1950s and 1960s too. Today the political terrain in Bengal is claimed by three broad fronts. While only the Communists have been able to make and sustain success, the principal opposition to the Left Front comes from the Congress Party, first spearheaded by the brilliant Siddhartha Shankar Ray and then represented by the erudite Pranab Mukherjee. The split of 1996, when Mamata Banerjee, the feisty Congress virago left the party to form her own Trinamool Congress, destroyed any chances there may have been of unseating the "red brigade". It is her party which formed the "third front" of Bengal politics, in an uneasy alliance with the BJP.

In 2000, however, it appeared that a *rapprochement* between the mother party and Mamata were possible. Jyoti Basu, after successfully leading the Communists for almost twenty-five years and having been the Chief Minister of West Bengal for twenty-three, decided to announce his retirement from state politics. Many believed that it was the personality and demeanour, abstemious and brooking no nonsense, of this quintessential "bhadralok" which ensured both popularity and recognition for his government in consecutive elections. In his departure from the scene, Mamata Banerjee, above all, sensed that some ground could be recovered from the Communists. A vaccuum of leadership was cited, as is often done when a political successor does not appear familiar to political pundits working on assumptions. Basu's heir-apparent, Budhadev Bhattacharya was by no means a newcomer, either to politics or administration. In 1977, Bhattacharya joined the cabinet as Minister for Information and Cultural Affairs, since then he held various portfolios, most notably the Home (and Police) Ministry and finally became Deputy Chief Minister to Jyoti Basu, taking over from him in November 2000.

Sensing that a change of guard necessarily amounted to insurmountable tasks incorporating organisational difficulties and a lack of recognition, Banerjee came up with the idea of a "Mahajot" or Grand Alliance to fight the Communists in the 2001 Assembly Election. This would involve a coming together of her Trinamool Congress, the Indian National Congress itself and, bizarrely the BJP against the Left Front. Her choice of the BJP was subject to compulsions of partnership at the Centre in the Lok Sabha. She continued to be a member of the BJP-led NDA. Simultaneously, she cultivated the understanding of the formidable PCC President A.B.A Ghani Khan Chowdhary, the septugenarian and erstwhile ruler of Malda and Indira Gandhi's Minister for Railways in the 1970s. Barkatda, as he is popularly known, is a senior figure in the Congress Party. He is one of its longest serving MPs and something of a father figure for the Congress in West Bengal. In character he is something between Malaysia's "Tunku" Abdul Rehman, inspiring fealty from his supporters, and a latter day Kamaraj, revered and respected by those he represents. Chowdhary gave his full support to the move, regularly flying down to New Delhi to meet Sonia Gandhi over the matter. Another prominent figure who enters the scene now is Somen Mitra, a senior leader in the Bengal unit of the party with a significant following among the Congress legislators. Thus the pressure grew, emanating from a significant quarter of the West Bengal Pradesh Congress Committee (WBPCC). State leaders had protracted meetings with their national counterparts in New Delhi. The BJP, as far as the Bengal Congressmen were concerned, was a lesser evil than the Communists, whom they had been fighting for twenty-five years. In a letter to the Congress President, the State General Secretary, Sultan Ahmed wrote:

> The failure to assess the grassroot sentiment has immensely damaged the goodwill of the Congress and given the impression that the Congress as a party is not willing to fight against the CIP (M).... While the argument forwarded by the AICC that the party cannot have any direct or indirect alliance with non-secular political outfits is not disputed, in reality we find that the Congress nominee got elected to the post of deputy mayor in New Mumbai getting open support of Shiv Sena councillors who are allies of the BJP.

It is shocking to see validations and justifications being given, by citing irrelevant records, to create an atmosphere of acceptability for the BJP in the Congress Party. Meanwhile, Mamata Banerjee's protests grew more urgent by the day, her supporters within the Congress more trenchant over their position. The other group in the Congress, represented by Priyaranjan Das Munshi, an outspoken Congress MP in the Lok Sabha, had no such considerations. He took the position that while an alliance was possible with the Trinamool itself, it was unacceptable to forge an understanding with the BJP. These, in fact, were the feelings of the, so far, reticent Congress President Sonia Gandhi too. Kamal Nath, the man deputed to "sort things out" with the demi mondes of the Bengal Congress, understood this well and pursued this line cogently in all his discussions with the pro-Mahajot group. It was still mid-May and Mamata Banerjee had her eyes set on the Municipal elections and the June 9 Lok Sabha by-election for the late Gita Mukherjee's Panskura seat. By fighting the election en alliances with the BJP (of which she was already a part) and the Congress, Banerjee hoped to use the result as an indicator for the potential of a Mahajot. Even had the Mahajot lost, a joint candidate would have ensured a higher vote in their favour and thus an espousal of the proposed alliance. Sonia Gandhi did not appreciate this view and Congress fielded its own candidate for the contest, affecting a serious setback for the concept of the Mahajot. Nothing could have been more sagacious and nothing helped her authority more.

The demands to join the Mahajot in West Bengal were the result of frustration, both on the part of Mamata Banerjee who has built a career out of "Commie-bashing" and of a section of the state Congress. Twenty-five years of Communist rule have exasperated the opposition. The Left Front government represents for these groups an elective dictatorship whose continuation in power thwarts the political progress (in whatever measure) of the opposition. Therefore the concept of the Mahajot in West Bengal appeared to lead to a "promised land", and "greener pastures", it signified a possibility to the end of Communist predominance. The pro-Mahajot Congressmen of West Bengal could not appreciate the enormity of the consequences their proposals entailed. Their political vision, limited to Bengal, was insensitive to the politics of the rest of the country and politically vacuous. Simply put, it was impolitic. For the Congress Party to join hands, however far stretched, with the BJP would amount to *ideological harakiri*. Simultaneously, Sonia Gandhi's personal distaste and arrant dislike for the BJP and its ideology would never allow her to give way to them. She was also shrewd enough to appreciate the value of keeping the Left Front mildly congenial for future partnerships at the Centre. Historically too, the left and the Congress shared a greater concentricity than either could with the BJP, in terms of their socialist legacies and anti-fascist ideologies. Most importantly, however, and this is a point which has not been given enough recognition in any analysis of this entire episode, Sonia Gandhi was astute enough to realise that any pact with the BJP would amount to a surrender of principles on a national scale. If there is any single issue over which Sonia Gandhi has demonstrated both a firm understanding and a strong willingness to act in her career so far, it is the necessity to blunt the right-wing. She was able to recognise the vast damage Rao's accommodation of the BJP and its associates caused both to the Congress (in electoral terms) and to the polity as a whole. She required no tutelary to guide her over the pro's and con's of the Mahajot matter. Even under immense pressure from a recalcitrant state unit, which threatened to split for a second time in five years, as leader of the Congress Party she remained firm. That the pro-Mahajot Congressmen coalesced to their leader's view saw her prerogative and authority greatly enhanced. While the Congress had jay-walked into the BJP trap under Rao over the Ayodhya crisis, Sonia Gandhi was determined that this would never happen under her. Just when her leadership appeared threatened by internal dissent and almost provoked splits within the party, she was able to turn things around by resolving the Bengal crisis. A crisis and its resolution restored the confidence of her party leaders. Nonetheless, while she had demonstrated great dexterity over the handling of this issue another crisis had lingered on and ended in a not so successful conclusion.

UP : Fear and Loathing in Lucknow

The politics of Uttar Pradesh revolves around how much control is retained and how much opposition detained in the process of establishing authority, whether individual or corporate. Similarly the success of a political party depends largely on how strong a grip it can exert over a single caste or community group and a corresponding weakness in one's opposition in fermenting such *en bloc* sustenance. Usually this weakness in others is engineered, though in the case of the Congress Party it has arisen as a consequence of its own floundering political strategies with only a little help from its rivals. The Muslims left the party because it did not appear to protect the Babri Masjid. The upper castes jumped ship because the Congress did not replace the Masjid with a Ram Mandir. And finally, the Scheduled Castes abandoned it for charismatic leadership of their own community leaders in the wake of the reservation policies of the early 1990s.

With its traditional voters gone, Congress leaders took to conducting adversarial politics within the confines of their own state unit. State leaders looked for dominant patrons at the Centre. These "alpha-males" in turn advanced association and accoutrements to their respective proteges and gave them license to operate as they wished in the state, provided that they would remember the source of their reserves. When Narayan Dutt Tiwari and his followers left the mainstream Congress in 1994 to form the Tiwari Congress, a number of second rank state leaders had an exclusive and near-total control of the UPCC. Jitendra Prasad, the PCC President at the time, cultivated and groomed them. In 1996 the alliance with the BSP, which gave away three hundred of the total four hundred and twenty odd seats, was cemented with a view that it would throw up an obsequious and ultimately captive legislature party in the Assembly. Prasad's calculations proved prescient. Of the thirty odd legislators elected to the Assembly after the 1996 assembly election, over half succumbed to his authority due to a mixture of fealty, foibility and fear in varying measures. Pramod Tiwari, the leader of the CLP was isolated and hectored whenever the opportunity provided for such enterprise.

An enterprise is what the UPCC became. Properties of the UPCC, like the National Herald building were almost signed off to seedy building, contracters through dubious procedures. Organisational elections to the PCC in 1997 were disengeniously orchestrated, with the selection of returning officers and the PCC list itself being drawn up by a cabal rather than a committee. Select members of the press-core were fed selective stories, beneficial for the reigning establishment, burlesque about its competition. Above all, the split in the legislature party in 1996 which led to the formation of the Loktantrik Congress under Naresh Agarwal was a final proof of profane power games being played out for individual rather than party amelioration. It would appear that the proteges had outgrown their mentors. Meanwhile, a furtive and insidious development occurred which brought the Congress in the state closer, if not in partnership, to all its political rivals in the state. Voices demanding an "alternative acceptable leadership" to Narayan Dutt Tiwari began to be heard. The 1996 split had coalesced a group of Congress dissidents within the ruling BJP, a second section was strident about alliances with the SP while a third, comprising legislators and former ringleaders, urged for organisational changes at every level so that all opposition within could be uprooted.

In 1998, Sonia Gandhi replaced Sitaram Kesri as AICC President and Jitendra Prasad, enjoying his position of pre-eminence as party vice-president, lost a benefactor. Kesri had owed much to Prasad, not least of all the favour that Prasad had done him of assuring a strong register of votes from UP in the AICC leadership election. With her arrival the balances guiding patrimonial politics, particularly in UP were overturned. Jitendra Prasad was removed as vice-president, Sitaram Kesri confined to membership of the CWC. As for providing alternative leadership to UPCC, Sonia Gandhi picked her own man for the job, thus in a way accepting the demands of the dissidents for a change but supplying a candidate who was acceptable in her eyes but not convenient for their equations.

Salman Khurshid's tenure as UPCC President certainly provided for a tempered mutation to the pre-existing atmosphere of Congress politics in the state. His operative style has been variously described as confrontational, cantankerous and constrained. However, it is for his critics to judge whether a quiescent or pliable leader could have cut swathes of progress in the prevailing atmosphere of the UPCC. That he did not receive adequate cooperation from the malcontents in the Congress, despite repeated attempts to involve them in participatory politics, is true. Writing to Sonia Gandhi the state president observed:

> Their standard strategems include whisper campaigns, planting stories in the media, undermining the work being done by the UPCC to revive the Congress. Being critical of every step and talking negatively to demoralise ordinary workers is routine behaviour. They have an unreasonably high expectation of being offered greater participation in decision making, but with little inclination to cooperate. Due to the large-scale manipulation in the last party elections there is acute resentment against the main protagonists. Over the months, standard attempts to soften them and reach out to them were seen by ordinary workers as unreasonable appeasement. On the other hand, they projected our courtesies as a sign of weakness. In UP appearances play a very crucial

role and any projected signs of weakness hit the morale of workers very severely.

For their part, these dissidents continued to indulge in a cannibalistic form of politicking which abated further progress which he could have made. Despite the internal instances of surreptitious sabotage, Khurshid went about fulfilling his brief in a practised, and as far as possible, conciliatory manner. His schedules were laborious and itinerant. In the first few months of his charge, he had covered the entire state, holding meetings in each of its hundred odd districts. A system of preparing alerts and bulletins for the Congress President in New Delhi was established whereby Sonia Gandhi was kept informed of developments. These were rather different to the run of the mill committee minutes or observations of the AICC representatives. They included detailed notes and exhaustive enumerations about the ground situation. The disturbing aspect of his style however, as far as the dissidents were concerned, was the truculent and trenchant line which Khurshid took against Mulayam Singh and his SP. Over the years, the SP had grown complacent about any threat from the Congress Party which in turn provided a rather flaccid response to the SP considering that it was a principal rival. Salman Khurshid made his battle with Mulayam Singh an *affaire d'honneur* to be fought until death. The tactic was a pertinent one because the Congress by this stage was competing with Mulayam Singh for the Muslim vote which had gone over to him. The installation of a Muslim PCC chief was primarily done to inject confidence into the lingering bitterness of the Muslim community and thus register a political reconversion in their minds. The other less obvious but equally valid assumption was that the upper castes, disgruntled with the BJP for various reasons, would begin to retreat towards the Congress once they saw it had secured the support of another strong vote-bank like the Muslims. This provoked an equally vehement attack upon the BJP, at times emotive because it appealed to previously embitterred Muslims, immensely important because it persuaded the frustrated upper-castes, particularly Brahmins. How far the strategem worked has been looked at earlier in this book. Post-elections the chorus for leadership change began to reverberate again. The infinite cost of time and pride spent in reviving the UPCC had given some fullfilment to Congress workers. However, that seemingly inextinguishable bolus of dissenters did not share this enthusiasm. With the leadership election in the winter of 2000 on the horizon, they now raised the bogey of revolt. Jitendra Prasad's own efforts, now out in the open, to challenge Sonia Gandhi appeared threatening enough to the party high-command. Mysteriously, this gave way to the removal of Salman Khurshid and the appointment of a new "non-controversial" UPCC President. How this came about is a bizarre story, the sources are often unreliable and sometimes untraceable. It would appear that party leaders, among them Madhavrao Scindia and Arjun Singh, were persuaded to believe that Khurshid would not be able to secure a strong enough vote from the UPCC members for Sonia Gandhi and thus Prasad would be able to make a stand from Lucknow. This in turn would prove embarrassing for the central leadership and for Sonia Gandhi herself. Thus a policy of appeasement was put into play, on exactly whose suggestion it is unclear. The little known Congress MP from Kanpur, Sri Prakash Jaiswal was installed as the new president and Salman Khurshid shifted to New Delhi as Chairman of the newly formed Department for Policy Planning and Coordination. To a vast number of party workers in UP this appeared to be the height of malapropos. Working on the assumption that Jitendra Prasad enjoyed unchallenged support in the PCC, the central leadership effectively subsidised support to a group of ungratifiable stirrers. That Prasad's group was ineffective, even weak, was proved by the subsequent results of the election. Nonetheless, Congress leaders were working on the Hobbesian principle, cited by Mani Shankar Aiyar, that "between 'electibility' and 'suitability', the party falls between two stools. The present system ensures stability and consistency of opinion in the party high command. It does not give enough scope for innovation, imagination, the spark that can light a people's heart." More noteworthy, and arrantly damaging was the fact that Khurshid's removal put a stop to the momentum building up in favour of the Congress throughout the state. At the same time it exerted pressures in places where there were previously none.

Death of an Airman

There was an atavism about Rajesh Pilot's politics, for he was instantly comparable to Chandra Shekhar in the image of a bucolic "Young Turk". Unlike the former Prime Minister, however, Pilot was able to ingratiate himself with his compeers and often enlist their admiration. Nor was his "dissidence" an aberration for he was always vocal on important issues, often bellicose on party political matters and willingly audacious when it came to questions over party leadership. That was in the nature of this Gujjar strongman who represented, for almost ten years, the avant-garde of the Congress Party. This image did not desert him even until his death in a car crash in Rajasthan on June 11, 2000. Just weeks before he had declared his ambitions on BBC's "Hard Talk" admitting that there was nothing wrong if he aspired to become Prime Minister. In a party where suspicions rise sharply over the mention of ambitions this aroused certain misgivings. His decision then to attend Jitendra Prasad's Jhansi rally in May, a thinly veiled show of strength against the state Congress leadership and therefore Sonia Gandhi herself lent credence to the theories that he was manouvring himself to challenge her. Nonetheless, challenge was what Rajesh Pilot did best. In 1996, while it was apparent to everyone in the Congress that Sitaram Kesri was bound to emerge the victor in the party leadership election, Pilot continued to see things his own way. Days before the election on June 9, 1997, Pilot lambasted Kesri and Pawar, the other candidate, in an Interview given to *India Today* declaring:

> Kesri cannot lead, he is amoral; he has no transparency. Sharad Pawar was Chief Minister of Maharashtra. I think the Congress lost there for the first time in 50 years. Both of them have been tried out. I am the only one in the list of three who has not been tried.

Even though he lost the leadership election, this defeat did not detract from the influence he possessed among the workers and the goodwill of the public at large. Pilot was one of the few ministers of the Rao government who escaped with his reputation nearly intact while his ministerial colleagues faltered for a variety of reasons. His strength lay in his popularity among the backwards and principally among the Gujjars of western UP and Rajasthan. While his death robbed him of another chance to make a bid for the leadership there were others who took up this "cause".

The Leadership Election

"Coteries do not serve the party. They encircle the leadership, insulate it from the workers and block channels of intra-party communication. For their own vested interests the coteries slander all those who refuse to be browbeaten. They misrepresent all discussions and differences as proof of disloyalty. Coteries are a cancer that eat into the vitals of all political parties : we must save the Congress from them."

One would be forgiven for mistaking this passage for the ponderings of an exiled revolutionary, far from home, divested of his attachments and identity with his motherland, raging against a machine of an establishment he blames for snatching away his privileges and way of life from him. Nevertheless, thus spoke Jitendra Prasad. In a pamphlet distributed to not enough Congress delegates, as it turned out, Prasad spoke of his disillusionment with the "Congress system". He was at pains to emphasise that his candidature for party president was not a signal of any personal animosity against Sonia Gandhi but an attempt to demonstrate "how inner-party democracy should function." Prasad's political profile was itself the very definition of what a coterie member should be. He began his political career as a member of the Uttar Pradesh Legislative Council in 1970 and entered Parliament the following year in the Indira wave representing Shahjahanpur in UP which he represented for 17 years (not consecutive) in the Lok Sabha. While his career witnessed sharp elevations and downfalls, among the numerous posts which he held at one time or another were the coveted appointments of Political Secretary to both Rajiv Gandhi and Narasimha Rao. All these accumulations of political laurels are a tribute to the shrewd agility and political acumen of a man who had come to epitomise survival in the murky labyrinths of power politics. Nonetheless, it was Kesri who elevated him to the office of Vice-President in June 1997, a position he held on to until April 1998, when Sonia Gandhi dissolved it. He could never rise above it and finally sank struggling against a leadership apparatus he had helped to create, in more ways than one. Until Sonia Gandhi removed him from the post of Vice-President, Prasad had been at the most central of coteries. He had all the experience needed to analyse the fallouts, positive or adverse, of running a political organisation from the comforts of a silent, largely unseen inner circle of hand-picked backroom boys. Indeed he had been an engineer of many of those predominantly adverse fallouts. Prasad was adviser to Narasimha Rao when the Babri Masjid was demolished in 1992. It was he who had suggested continuing support to the Mulayam Singh government in Uttar Pradesh in 1994. In 1996 as President of the UPCC, he had engineered the alliance with the BSP which gave away 300 of the 425 seats in the UP Assembly to that party after very little consultation with other party leaders. In his loyalty to Rao, he appeared staunch; "He is my leader and it is my duty to stand by him in every situation."

While in politics it is all to easy to "loyally" switch allegiance from one persona to another it is perhaps even easier and far more prudent to change principles and alternate between a varied repertoire of survival strategies, particularly when principles are denied the sweet nectar of reward, in whatever measure that may be granted. Each time that a transfer of power occurred within the party, JP, as he was often called, gravitated with swiftness towards the emerging successor. His decision to stand for the party election was by no means a sudden, desperate act of challenging the leadership in a final and glorious showdown. Nor was his "death-train" accompanied by any loud fanfare or baggage from the rest of the party. As a very senior member of the Congress, Prasad was entitled to holds views, even if they differed from the vast majority of the party. He was even franchised to put them to a contest with Sonia Gandhi which is precisely what he did. Prasad was clever enough to realise that it was a battle he could never win, but that was not the point he was making.

Prasad wished to make a dent, perhaps have his injuries registered within the party and outside, certainly he wished to demonstrate to Sonia Gandhi as well as the rest of the party, his clout over the party organisation. He sought to portray himself as the victim of the designs of a few favoured elite within the party. This strategy, at first sight, appears to be a viable one. Certainly it would find favour with the innumerable other discordant Congress leaders and dignitaries who, at one time or another, may have felt slighted or isolated by the actions of the small and influential body of a coterie. While he may have been clever, he did not appear to realise that even he, with all the experience of inner party politics at his command, would be unable to "reach out" to the electoral college of the Congress Party when the choice for them lay between him and Sonia Gandhi. It cannot be that Prasad did not see this, but he was vain enough to conclude that he would be able to draw away a sizeable chunk of malcontents and subsequently secure enough support to maintain a power base of his own within the party. The theme of the death-train is once more evident in the choice (or were there no alternatives) of his confidantes at this juncture. Every evening, for a few weeks preceding the party poll, a group of Prasad loyalists would dutifully assemble at his Teen Murti Road residence.

The calm of Lutyens' Delhi on balmy evenings, the pervading atmosphere of conspirators meeting after dark to plot designs while time hung heavily, must have provided Prasad and his group with a tinge of misapprehension of their own chances. After all this was a tightly knit group, meeting together in those whitewashed bungalows originally designed for guardians of the British Raj, exuding both comfort and a buzz of power. Discussions over sumptuous snacks, moving between gossip and serious discourse in these surroundings led him and his motley collection of friends to misread the mindset of the Congress Party. A cursory glance at the list of invitees to these reclusive soirees would reveal that Prasad's court attracted people who themselves formed only a part of the fringe groups in the party which are gleefully labelled "dissidents" by the Indian media. Of the notables was Begum Noor Bano, two-term MP and a member of the Royal Family of Rampur, Khan Gufran Zaidi, a septugenarian but still active Congress MP from the Rajya Sabha and Sujan Singh Bundela, Congress MP from Jhansi, whom Prasad wanted to contest the forthcoming election of UPCC President against the official party candidate Jaiswal. Neither of these had any regional base of their own to speak of, although it must be said both Bano and Bundela exerted strong local influence in their constituencies. They brought with them their own second line lieutenants and acolytes who contributed to making these soirees a seemingly busy and crowded affair. The untimely death of Rajesh Pilot in an accident had snatched away the most potent ally Prasad could have hoped for in such circumstances. To speculate on his chances of success had Pilot been alive, is difficult. Certainly it is probable that Pilot would have extended his patronage to Prasad. It is even more plausible to suggest that Pilot may have himself stood as a candidate against Sonia Gandhi, if the last few actions of his life are anything to go by. Certainly that would have embarrassed the leadership, not merely the act of a senior and highly popular leader standing against an adored incumbent but the possibility of him striking up a respectable number of votes even if Sonia Gandhi won the election. In the circumstances, Rajesh Pilot's absence would certainly have been felt by Prasad and his team.

It would be foolish to ignore the pool of talent, however miniscule, which JP had assembled around him. He had always been in awe of and admired the power of the press and had, therefore, cultivated around him a bolus of journalists and correspondents who would dutifully grant him lines in the broadsheets and magazines during this period. This created, not only for him and his group but for the rest of the party and the public at large, an illusion of strength which did not correspond to reality. Nevertheless, whatever influence a national press may or may not exert over the polity it is rarely in their power to alter the course of events by way of selective leaks and plants. Nor can the press sustain a superficial campaign mounted on the brittle support of past generousity by an individual against the tide of *realpolitik*.

As with everything, Sonia Gandhi took a serious view of the emerging developments. However, she was unperturbed by these developments. Her confidence was generated both by practice and by the justifiable assurance that the party could not desert her. The practice had come by her experience and handling of the leadership crisis of 1999 when the combination of three CWC members, Pawar, Sangma and Anwar had been thwarted and sent packing by the censure of the entire party. With the exception of certain numbers of the party organisation in Maharashtra, no one else had risen and joined the revolt. None would do so now. This view was not borne out of any complacency on her part. Sonia Gandhi understood well that Jitendra Prasad had left himself open on three flanks. The first was Uttar Pradesh, she had finally accepted the demands of many party leaders and removed Salman Khurshid, her personal choice, as the UPCC President. The grandees had persuaded her that Khurshid could not be guaranteed to deliver votes in a leadership election from Uttar Pradesh which comprises the highest number of the electoral college of the AICC and the PCCs. They also argued that Prasad would be assuaged were she to install a "non-controversial" President instead of Khurshid who shared a very unsettled relationship with Prasad. Reluctantly, Shri Prakash Jaiswal, a little known MP from the industrial city of Kanpur, was appointed the new PCC President. This stumped Jitendra Prasad who, although happy to see the last of Khurshid, now had to contend with a man not of his own choice. Madhavrao Scindia and N.D. Tewari, among others, were now unable to explain the emergence of Prasad as a candidate despite the realignments they had engineered in Uttar Pradesh. This proved to be the first blow to Jitendra Prasad's ambitions. He was isolated in his home state because for leading members of the party, delivering votes from UP now became tantamount to their own political survival. As a result, Prasad faced not merely Sonia Gandhi but the combined forces of Scindia, Tiwari and Arjun Singh who were obliged to cut him down for the survival of their own credibility.

The second and more obvious rout he faced was at the national level. Despite a long innings in party politics and a stint as the AICC Vice-President, the depth of Prasad's political contacts was deepest in northern India, from where he came and which he represented. Like his former master Rao who was more comfortable with politics in his native southern India, Prasad did not possess a grasp over the motivations and machinations of politicians and politics outside his home turf in the Hindi heartland. In state after state to which he travelled to garner support for his candidature, Prasad was met with lockouts and disinterested Congressmen and women. He took to the recourse of complaining of a conspiracy against him, of an authoritarian central leadership working against him through pressure tactics and manipulations. He did manage, however, to portray that regional satraps, disenchanted with the central leadership, privately supporting him and would deliver the goods. Such theories were percolated from the AICC, too. The usual suspects, big names like J.B. Patnaik from Orissa, Karunakaran in Kerala and Vijaya Bhaskar Reddy from Andhra Pradesh, were floated from time to time as being sympathetic to his cause. This only persuaded them in turn to further distance themselves from charges of dissidence which are all too quickly hurled at politicians in the Congress Party. Thus this strategy of projecting the support (real or superficial) of party big wigs from the states backfired on Prasad. Potential supporters also turned against him when it was circulated that Prasad was being funded and supported by the apparatus of Sharad Pawar's NCP to embarrass the Congress leadership. It was this rumour which created a seriousness within the party, for no one, not even the most cynical dissident in the Congress, could bear the thought of being humbled by the forces of Sharad Pawar. So far, the attitude of the average party person had been complacent and at times conciliatory, now it became hardened as some began to doubt whether this really would be a one-sided contest.

The third and final flank which Prasad and his team did not even consider was that most fundamental rule of power politics. The importance of credibility coupled with the ability to deliver rewards. This abstraction is singularly the most important and valued currency in the bazaar of power politics. Prasad could not combine credibility with deliverance. It was this fact alone which assured Sonia Gandhi of an overwhelming victory in this leadership election. Had she even been complacent and careless and made no attempt to arrest developments early on, she would still have emerged victorious. Needless to say, Prasad could not even manage to embarrass her because his bag of goods was light and exhausted from years of political expenditure. Writing for an online journal as a response to Jitendra Prasad's declaration, Salman Khurshid outlined the mood of the party in a manner which is difficult to improve upon:

A few days ago, Jitendra Prasad, a member of the highest policy making body of the Congress Party, announced his candidature for the post of Congress President. In a document that pretends to be a manifesto of sorts, entitled, "Why I am a candidate", he has expressed his reasons for doing what has seldom been done in the history of the Congress......Jitendra Prasad has yet to substantiate his expressed concerns with specific models and articulation that would give his issues political life. Yet he offers himself as an improvement on the present leadership of the Congress. Of course he liberally castigates the "coterie"......JP regrets the Congress is a loser. He hates losers although he will soon be one himself......He says he has realised how wrong he was. He has not sought forgiveness, just support to be president......It is imperative that we conceive an ideology that will combine contemporary economic reality with a transparent and effective commitment to empowerment of disadvantaged groups. We have to strive for good governance, compassion, decency and change. I believe that Mrs. Sonia Gandhi represents all of that in far greater measure than any other leader, both in the party and outside. That a large number of young Congress leaders and workers who describe themselves as the sunrise Congress support her despite our defeat in elections is a significant political statement. We want debate and we want change but we do not believe that we will succeed without Mrs. Gandhi. That is why we are not candidates in this election. That is why we do not support JP the candidate. That is why we support Mrs. Gandhi.

Most Congress members who had a voice in the leadership election would have understood exactly what Salman Khurshid was speaking of even if they could not articulate their concerns in the same manner. Many would sooner have empathised with the sentiments voiced by Khurshid in his article than with the contents of Jitendra Prasad's leaflet. Many were able to recognise now that what had begun with a minor exchange of fire between the "dissident" Prasad and the "loyal" Khurshid had expanded into a full scale battle between Prasad and Sonia Gandhi herself. Consequently, they were obliged to take sides and this often assumed ugly proportions. On the day when Prasad arrived at the AICC to fill in his nomination forms, he was greeted not merely by discordant glances but fists and a violent upsurge which found some of his supporters lying injured among flowerbeds, others with their clothes torn. Naturally the television and press cameras gleefully clicked away and the unsettling visuals were prominently displayed in every newspaper the following day. Observers questioned if this was what inner party democracy meant in the Congress Party.

Ram Niwas Mirdha, the man in charge of formulating the election schedules, the party's resident Election Commissioner if you like, had set the counting of the ballot for November 15. From the morning of the day itself, the AICC was transformed into a *melange* of colour and celebration. Part circus, part a reflection of a political HQ which it is, the AICC was crowded and overflowing with party workers, leaders and dignitaries. It would have seemed, to those unfamiliar with the political culture of the Indian subcontinent that this was some medieval gathering, arranged to rejoice and celebrate the coronation of a royal rajah. Elephants dressed in glitter, dancing stallions, and acrobats moved among Congressmen walking in and out of what apparel to be a club, dressed in the starched white apparells of the Indian politician. The scent of marigolds and roses mixed with the jasmine perfumes emanating from the AICC's lawns, which in turn were overborne by the smell and sounds of bursting firecrackers. Meanwhile, a hundred or so members of the party's Seva Dal, or cadre, stood stiffly and uneasily in their uniforms, titillating between a desire to join the celebrating masses and performing their duties of enforcing discipline upon those who entered or left the AICC compound which was practically sealed for the day. Within was a collection of Congressmen and women which varied from Chief Ministers to party workers, members of the AICC and other PCC delegates who had assembled to witness the result of an election few ever got to see. This was only the second time that the party had held an internal election to choose its President in 50 years.

The counting progressed all through the day. Prasad's supporters had estimated that he would secure around 300 votes, whatever the odds. Meanwhile, Sonia Gandhi and her team were, of course, confident of victory. However, some Congressmen, predominantly die-hard supporters of the Congress President, through a combination of naivety and a fear psychosis, despaired of the final result. By the late afternoon, journalists began making and taking soundings in various parts of the AICC forecourt. Anyone making a comment on the progressing counting was immediately surrounded by a gathering of strays equally intent on making up their own minds through this informed gossip. By 3 pm it was all clear, Prasad was struggling to reach a hundred votes out of the 7000 or so already counted. By the time the result was announced a few hours later, the AICC compound had been stormed by enthusiastic party workers and leaders all anxiously awaiting the arrival of Sonia Gandhi to make her speech of thanks. The entire paraphernalia which accompanies such celebrations in India grew; hot air balloons were hoisted over the grounds, the bands and acrobats previously playing outside on the Akbar Road were now ensconced inside, as loud as ever.

Few were left unsurprised by the result, it was a staggering defeat for a man who had once held the party in his grip. Of the 7771 votes cast, Sonia Gandhi had secured 7448, Prasad had fizzled out at 94, not even making it to triple figures. Few had thought that the magnitude of his eclipse would be so dark and overwhelming. In 1997 it was Prasad who had almost singlehandedly secured over a 1000 votes for Kesri against Pawar and Pilot. He admitted defeat and congratulated Mrs. Gandhi, still insisting, however, that his struggle for inner party democracy would continue and called for "immediate steps to review the entire process of organisational elections."

Sonia Gandhi for her part was greeted by loud acclaims and cheered when she did appear in the evening to deliver her speech. After the occasion, she exchanged views with journalists and calmly remarked with a very perceptible grin on her face that Prasad had done "rather well" to have got the votes he did. When questioned about inner party democracy, she responded with an uncharacteristic but light-hearted retort:

> The press now says that there are two or three coteries, which is an improvement because initially there was only one.

As party men and women lined up under the ancient bargat tree inside her 10 Janpath residence all through the evening, she met each and every one of them, thanking those she recognised. The more private visitors, who no doubt deliberated the fallouts of the day, met with her in her study. This was the much maligned coterie back at work. The subjects under discussion ranged from reporting back on how the election had gone to the future course of action regarding Prasad and his support base. Sonia Gandhi received them and their views with the freshly acquired confidence of a party leader who has just been elected to their post by a more than absolute majority. To most, like veteran thespian and party MP Sunil Dutt, she smiled and nodded her head expressing thank yous. With others such as Madhavrao Scindia who came in loaded with paperwork, she devoted more time over discussions on a wide range of matters. The coterie had its own way of congratulating its elected leader for Sonia Gandhi had secured a first for her family. She was the first member of the Nehru-Gandhi dynasty to have been elected its President in post-independent India.

The following week *Frontline,* a national magazine, articulated the summum bonum of the entire exercise of Congress Party organisational polls and what they meant for Jitendra Prasad:

The defeat means virtually an end to Prasad's hope of emerging as an alternative power centre in the Congress (I). The abysmal performance marks a "historic" low for Prasad, whose political career is almost four decades old. Never before had his support base in the Congress (I) shrunk so much, particularly in his home state of Uttar Pradesh.

The legitimacy aqcuired by her victory in the leadership election gave Sonia Gandhi a more tenacious grip over the Congress than any of her predecessors in that office. Furthermore, election victories in the election going states in the following year would only supplement her strength. Her opposition within the party had disintegrated. Jitendra Prasad's death in January 2001 from a brain haemorrhage, while climactic for him, did not add comfort but nor did it invoke any sadness in the party as a whole. A new CWC was constituted, orthodox and convenient in composition. The only suitable epithet for Sonia Gandhi as she saw in the New Year in 2001 is provided in the following observation made many centuries ago:

> Everyone sees what you appear to be, few really know what you are, and those few dare not oppose themselves to the opinion of the many, who have the majority of the state to defend them; and in the actions of all men, and especially of princes, which it is not prudent to challenge, one judges by the result.

Blood, Sweat, Toil and Tears

Reaching Out – The Lost Generation and the Generation that Lost – Gujarat Torched, India Enflamed – Himalayan Respites

Reaching Out

With the exception of Madhavrao Scindia's death, 2001 was, arguably the easiest year for Sonia Gandhi as the Leader of the Opposition. The defeat of the 1999 Lok Sabha election, the challenge to her leadership in 2000 and the initial difficulties within Parliament were now behind her. The sins of Gujarat, the travails of the POTO[1] legislation and electoral difficulties lay ahead. The year 2001 allowed settlement and conciliation.

One of the most serious issues which demanded the attention of the political classes in India at the time was the NCERT's[2] National Curriculum Framework for School Education in November 2000. There were provocative and controversial ancillaries to this framework. In the process of arguments over the very future of primary education in India the matter became addled with Constitutional amendments and provisions, nomenclature, and Sonia Gandhi's own strident opposition to what has come to be known as the 'saffronisation of education.'

The Constitution Amendment Bill which only just preceded the bid for 'saffronising' school curicula aroused certain misgivings too. In her letter to the Prime Minister which was intended for publication Sonia Gandhi wrote to urge greater inclusion for those not covered by the government bill. 'There are certain aspects of this issue,' she wrote, 'which have been touched upon in the past by the Standing Committee related to the Department of Education, which do not appear to have been adequately covered in this Bill.'[3] She went on to urge for the retention of

---

1. Prevention of Terrorism Ordinance.
2. National Council of Educational Research & Training.
3. LOP's letter to Prime Minister. November 23, 2000.

Article 45, which faced deletion due to the provisions in the new bill. The government had argued that the Directive Principles, that is the principles governing State action, which incorporated Article 45, would have no use once the state made education a 'Fundamental Right'. Sonia Gandhi's objection was straightforward:

> Article 45 under the Directive Principles need not be deleted merely because education is being made a fundamental right. The Directive Principles embody the objectives of the State. There is no conflict between the Fundamental Right and the Directive Principle. Both are complementary to each other. Further, Article 45 gives a directive to provide free education for all upto 14 years. It takes care of the 0-6 years age group as well, which the Bill does not do.

Four days later, V. Krishna Ananth, writing in *The Hindu* found in her letter 'an attempt to distort the issue rather than any serious concern for the disprivileged.'[4] Taking recourse in convoluted language, '...the Leader of the Opposition (LOP) refuses to recognise that the very spirit of Article 21 is that the rights guaranteed so, are enforceable by means of writ jurisdiction' and accusing her of 'exposing....her ignorance of constitutional provisions.' It was unfortunate to see the government hit out on what was a critical issue through the lines of the media. The opposition to her remarks was a demonstration of the kind of 'blockage' waiting to come.

To Sonia Gandhi and almost all liberal-minded opinion in the country the government was devolving its responsibility from education. In an internal document circulated by her office, her Parliamentary Secretary wrote, 'Now that the Bill has been drafted, LOP has simply pointed out some lacunae to make it foolproof. There can be no objection to that by the media. LOP is merely saying that if we have to pass such a Bill, it should at least be made more effective.' It was with regard to the other provisions put forward by the Minister of Human Resource Development that the truest intentions of the NDA government and Sonia Gandhi's

---

4.   V. Krishna Ananth. 'Sonia and the Right to Education.' *The Hindu*, November 27, 2000.

hardest resolve to fight them surfaced. In his letter to Sonia Gandhi, the Minister for HRD, Dr. Murli Manohar Joshi, an unapologetic BJP hardliner and self professed architect of Hindu revivalism, pretending innocence wrote:

> The National Council of Educational Research and Training (NCERT) as an apex body of professionals in the field of school education took the initiative in the matter...After this yearlong process of consultation to arrive at a national consensus, the NCERT brought out a new National Curriculum Framework for School Education in November 2000...I take this opportunity to impress upon you the need for considering this document in your party and among legislators who may like to help and guide the respective state governments in implementing the curriculum framework in a desirable manner for the betterment of the state, in general and for improving the quality of education in the state, in particular.[5]

Speaking at the discussion of the 'saffronisation of education' Sonia Gandhi deplored the attempts by the government to push through what was clearly a partisan and anti-diluvian flavour into the educational process as a whole. Her speech, bruising as it was for the government and widely interrupted by BJP MPs in particular, may be construed as her reply to Murli Manohar Joshi:

> This debate has been necessitated by continuing efforts, overt and covert, to divert value systems in education into channels that do not reflect the consensus of the nation on the nature of our nationhood. She was disturbed at the attempt to launch a national curriculum which was based on the perception and prejudices of some people, of some ideologues of a certain persuasion instead of the nation as a whole.

It was the following part of her speech, however, which really tore the BJP's underbelly, leading to interruptions and points of order. Without distraction and with remarkable equipoise, Sonia Gandhi declared, 'to mix communal ideology with history textbooks and scientific facts is tantamount to playing with fire. In a country as diverse and complex as

---

5. Murli Manohar Joshi's letter to Sonia Gandhi, Leader of the Opposition. February 8, 2001. The italics are the author's.

ours, such an approach is not only incorrect, but also fraught with dangerous consequences.' The challenge was now inserted, 'The 'saffronisation' of education at all levels will be resisted by the Congress Party – I say this with all the strength at my command – and I am sure that it will be resisted by all secular forces represented in this House and outside....' Her final lines were reserved for Murli Manohar Joshi who had so coolly and nonchalantly written to her earlier in the week, and for a *blasé* Prime Minister himself, '...we hope this debate will put the Hon. Minister of Human Resource Development on notice that he cannot substitute a National Agenda with the hidden agenda. We also hope, this debate will alert the Hon. Prime Minister to the need for continuous vigilance to ensure that the hidden agenda, his Party agenda after all, is not smuggled through the back door in the mistaken belief that no one is watching, because Mr. Speaker, Sir, we are watching...'

It was an unprecedented aggression, it was dramatic and for once it had remarkable consequences. Her intervention in the debate was perhaps the most popular assertion she had made since becoming an MP. 'saffronisation of education' became unpopular in the public mind, it also became another well-defined front that separated a united opposition against a beleaguered government. The government already had considerable cause for its *angst.*

By the time the full consequences of the Tehelka expose were revealed, Sonia Gandhi was already addressing the 81st Plenary of the Indian National Congress in Bangalore. In brief, Tehelka, a media company, had carried out a sting operation to test the level of corruption prevalent in the Defence Ministry. They had successfully offered money or incentives to senior members of the NDA leadership and members of the defence establishment to procure 'phoney' orders for an arms company. All this had been recorded on camera; It was a groundbreaking revelation. No less than the President of the BJP, Bangaru Laxman was 'caught on camera' stuffing his table drawers with bundles of money. Furthermore, the Tehelka team had sought and got an appointment with Jaya Jaitley, a senior member of the Samta Party whose leader, George Fernandes, held the Defence portfolio in the cabinet. The meeting took place in a no less grand and important a place than the Defence Minister's private residence. It was the most illustrative and cogent example yet of scandal and financial sleaze in the highest echelons of the Indian government, relayed directly into the homes of millions of Indians via excited news networks. The government had no choice but to be defensive. Yet among the politicians, only Bangaru Laxman, the President of the BJP found his head had rolled. The transcripts had implicated many others. George Fernandes did resign subsequently under the tremendous pressure generated by the opposition but casually strolled back to his vacant portfolio shortly afterwards. The irony of a purportedly nationalist party covering up a serious debacle concerning national security, was lost only on the members of the government. The entire episode was loopholes to be filled. Sonia Gandhi's own view on the matter deserves citation because it is critical for this particular study. Her first reaction, made in Bangalore, was perhaps the most articulate and well- formed opinion she gave on the issue. Her own subsequent conclusions, enunciated many times, did not again match up to her first interjection. 'Last night, we saw the sad spectacle of a Prime Minister defending the indefensible to remain in power,' she told the AICC, "The Prime Minister and his colleagues have surprisingly accused the media of conspiring with their political opponents. Yet he admits that there is a cancer in the government." Honing in on the BJP itself, she thundered:

> The BJP leadership is issuing certificates of integrity to its leaders and Allies in the same breath as they pronounce piously their intentions of holding an inquiry. We do not expect moral stature from these people. We have always known what they are all about. But we certainly did not imagine that they would descend so low and that they would make commerce of national security. This has shocked all of us. This has shocked the whole nation. We owe to our people, to our soldiers, to the memory of our martyrs that we demand the departure of this government on moral grounds.

This strongly worded speech was not bettered by Sonia Gandhi herself, but it did not make the connection between the determination of the Party with the actions that such an issue demanded. The government scarcely moved, the issue subsequently fizzled out, but the issue did not die.

During the summer of that year, Sonia Gandhi undertook a tour of the United States. This was important for two reasons. First, she was representing India at the UN General Assembly on HIV/AIDS, in New York. Less well defined, though equally important, was the need to demonstrate her outlook and, in the same vein, represent India to the rest of the world. The trip also provided a breather from politicking back home. George Bush had been newly elected President of the United States but Sonia Gandhi refused to be drawn into the controversial election in any serious way. In one of her first major speeches on American soil, she immediately struck a rapport with her audience. '...these days, the areas of communality between India and America have expanded' she remarked.[6] '...During the recent Presidential elections in America, many Indians felt that we should offer our electoral technology to you. Given what is happening in California we can even offer consultancy on how to manage power cuts. We have also great expertise in dealing with what we call defections and what you call shifting political alignments.' The audience was in splits.

The immediate objective of the tour, the address to the UN General Assembly, was another coup. Exhuding élan and an understanding of the issues involved, she called for the thrust of the global effort to tackle prevention and not remain restricted to the high-risk groups. Her speech lacked the fetid 'poli-speak' of the bureaucratic mind which Indian leaders abroad find increasingly preferable to resort to. At all times conscious of the need to keep the issue beyond politics, she assured the UN of 'our deep commitment in India at the highest political level to do everything we can to control this epidemic.'

It was not the only time that Sonia Gandhi stood by the Indian government. On the morning of December 13th, Sonia Gandhi's cavalcade

6.   Address to the Asia Society and Council on Foreign Relations. New York. June 26, 2001.

was stopped and diverted en route to Parliament House. It transpired soon afterwards that terrorists had 'laid siege' to Parliament itself and were involved in a gun battle with security forces. Her defence of democracy speech, made in the wake of the December attack on Parliament, described the attack as not merely an offence against the edifice of Parliament. She also went on to say:

> It was an attack on a magnificent institution, the symbol of all those values that we cherish, the symbol of our parliamentary party. Democracy, in our vicinity, the meaning of this word, the meaning of democracy, can never be understood. In our vicinity, they can never pride themselves in such an institution. On a number of occasions, when attempts were made to establish democracy, those attempts have been invariably stepped upon and crushed by the heavy military boot.[7]

The violent end to 2001 may have induced a sense of foreboding in some. Having assured the government that the Congress Party would 'back the government in its effort to track down and bring to justice terrorists who threaten the nation's intergrity...' Sonia Gandhi and the nation at large turned their attention to the forthcoming assembly elections, which were scheduled for the first quarter of 2002. No one could have expected that for India, the bloodiness had not even begun.

The Lost Generation and the Generation that Lost

"The glories of our blood and state
Are shadows, not substantial things;
There is no armour against Fate;
Death lays his icy hand on kings:
Sceptre and Crown
Must tumble down,
And in the dust be equal made
With the poor crooked scythe and spade."

Death the Leveller – *James Shirley*

---

7.   Discussion regarding the December 13th terrorist attack on Parliament. December 18, 2001.

The Congress Party had every reason to be disappointed with its progress in Uttar Pradesh. Madhavrao Scindia felt particulalrly frustrated because it was his handpicked candidate who was at the helm of affairs in the state now, and had been for the last 11 months, but no progress had been evident. Now, with the Parivartan Yatra on schedule and running throughout the length and breadth of the state, the Congress appeared to be finally preparing for some pre-election exercise. As a senior leader and General Secretary of the party, Scindia was asked to do his bit. Such periodic requests notwithstanding, he felt obliged to do something for his protégé Sri Prakash Jaiswal, the state President, who failed in what is always described in the Congress as "sending the right message across". Whenever he ran into a Congressman from UP, the Scindia, a former Maharaja of Gwalior, would initiate the conversation with a persuasive, "Jaiswal's doing a good job isn't he?", thus pre-empting any other opinion. At the same time, Scindia would work hard through his contacts in the media to get Jaiswal a good press. An entire year had gone by since he had played his hand in UP. Matters hadn't improved and the No. 2 of the Congress Party, its Deputy Leader in Parliament and a popular figure around the country, began to feel under siege from criticism and backbiting. Though he was immensely popular among the party workers, in a way that few leaders are, Scindia had few friends within the party hierarchy. He was trusted by the Congress President herself and was liked by many of the backbenchers in Parliament. That did not, however, grant him respite in his native Madhya Pradesh where individual alliances are brittle and short-lived, sustained periodically by opportunities for confrontation between individual leaders. There had been a time when Scindia could have been the Prime Ministerial candidate of the Congress centre, supported by a group of newly elected and young parliamentarians, immediately after Rajiv Gandhi's assassination in 1991. Even then, he had forfeited the opportunity, deliberately confessing that he lacked the "killer instinct". Nonetheless, his popularity in the early 1990s had shored up a heap of trepidation with the Narasimha Rao establishment. Rao eventually hounded him out of the party on charges of corruption when the maelstorm of the Jain Hawala case broke out. A very brief period in Gowda's United Front Government served between his departure from and return to the Congress where he was rehabilitated by Kesri. With the arrival of Sonia Gandhi, which in some ways he had aided, he was comforted. Rank, privilege and prestige were made available. He was dependable and reliable. Moreover, few others could serve as an effective bridge between an aloof Congress leadership and the rest of the opposition. Only Scindia, among those who could, remained steadfast and loyal to Sonia Gandhi personally. At 56, he was young. There has been speculation whether he could have made a future Prime Minister, in case Sonia Gandhi ever declined the chance. His sympathisers argued for his candidature. With his experience gained through nine unbroken terms to Parliament (1971-1999) it was certainly possible. Such speculation was immediately dismissed by his detractors as a threat to Sonia Gandhi's leadership. While he never personally circulated these themes they were nonetheless highlighted by other party leaders to undermine his influence. In turn, mass support was turned against him when it was spread that he could, in the future, pose a challenge; certainly there was no evidence to suggest this but conspiracy seldom requires evidence. An idea is floated, it is disseminated with largely adverse fallouts for those it is addressed to, possibilities are highlighted on the basis of events which, on face value, suggest a threat, consent to such ideas is eventually created. Among these engineered plots, usually the work of his senior colleagues, Scindia's own dexterity diminished, for parries of manipulation and intrigue were not the strongest weapons in his political armoury. He himself did little to dispel doubts, often he remained unaware. He did not consider himself a candidate for party leadership any more, preferring to play the role of a strong and loyal vassal in strengthening his chosen leader.

One evening in August 2001, Scindia invited a friend to his New Delhi home. The visitor, a keen observer of Congress Party affairs and a close confidante of many of the party's leaders, often dined with the Deputy Leader. They discussed various matters including the situation of the party in UP. Over dinner, Scindia raised the subject of Congress

237

leadership, and the choice of a Prime Ministerial candidate when the time came. Both agreed that Sonia Gandhi was the first and natural choice. Scindia's reasoning was that, "She's good enough for everything else, we get her to win us our seats so why can't she claim what's rightfully hers?" It was a sensitive subject which few spoke about in party circles except in the most closeted company. A testimony to the lack of confidence within the party in presenting a undisputed Prime Ministerial candidate to the country. His visitor agreed with the general principle but argued that there was a possibility that she herself could choose to decline an offer. "So who is the alternative?" asked Scindia. "Well I'm afraid its not you," said his companion. Scindia nodded in approval without a a flicker of disappointment on his face. He knew this all too well and by the end of the evening both agreed on the name which Madhavrao Scindia pronounced as a viable alternative candidate should the need ever arise.

On the day of his departure for Kanpur to monitor the Parivartan Yatra there, Scindia invited four other journalists to travel with him. He was scheduled to address various meetings along with Jaiswal in the city and flag off the party processions the next morning. It was a tight schedule the Deputy Leader found himself in, this was the only day available. The eight seater Beechcraft belonged to the Jindal Group, an industrial conglomerate, and was often hired out to politicians and business leaders. It had been made ready to ferry the group's chairman the following weekend, that event had been postponed and the plane was now put at the disposal of Madhavrao Scindia and his entourage. The sky was clear, it was midday, lunch had been packed to be consumed on the journey. The plane took off towards Kanpur traversing diagonally the UP "badlands" of Etah, Mainpuri and Farrukhabad. A similar VIP flight had returned midway with the UP Chief Minister Rajnath Singh due to bad weather in this notoriously unpredictable weather belt. Scindia's aircraft cruised along nonetheless. In Kanpur restless crowds waited at the aerodrome for their leader. At about 2 pm a rumour circulated that the aircraft carrying Madhavrao Scindia had made an emergency landing near Aligarh owing to inclement weather. Before anyone could find out what was really happening, Star News announced that it had crashlanded somewhere in Farrukhabad district. The news was varied but consistently coming in. It was only a few minutes before the television confirmed that the aircraft had crashed somewhere in Farrukhabad district with no survivors. Death had come to Madhavrao Scindia in isolation, when none expected it. With his death, unnacountable and shocking as it was, an entire generation of Congressmen was obliterated. Once more, the sudden demand for sacrifice, of promise, of youth, charisma and nobility had been paid by the Congress. This was the third generation of Congress leaders to have been accosted by surrender still in the tracts of buoyant careers. Tragically, this last generation which included in its ranks Sanjay Gandhi, Rajiv Gandhi, Rajesh Pilot and now Madhavrao Scindia, was irreplaceable. Already weak and uncertain, Scindia's death dealt a body blow to the Congress. In shock, the party surrendered to the sad circumstances of destiny. It lost its will to question such injustice, such flashes of an unforgiving fortune which demanded as tribute the lives of its best loved. Politics would continue, factionalism, dissent, victory, triumph and failure would all go on and be played out but to all his critics and his party, which often displayed a hostile will against him, Madhavrao Scindia avenged his deprivations through his death, by simply not being available any more, at a time when the Congress really needed him.

Gujarat Torched, India Enflamed

'On November 7 (1938), a seventeen-year-old German Jewish refugee by the name of Hersschel Grynszpan shot and mortally wounded the third secretary of the German Embassy in Paris. On the night of November 9-10, shortly after the party bosses, led by Hitler and Goering, had concluded the annual celebration of the Beer Hall Putsch in Munich, the worst pogrom that had yet taken place in the Third Reich occurred. It was a night of horror throughout Germany. Synagogues, Jewish homes and shops went up in flames and several Jews, men, women and children were shot or otherwise slain trying to escape burning to death. According to Dr. Goebbels and the German press, which he controlled, it was a 'spontaneous' demonstration of the German people in reaction to the news of the murder in Paris.'

The Rise and Fall of the Third Reich – William L. Shirer

On the morning of February 27, the Ahmedabad bound Sabarmati Express had an unscheduled delay of 20 minutes at the Godhra railway station. Soon after it began to move it stopped again at Signal Falia, less than a kilometre outside the station. Within minutes two carriages were on fire resulting in a horrific death for 58 passengers. The casualties included 26 women and 12 children. The train had been carrying a boisterous group of Sangh activists returning from Ayodhya. The district collector Jayanti Ravi insisted 'the incident was not pre-planned, it was an accident'. At 7:30 pm that evening the Chief Minister of Gujarat, Narendra Modi declared on national television that what had occurred at Godhra was, 'a pre-planned, violent act of terrorism'. Meanwhile, instead of carrying out preventive arrests or any damage control exercise, the administration moved the charred bodies of the victims to the Sola Civil Hospital in Ahmedabad and, in an exhibitive fashion, laid them out on ice slabs in front of a naturally hysterical crowd of hundreds of relatives and onlookers. These are the facts of what occurred. Who burnt the train carriages and why is still a subject of a national level inquiry. Was it an irate Muslim mob? Was it foreign agents trying to create trouble? Indeed, was it the Sangh and the BJP which masterminded the whole operation themselves or could it actually have been an accident after all? Although these questions are largely unanswered even today, what occurred in the immediate aftermath of the Godhra tragedy can only be described as genocide; a well-planned, sinisterly well-executed, flawless and authorised exercise of mass murder. L.K. Advani, the founding father of parliamentary fascism in India, was to describe it as 'a blot on the government'. A month of unmitigated horror unfolded for Gujarat's Muslims following the Godhra incident. It is impossible to be dispassionate about the events that occurred but they are so well and highly documented that repeating them here in brief will not convey the scale of the genocide.

Unofficial estimates put the number of those killed (excluding the victims at Godhra) at almost 2000. In the first 72 hours of the violence, 230 religious places, including mosques and shrines, were gutted or destroyed. Over 150,000 people were made refugees overnight in their own home. A primary estimate of economic losses for the Muslim community of Gujarat put the figure at Rs. 3800 crores. Members of the BJP government in Gujarat physically led the carnage, members of the BJP government at the Centre stoked it by their indifference. In a chilling statement, Narendra Modi, now lionised by his party, stated, 'every action has an equal and opposite reaction'. Dr. Jaideep Patel, Joint Secretary of the Gujarat VHP and a senior Sangh functionary, was more in line with the traditional fascist excuses, 'The people came spontaneously,' he said, 'and there were 15-20,000 of them. So let the police arrest 15-20,000 people,' challenging the administration which had already been infiltrated with Sangh volunteers and sympathisers. Alternatively, Arun Jaitley, the senior BJP leader, sometimes even described as suave, condescended to defend the police actions. Two days into the pogrom, on March 1 he declared, 'Yesterday the police arrested 700 people. In Ahmedabad alone they fired 300 rounds. Therefore, to say they were mere spectators is simplistic. If somewhere there has been dereliction of duty by particular officers then I'm sure we'll take all measures against them'. He was absolutely right on the latter count, for dereliction of duty to him, as for other members of the BJP, presumably meant impeding the destruction and violence. As a result, any officer or serviceman who acted against the rioters was transferred. The 300 rounds fired in Ahmedabad thus found their target; they killed 40 people, 36 of them Muslims, even though they were the targeted community. It was no wonder then that the former Chief Secretary of the Government of India, T.S.R. Subramanian commented to *The Indian Express*, 'There is no civil service left in Gujarat'. The Governor of Gujarat, himself a Sangh sympathiser, did not even see fit to submit a report on the situation to the Central government.

Just two years before Sonia Gandhi had written to the President of India terming the decision of the Gujarat government to allow civil servants membership of the RSS as an 'obnoxious decision which must be reversed if we are to safeguard the principles enunciated by our founding fathers in our Constitution'. The pressure she had mounted persuaded the Gujarat government to rescind their directive. Clearly it had not dented their resolve in the long run.

In the political scheme of things, against which the entire fallout must unfortunately be judged, the BJP had succeeded in nothing short of a balkanisation, along religious lines. Gujarat had been months away from an election. The pogrom of the Gujarat government, the inaction of the Centre, the violence perpetrated by the Sangh, the vitriol and misinformation churned by the vernacular media and, finally, it must be said, the ineptitude of the state Congress unit, gave the BJP an unprecedented advantage over Sonia Gandhi in the elections which took place at the end of 2002. In its issue covering the Gujarat tragedy titled 'Genocide', the outspoken *Communalism Combat* magazine took the following view:

> Since 1998, the year the BJP rose to power in the land of Gandhi, the apostle of peace, when not engaged in practising hate, the cadre of the Sangh Parivar are fully occupied in preaching it. When not busy burning the Bible, or a yet to be born child sliced out of a mother's womb, they distribute pamphlets intended to poison minds.

The first movements of the political conflict that erupted in Gujarat found both Sonia Gandhi and the BJP in their natural element. She had been one of the first leaders across India to have condemned the Godhra massacre, it came naturally to her to take on the right-wing. On the other hand, the BJP had perpetrated the violence which followed, keeping in line with the traditional politics of all fascist formations, as quoted at the beginning of this chapter. The BJP too, was comfortable doing what it has always done best, stoking the flames of communal discord and carrying out state-sponsored violence against its own citizens. The methods and motivations which guided the Nazi holocaust against the Jews of Europe in the 20th century were put to use by their political descendants in the

21st century, against the Muslims of Gujarat. The method, the manner, and even the justifications of the BJP, word for word, action for action, bore an uncanny reflection to those of their Nazi forbears.

The opposition was in discord, there was no unity. In the campaign that followed, Sonia Gandhi failed to win the election, the Congress Party lost its voice, the BJP triumphed, secularism became a term of abuse and Hindutva appeared to have succeeded in its biggest test. Narendra Modi, supported by his party leadership, concluded at the end of the violence, which finally subsided in late April, 'The five crore people of Gujarat have shown remarkable restraint under grave provocation.' Ironically, it was after this defeat that Sonia Gandhi found herself. Gujarat became a defining issue. Its violence, which had defiled a nation, became an inspirational resolve on her part to continue the fight for secularism, long after the fight for Gujarat had subsided. Anyone else with even a residual evidence of egocentricity would have melted away in the face of the personal abuse and provocations that were directed at her. Frustrated as she must have been, repeatedly, by the disorganisation and weaknesses of her own party, during the campaign she continued to fight, specifically in the name of secularism, both within Gujarat and outside it. For her and the 'secular side' as a whole, winning the Gujarat election was more important than how it could be won. The message of the Gujarat victory and the implications of the BJP's possible defeat was the only cause worth projecting. Enclosed in this determinism, she stumbled with tactics. Sonia Gandhi lost the Gujarat election because she did not allow this personal instinct to guide party strategy. She failed that battle because her own colleagues succeeded in convincing her with their outlook.

This is what happened. Between fascism and liberalism lies a practical spirit which can moderate itself, from being authoritarian to becoming humanitarian as the situation demands. Like Pandit Jawaharlal Nehru, Sonia Gandhi does not possess even a shadow of this spirit. For Nehru there could be no compromise or co-habitation with the right-wing. His politics were unarguably and uncompromisingly secular, egalitarian and humanistic, more importantly his politics were divorced from any religious overtones. That is also the spirit of Sonia Gandhi. This is why repeated attempts by Congress strategists to inculcate a temporary energy of religious innuendo into her campaign did not find any practical success on the battlefield of Gujarat. The appointment of Shankersinh Vaghela as the chief of the Gujarat campaign, the significance of launching the campaign from the holy temple sanctuary of Ambaji, the baggage of religious symbols, the absence of Muslim campaigners and the general implications of a religious movement were hardly likely to stir up the masses of Gujarat, already intoxicated by Modi's 'heroism' and the BJP's symbolism had become too entrenched in the psyche of Gujarat to be confiscated by an otherwise secular Congress Party. In a scathing attack on the Congress strategy, titled 'Congress is the BJP's B-Team in Gujarat' the editor-in-chief of *The Asian Age*, M.J. Akbar wrote:

> The Congress under Sonia Gandhi has decided to abandon secular politics in Gujarat and imitate Modi, albeit without Modi's unique extremism. It is a difference of degree not content. No wonder Jawaharlal Nehru's face is missing from the lineage of Congress leaders on Congress posters, although Sonia Gandhi's is included: Nehru called dams and steel mills the temples of modern India. Nehru would never have buckled, as his successors have done.

Prescient though his observations were, to an uncomfortable degree, Sonia Gandhi herself could not have been accused of abandoning secular politics. In April 2002, she presided over the Congress Chief Ministers' Conference at Guwahati. The violence in Gujarat had not wholly ended. Her instructions and outlook at this juncture were enunciated in her opening speech at that conference. It is important to quote this excerpt at length because between this speech and the article quoted above, the tactics and strategy of the Congress Party had altered conspicuously. What did not alter however, was her instinctive and personal perspective:

> We are meeting against the background of one of the darkest periods in our post-independence history. The images I have seen, the stories of utter despair and desolation that I have heard during my recent visit to Gujarat will not leave me for a long time to come. How can it be said that

these atrocities were perpetrated by people of one religion or the other? .
The perpetrators of these atrocities have violated all tenets of all religions.

In a more politic vein, she attacked the Vajpayee government for its
unflinching support to Modi and its victimisation of those officers who
had tried to curb the violence. Although strong in her complaint, she
registered it as the Leader of the Oppostion, duty bound to oppose the
ruling government.

It was after having delivered a singular condemnation of the Central
Government that the Congress President delved into the definition of
her political philosophy. She constructed her outlook before the present
Congress leadership in a speech that should have been made before a
crowd of millions. The 'Battleground for Secularism' speech is the
expression of her approach, it is the most serious understanding
communicated in recent years of India's pluralistic culture by any
politician. Within it she also deciphered, comprehensively, the method
of the BJP. It was clear and cogent, unconvoluted by any vicissitudes of
form or politeness. It was what India needed to hear:

Secularism is India's destiny. An India that is not secular will simply not
survive. This is the time for each and every one of us to reaffirm our faith
in secularism. The debate on secularism is the ongoing battle between an
overwhelming number of Indians, steeped, in their own religions yet
tolerant and respectful of other faiths, and a handful of Indians, self-
appointed guardians of their own faiths, fanatically convinced of their
own righteousness. The overwhelming number of Indians want to live
in peace and goodwill. A handful of Indians seek to disturb that peace by
their bigotry and narrow mindedness. The overwhelming number of
Indians want to move forward, to look ahead. A handful of Indians want
us to be prisoners of a past invented and interpreted by them. This is the
real battleground of secularism. It is to rescue and protect India's great
religions from the zealots of obscurantism, from the merchants of
fundamentalism, from the purveyors of hate and poison. It is this vision
of secularism that the Congress has always stood for and practised. It is
this vision of secularism that is in danger. The Congress alone represents
the overwhelming number of Indians of all faiths who want to live and

work in an atmosphere of peace and amity, in an environment of mutual accommodation and acceptance.

So what changed between the conference in Guwahati and the campaign in Gandhinagar that altered, if only overtly, the approach of the Congress to the Gujarat election? At the time, Prime Minister Atal Behari Vajpayee was telling the BJP National Executive in Goa that, 'wherever there are Muslims, there is a problem. The kind of Islam being perpetrated in the world today is a violent, intolerant Islam that has no place for tolerance.' In his understanding, there was no role of the state or for him as Prime Minister in providing preventive relief or action for Gujarat, to him the tragedy of Gujarat 'could have been avoided' if the burning of the Sabarmati Express had not occurred. No mention was made of the role of the state in creating or subsequently containing the public agitation. Contrast this with Sonia Gandhi's directives to her Chief Ministers at Guwahati. 'Let me make it absolutely clear', she declared, 'any individual or any organisation preaching or practising the politics of hate and threatening the very existence of our secular fabric must be dealt with without fear or favour according to law. My directive to you from this Guwahati Conference is that there must not be any compromise, under any circumstances on this under a Congress Government.' Here then was a clear division between the BJP and Congress. Both appeared committed and inflexible in their respective stands. Both represented the spirit of their own respective ideologies. Within Parliament too there was no abatement in the deep tension between the Prime Minister and the Leader of the Opposition. During the debate on the POTO legislation, she thundered at Vajpayee, 'Your moment of reckoning is coming'. In his book, *Sonia : A Biography*, Rashid Kidwai notes the mood of Sonia Gandhi around this time:

> For political observers, Sonia's speech stood out against that of the Prime Minister. Hers was a passionate appeal to Vajpayee not to let political considerations bring into existence a draconian piece of legislation that had the potential to violate basic human rights, especially at a time when the polity was divided owing to the Gujarat communal riots and the

Ayodhya agitation. In contrast, the Prime Minister's speech lacked substance. It was a personal attack and had a laudatory tone about his own long stint in Parliament, which did not go down well with many seasoned parliamentarians like Chandra Shekhar, Somnath Chatterjee and Jaipal Reddy.

The divide was complete, a Prime Minister on the defensive, a Leader the Opposition confident and assertive. Moreover, the divide was nambiguous.

The run up to the election, long as it was due to the exigencies of rehabilitation and the return to normalcy, slowly eroded this divide. Principles changed into practicability. Congress thinking on the ground began to believe that the Muslim vote in Gujarat could be taken for granted and that the direction of the campaign should aim to garner the Hindu vote instead. In doing so, the lieutenants of the Congress walked right into the hands of the BJP. Instead of persevering with the aggressive and well articulated model proposed by their leader, they sought to convince her of minimising or down playing this and taking on the BJP on their own turf of Hindutva. The fever of the prevalent feelings in Gujarat, the fear psychosis that this fever engendered and the subsequent unwillingness to convert the public mood in the state, meant that a secular campaign took a back seat. Perhaps, had the results of the election campaign been any different, commentators and historians alike would have diluted, even altered, their criticisms of the Congress strategy. With hindsight, it seems preposterous that the party could have employed the tactics which it did. Nonetheless, the privilege and comfort of retrospective analysis was not available in the searing political heat of the Gujarat campaign.

Yet, what is astounding is that Congress came close to scoring an upset in the election. This is an aspect of the whole campaign which no onlooker has given time, attention or credence to. It is not a matter for argument. The statistics, without the manipulation of figures, speak for themselves. Of the 182 seats to the Gujarat Assembly the BJP had a clear win in just 92. Additionally, Congress lost 19 seats as a direct result of Sharad Pawar's NCP and Mulayam Singh's SP participating in the election.

The votes they received were just a little more than the margin of defeat for the Congress candidates in those 19 seats. In a further 15 seats the BJP won by a margin of less than 5000, unconvincing figures for a party that had created an absolute polarisation. In communally sensitive Surat and Bhuj the Congress candidates overturned majorities of 22,000 to wrest the seats from the BJP. In L.K. Advani's own Gandhinagar city seat the Congress candidate won by 20025 votes. Much had been made of how the tribals in Gujarat had switched wholesale to the BJP. Yet of the 26 seats designated as Tribal dominated, the BJP won 13 and the Congress 11, not an indication of any absolute switch over. In the three temple towns of Somnath, Dwarka and Ambaji, the former two being regarded as repositories of Hindu culture and learning, the Congress triumphed. However, in the larger outcome, these singular victories were swamped out as isolated cases. On paper the results were clear. Of the 182 seats the BJP won 126 and Congress 51. It appeared on that dark winter day of December 15, when the results finally came in that Modi and mayhem had defeated Sonia and secularism for good. Appearances can be so deceptive.

Himalayan Respites

Taken in isolation, the result of the Gujarat election could have spelled disaster for the Congress Party and its leader. As it turned out, the battle of Gujarat was only one decisive encounter the party lost in a string of otherwise uninterrupted victories. At worst, defeat in the hard fought Gujarat campaign of December dampened the euphoria of winning the Jammu and Kashmir elections that preceded it.

Demonstrating remarkable precience and much against his personal wishes, Sonia Gandhi had appointed Ghulam Nabi Azad President of the Jammu and Kashmir Congress unit. The usually unflappable and indefatigable Azad had been apprehensive, not least because of security concerns. His chagrin was understandable, having been successively responsible for the affairs of important states like Karnataka and Uttar Pradesh and enjoying the status of a power-centre in his own right, he was now answerable for and in charge of effectively just four parliamentary seats. The appointment had been an unmitigated downfall for Azad. It demonstrated Sonia Gandhi's willingness, usually restrained, to exert control over 'party bosses' and individuals whose politics were caliberated to consistently survive leadership change at the top. There was little need, as such, for Sonia Gandhi to turn to coercive methods in enforcing her prerogative over the party. Yet for weeks after Ghulam Nabi Azad was transferred to this state, workers and leaders in Party offices throughout the country spoke of her sudden willingness to turn tough on senior leaders. For some commentators it was tempting to draw an immediate parallel for this action with Indira Gandhi's leadership style. In reality the contrast could not have been more diffuse, for Sonia Gandhi authoritarian incorporation has never been the modus operandi of exercising power. Instead, it is a tool the use of which is seldom called for. When coercion does guide her instincts, the subsequent decision is irrevocable. And so it was with the decision to send Ghulam Nabi Azad to Kashmir. Whatever the initial lever of influence may have been to appoint him President, the results of the Jammu and Kashmir assembly elections redeemed her will. Congress, which had lingered on as a shadow in the politics of the volatile state since the 1980s, emerged the second largest party in the assembly, prompting Azad to describe Sonia Gandhi as 'a visionary'. He had cause to be elated. Among critics, supporters and commentators, the Jammu and Kashmir victory restored the perception (almost legendary) about Azad's 'golden touch' and his ability to deliver, and thus survive. More importantly, it was Sonia Gandhi's decision-making and instincts which received unprecedented laurels. Not so much due to the victory itself but because of the consequences of that victory.

October is always a balmy month in New Delhi. The post-monsoon, pre-winter climate induces a natural congeniality amongst the inhabitants of this otherwise hyper-strenuous, halfway house that poses between a cosmopolitan capital city and a bureaucrat's dishevelled fantasy. It was an October evening and the CWC had earlier passed a resolution, half bewildered, half stumbling in adoration, authorising Sonia Gandhi to decide on the details of government formation in Jammu and Kashmir. One of the distinguishing traits of Sonia Gandhi's temperament is that a mood of confidence is clouded by a more apparent air of insouciance, in her posture and her speech. On that clement evening too she emerged from her bungalow into the patio full of eager, awaiting journalists, smiling and assured. The corollary to this unusual display of disposition was a (as yet unknown) pact that she had secured with Mufti Mohammed Sayeed, leader of the PDP, a regional party with the largest number of victorious candidates in the election. On its own the PDP did not have enough members to form a government and journalists, Congress leaders, the opposition and members of the PDP itself, expected the Congress President to demand a heavy price for her support to the Mufti and his party.

Through sheer intellectual energy, Sonia Gandhi had steered a consensus earlier that evening to allow the PDP to lead the government in Kashmir, with minimal dissent or diversion. The cause of restoring confidence and peace in the much troubled valley had unarguably remained foremost in her mind. For the first time in a long time, the Congress leadership had forsaken its prerogative to lead another state government. With Kashmir under its belt, the party would have had its government in 15 states throughout India. Instead, consternation was minimised, her personal authority unopposed and concord seemed restored between a regional party and Congress. The earlier conscience-stricken Ghulam Nabi Azad was visible as a picture of consanguinity as he stood alongside Mufti Mohammed Sayeed while Sonia Gandhi virtually declared the formation of Kashmir's new government. The pictures coming off the national network and through the television screens into homes across India showed Sonia Gandhi as a wise, resolute and progressive leader, in sharp contrast to the traditional mould of wily, opportunistic and grudging politicians which the Indian public has grown used to seeing. It was certainly a boost for Sonia Gandhi personally. The ruling BJP-led NDA government appeared to be under pressure.

It took the genocide of Gujarat to break this run. However phyrric the election victory of Gujarat may have been, the BJP leadership felt that the results there restored to them their core support as well as the hard right ground. Jammu, predominantly Hindu, had voted overwhelmingly for Congress, giving it a landslide. Gujarat changed the psyche created by Jammu.

While 2002 had given Congress stunning victories, most notably in Punjab and Jammu and Kashmir, the fires of Gujarat burnt down this optimism and hope within the party by the end of the year. For Sonia Gandhi, however, an important lesson had been learnt; fraternising, even casually, with elements of Hindutva, even its imitation, was worthless to the cause of Congress. Her espousal of the secular agenda, the Congress Party's contribution to this and a stronger than ever dislike, verging on abhorrence, for fascism in all its forms, became entrenched in her mind. What she had witnessed in Gujarat, the Congress Party's unsuccessful attempt to dislodge the BJP model and her own mental conditioning made her stronger about her own value system and its validity to Congress politics. It also became easier to separate the Congress' presentation from the BJP and its various wings. Post-Gujarat, Sonia Gandhi became singularly more committed to a 'secular and developmental agenda' for governance. Little of the personal anguish from the Gujarat election showed. On New Year's Eve, barely two weeks after the results, she called on Congress leader Salman Khurshid and his wife at the All India Institute of Medical Sciences (AIIMS) where their daughter lay unwell. Forgetting her political turmoil in the midst of their personal adversity, she lingered in the hospital room for quite a while keeping their spirits up.

The year 2003, like the preceding one, began well for Sonia Gandhi, indicating a regular cycle of victory proceeding defeat in an almost repetitive fashion. The voters of the hill state of Himachal Pradesh gave the Congress Party a landslide victory in February. The predominantly Hindu state (over 90 per cent of the state's population belonged to the majority community) resoundingly voted the ruling BJP out of power. For Congress and the secular wing, Gujarat had been contained, its effects neutralised. Sonia Gandhi was personally satisfied and her appreciation showed when the Congress decided to hold its party conclave in the amiable surroundings of the state capital Shimla.

While the politics of the Indian heartland remained in flux, Congress had lost by-elections in Rajasthan, Shimla induced a strong sense of recovery for the leader of the opposition. She arrived there radiating confidence, her vocabulary enhanced, speaking of 'moving towards a new political culture.' Throughout her three-day stay among the sunlight seeping pines of the hill station, Sonia Gandhi remained uncharacteristically vocal, some said even confessional. In her opening address to the party leadership and delegates on July 7, she spoke of 'a new air of expectation all round' and went on to describe her leadership style, in detail:

> I meet a very large number of people every day both from within the party and outside. There is never any shortage of advice on any subject. I listen to all of them. I consult my colleagues. They are men and women of wide experience. We may not always agree but I do seek a consensus. Ultimately the decision is mine.

This was the first time that Sonia Gandhi had spoken about her method and her practice of leadership in such detail. Yet very few observers including the army of 'Congress buffs' present, picked up on this analysis of Sonia Gandhi about herself. She could hardly have been speaking to the assembled congregation of the Congress leaderhip, for they were well acquainted with her style. The words were meant for others, possibly the accompanying baggage train of journalists, in order to prepare them for any major resolution which the Shimla Vichar Manthan Shivir would adopt. It preset the mechanics of the operating rules within the Congress Party. At the same time, Sonia Gandhi was giving a retrospective explanation to a much wider audience about her preceding decisions, particularly about Jammu and Kashmir,

> By nature, I not only want to do the right thing but I also want to do a thing right. It was not easy, for example, to decide what we did finally

when the government was being formed in Jammu and Kashmir eight months ago. But getting inspiration from what Rajivji himself had done in Punjab and Assam in 1985 and in Mizoram in 1986, I took the decision in the larger interest of our country.

There could be no lingering confusion, decision- making in the ongress Party lay in the hands of Sonia Gandhi, ultimately. On the fringes of the conclave, party-men took walks along the mall, a deceptive air of being 'en retraite' pervaded the scene as some observers thought of the whole exercise as a 'big party junket' where 'chins up' gatherings of self-congratulation were most in evidence.

Behind the scenes, within the walls of 'Oakover' and other Raj habitations, formulations were being worked out, speeches and resolutions being edited, drafts being called for. Policemen on duty were bemused to see solitary senior figures of the Congress Party making brisk visits to and fro with revisions and suggestions to the CM Virbhadra Singh's official residence, where the Congress President was staying.

As far as the political fallout of the Shimla Conclave was concerned, observers had remained expectant about a new policy regarding coalition governments. The official 'communique' was unnecessarily convoluted in this regard, the only decisive meaning which could have been drawn from it was a clear statement that Sonia Gandhi would lead any possible alternative Congress initiative. The AICC resolution, restrained by the norms of nomenclature and compelled by the rules of party-speak, was predictably phrased. It sought:

> the support of the people to bring India back on the path of progress with Congress under the leadership of Smt. Sonia Gandhi. We invite all progressive-thinking men and women, institutions and political movements who share our understanding of India's past, our concerns with India's present and our vision of India's future to join us in this historic endeavour.

The ancillary to this resolve was Sonia Gandhi's own vision of politics, a personal manifesto of her political objectives. It outlined a sensitive appraisal of the Congress value system, whereas the official 'Sankalp' or resolve had suggested a repetition of dogmatised word crunching. 'I see politics as being not just about fighting elections, crucial as they are', she said. The core of politics to Sonia Gandhi and, by association, to the Congress as a whole became, 'a process through which we identify ourselves fully with the people of the country, especially the poor, the disadvantaged and the deprived.' That mass of India, usually discarded after a ritual homage paid to it through high sounding phrases, was firmly established as the Congress constituency. Initiated in Shimla, the commitment to social empowerment would become the causus belli, the strategy for power of the Congress Party in the coming months. The final parts of her speeches in Shimla recognised the challenges of forthcoming elections. Sonia Gandhi tried hard to herald a re-statement of her party's political culture, she tried to re-orient a direction, the message from Shimla was progressive and far-sighted even if it was ineffectively relayed. Her words, seeking to evoke an intellectual continuity with the ideas of her forbears, deserved a better reception than they received at the time. 'I am convinced', she said, 'that the time is ripe for a massive renaissance of our political culture so that we build that society which combines compassion with competence, equity with excellence and integrates India's global leadership with local transformation.'

For the leader of opposition to speak in such a way seemed pretentious and unduly ambitious. Nevertheless, being the head of a party which now ruled over 16 states of the Indian Republic placed her in a special position. The term 'parallel Prime Minister' may seem far-fetched but in effect that is what she was. Congress ruled over a larger part of India than all its opposition combined. If the NDA spoke for the Centre, Congressmen were confident they spoke for the states. On a day-to-day basis the Congress Party and its leadership was responsible for the lives of a larger and more diverse proportion of Indians than any other political party in the country. In terms of intellectual energy, confidence and its outlook as a whole, the Congress Party in Shimla, in the summer of 2003 was in a battle-ready and positive frame of mind. 'These cool and comforting surroundings, surroundings that breathe history,' as she herself had exclaimed had worked remarkably on her mind. The nightmares of Gujarat felt far away, she got 'a refreshing feeling'. On the final morning of the conclave, Sonia Gandhi must have felt a rare exhilaration, at least the public display of her relaxed state of mind was unprecedented. Leaving her official bungalow on foot she walked along the pine-covered hillsides, on the curving roads leading away from the mall, unaccompanied by any crowds or ranks of leaders. So discreet and unexpected was her 'trip' that when she arrived at Woodville Palace, home of the Jubbal Royal family and host to a number of visiting senior Congress leaders, her arrival was a shock. There were no wailing sirens, no large security protocol, she walked along the lawns, admired the ancient deodar trees and lingered around the ivy-covered home. To the owner, Kunwar Uday Singh, himself a Congressman, she confided that she felt she had 'been here before.' This was not the Sonia Gandhi that people knew. The abrupt arrival of surprised party colleagues cut her wanderings short. It was time to return to New Delhi. At the end of the conclave, the feeling was that a sojourn had ended. What had been achieved, politically, was not clear. Meanwhile, important events awaited her attention in the capital.

'Say Not the Struggle Nought Availeth'

Debacle in the Heartland – In Shining Armour –
'Making Cosmos Out of Chaos'

Debacle in the Heartland

In retrospect, Shimla signified no major external occurrence in the so far placid story of the Congress in opposition. What was significant, in terms of politics, became evident within weeks of the conclusion of the party conclave. Post-Shimla, the interplay between government and opposition dramatically shifted gears and Sonia Gandhi, as Leader of the Opposition became the propelling agent of this new found confrontational overdrive.

On August 17th, Sonia Gandhi moved a no-confidence motion against the NDA government. The next day, she opened the debate, the first of its kind in the four years of NDA rule. The objective of bringing a no-confidence motion against a government which had a more than sufficient majority was not immediately palpable. Most commentators agreed, however, that it was staged to launch the campaign for the forthcoming assembly elections, and demonstrate Sonia Gandhi's combative intentions to the public.

While Sonia Gandhi's arguments were cogent and convincing, Vajpayee appeared all too climacteric, his peers in the government acidulous, the debate itself became banal shortly after Sonia Gandhi had spoken. The Opposition had demanded that the findings of the Central Vigilance Commission's (CVC) probe into allegations of graft during the Kargil War be disclosed. This was a serious issue with far-reaching consequences for defence procurement and military procedure, it went to the heart of security concerns. Grounding her attack with the formidable siegeworks of official papers of the CVC, the Comptroller and

Auditor-General (CAG) of India and the Public Accounts Committee, she arraigned the Government relentlessly, her manner astringent, she thundered,"Here is a government so lethargic that it is willing to risk the lives of our brave jawans, a government so irresponsible that it bargains with the martyrdom of our Kargil heroes." Substantiating her claims, she went further, "Operation Parakram lasted nearly nine months in 2002, involved over five lakh troops and entailed an expenditure of Rs. 8,000 crores. What did it achieve?" As always the apogee of her argument was secularism, only pitted this time against the thrust of the BJP's obscurantism. Reading out a 'charge-sheet', she accused those in power with "defiling the very essence of our nationhood" by jeopardising social and communal harmony. Unable to bear the abrasions any more, the Prime Minister, Atal Behari Vajpayee himself responded in a style which can only be remarkable for its brevity and its bathos. Wholly ignoring the issue under challenge the Prime Minister dismissed the fact that the information for the charges came from official documents. In his astringence, he attenuated his own argument by asking, "How can such charges be levelled without any proof in Parliament?" Rather than presenting a case of defence, or even launching his own offensive against the points raised by Sonia Gandhi, Vajpayee's objections appeared maudlin and ill-tempered, he criticised the vocabulary Sonia Gandhi used asking, "Should this be the way? Using abuses will not lead to a solution. It seems we are giving up parliamentary norms." Once the Prime Minister lost his nerve displaying a crazed animus, there was little more to be expected, neither from the government benches nor the opposition. The debate degenerated into a general caterwauling. In the end the outcome was what everyone had predicted and expected, the motion of no-confidence was defeated by 312 government votes against 186 of the opposition. A substantial number of opposition MPs did not even vote the motion to a score of numerical respectability. Towards the end of the debate, Sonia Gandhi reflected, 'When I talk of the country, they talk of my language and style. When I talk of the sufferings of the people, they level personal allegations against me'. She was right but the outcome signified a deeper defeat. As Leader of the Opposition, she had failed to lead a united challenge against the NDA. Her personal apophthegms, censorious and serious though they had been, with the desired acclamation by Congress members in attendance, still lacked the support of the larger opposition ranks. The motion moved by her had been defeated, but the effort to bring about unity within those outside government had been rejected publicly. While the BJP members were expected to raise the heat, which they did yet again, over her foreign origins, her vowels and her family, few expected members of the opposition to add to this attack. None other than Mulayam Singh Yadav intervened on behalf of the discredited and choleric Defence Minister, castigating the Congress by saying, *You did not even give him a chance to put his point across. This is not right*. The defeat in the two-day debate was only the beginning of the troubles for Sonia Gandhi's Congress.

While the Party had been deliberating upon the finer etiquette of politics in the cool climes of Srinagar and Shimla, a saffron storm had been brewing in the dusty stretches of the Indian hinterland. The BJP had literally been carving out its road to power in Rajasthan. Its leader, Vasundhara Raje Scindia, written off as a delicate and genteel Maharani, had spent the best part of the year cultivating recognition through an innovative, sometimes overly dramatic tour of the desert state. In Madhya Pradesh, the formidable Digvijay Singh had completed ten years in power and expected to win another term, his quiet confidence assured the Congress Party of some hidden strategy at play. Unfortunately, this time round there was none. The BJP in MP was led by the excitable god-woman Uma Bharti. Though few could see her as a serious choice for Chief Minister, her sustained activism at grassroots level was slowly draining support away from the Congress Party. In Chhattisgarh the most likely face of the BJP leadership, Dilip Singh Judeo, a Minister of State in the NDA government, had been censured in a very convincing case of financial corruption. Ajit Jogi, the Congress Chief Minister of this newly created and predominantly tribal state was expected to retain power. The optimism, justified as it turned out, was prevalent in New Delhi too, where Sheila Dixit had completed five years in power. Most of the achievements of her government had been the work of the Supreme Court, and judicial intervention, or so her critics said. The BJP had wheeled out Madan Lal Khurana, their 'Delhi face' for the last two decades. The stage was set for a winter election. Congress was the incumbent party in all four states.

On the day of the counting, Digvijay Singh accepted defeat with characteristic graciousness by 11 am. From 124 seats in a house of 228, Congress was reduced to just 39. The BJP was comprehensively triumphant with a final tally of 171. In Rajasthan the Congress Party could barely come to terms with the scale of its loss, the BJP surprised itself. In the 200-member Assembly, Congress had possessed 153 MLAs, only 56 survived the 'saffron wave'. The casualties included 29 ministers. The story was no different in Chhattisgarh, the Congress lost resoundingly. It was in Delhi that Sheila Dixit buoyed the mood of the party somewhat by winning a second term. Yet, this could hardly compensate for the loss of the heartland. A saffron crescent now carved itself across India, stretching from Rajasthan in the west to Jharkhand in the east. In between lay an unbroken stretch of BJP-ruled states. The Congress leadership had once more worked on estimations, not measures of the public mood. Each of the leading personalities in the respective defeated states had been given a greater degree of autonomy than any of their predeccessors, in selecting candidates, allocating resources, running the campaign and presenting policies. The various lobbies and the consequent level of factional inputs which they generated further contributed to the defeats. The most brazen example of this however was reserved for the formation of the Congress government in Delhi. Sheila Dixit, the lone winner in the four states had her selection delayed as Delhi's local leaders, aided by their respective leaders within the High Command tried to prolong her humiliation.

This fevered the party's general contretemps gravely and the unwelcome perception of an indecisive leadership placed Sonia Gandhi in some position of discomfiture. In the months preceding the elections, she had appeared combative, clear and confident. Some even saw an uncharacteristic preparedness for power. The defeat in the heartlands put those perceptions into abeyance.

While the Shimla resolve appeared redundant to many, including some around her, Sonia Gandhi did not think so. Addressing a conference organised by the *Hindustan Times* she reconstructed what to others may have been a tattered blue-print. 'The fundamental task we face is to create an all inclusive social architecture in which there is no place for bigotry, for intolerance, for obscurantism of any kind.'[1] In a polity where the decision-makers play policy weathercocks at the approach of defeat, Sonia Gandhi refused to modulate her recently defeated philosophy. Rather than be pressured into softening or hardening her party's stand, she preferred to hand it out straight to whoever was listening. Her departing words to that assembly of worthies were no different to what she had said in Gujarat, in Shimla or elsewhere. She believed India had to remain, 'an outstanding exemplar of an open, liberal, pluralistic democracy, committed to secular values, committed to combating religious fundamentalism of all kinds, committed to preserving and protecting its composite heritage.' Confrontation, and not any form of conciliatory co-habitation with its rival ideologies was to be her guide. In those last few days of the Thirteenth Lok Sabha, she remained in a minority even within her own party. It was perhaps this realisation, of fighting alone and fighting for her chosen stand, that spurred her to take to the country in the manner that she did. The Congress Party may have appeared meek and supine but it was not for nothing that Sonia Gandhi was a daughter of the House of Nehru.

In Shining Armour

For any government in office the prospects of a General Election are inevitable. It is the timing of these contests, almost always at that governments choosing, which must be married suitably to its political convenience. The BJP had never before been able to choose the moment

---

1.   Keynote Address on "The Indian Roadmap" to the Hindustan Times Conference on Peace Dividend in South Asia. December 12, 2003.

of going to the country by calling for a Lok Sabha election. The five years in office, which began in 1999 and would have culminated in the autumn of 2004, allowed the party to contest the election exactly when it wanted. The rest of the NDA was in concord. If it needed a push to take it into the election then the verdicts of the Rajasthan, Madhya Pradesh and Chhattisgarh Assembly elections provided it with that push. These victories in the heartlands of India had had little to do with the rest of the NDA. They had signified a battle between incumbent Congress governments in those states and the BJP at the Centre. Those state Congress governments had hoped that national issues of the day, primarily corruption, saffronisation of the school curriculum, the private misconduct of various central leaders, would help them in their states and become embedded in local politics. That was not to be, as we have seen in the previous part of this book. Now, fresh from these victories, the BJP had successfully managed to convince its junior partners in the NDA that registering those successes meant the mood of the country as a whole was behind the NDA.

A higher voter turnout in Rajasthan meant a higher degree of satisfaction with the politics of the Central government, this became the BJP's thinking and in turn was accepted by the rest of their coalition. It was the first mistake the NDA made as it approached the General Election. Allies such as the TDP, BJD, the Shiv Sena and others, were not the participating forces in those contests, yet they joined the BJP's celebratory mood as though its victories were their own. They cannot be grudged this, even with hindsight, for the entire confidence of the NDA rested entirely on the personality of its leader Atal Behari Vajpayee. This corporate condition, so settled as it was upon the minds of the NDA, was neatly enunciated by the BJP President Venkaiah Naidu who proclaimed, 'Atalji's contribution through the coalition experience is to make the BJP a factor everywhere. Today Vajpayee is the candidate everywhere.' This tendency, more marked than ever before, to make the leader an omnipresent, all encompassing attribute was the spirit of the BJP's first movements of the campaign. The NDA accepted this assertion.

In 2004 Atal Behari Vajpayee was the oldest Prime Minister to ever lead an election. He was almost 80. Yet, as an internal presentation made to the Congress Party's Campaign Committee itself believed, Vajpayee was, 'a Prime Minister at the peak of his popularity'. Nothing had damaged Vajpayee the leader in the public eye, or so it seemed. There was disquiet, even among some of his own supporters about his foster family's financial dealings and, coupled with his own poetic contradictions on almost every issue of consequence one would have expected some mud to stick, ostensibly none did. So it was with this seemingly unassailable head that the gigantic body of the government, aided by bright boys and smart software, not to mention the considerable weight of the administrative machinery, eased itself into the electoral battlefield, almost six months in advance of the time-table. The battlefield itself was of its own choosing, the timing of its own convenience and the issues an edifice of public posturings. Sonia Gandhi and her allies were nowhere even in sight. The vultures of the media, looking forward to a more vociferous and colourful bout wrote off the election as too one-sided.

In this euphoric and heady confidence that concentrated itself in the intellect of the government, outward thinking and, consequently, the flow of public ideas inwards diminished. Memoranda and inputs from public policy managers situated in New Delhi took precedence over the wisdom of grass-root party workers in their districts. In the same vein, brusque and brisk cellular phone conversation replaced the traditional and more direct discourse as a means for resolving dissent. Within a political culture where sitting together and face -to-face dialogue is the best guarantee of certainty, this was neither understood nor a means for minimising conflict. This development was something the Congress Party had had to face in the past but it now proved to be the curse of every incumbent government in India.

Nevertheless, the singular and most dramatic aspect of the entire election was the launch of the NDA's 'India Shining' campaign. This unprecedented dash of advertising replaced the manifesto, speech-making and long established word of mouth community interactions from the centre of election strategy. It was the boldest, most colourful, least imaginative presentation of a government's record in office, one which could have competed with the corniest facets of the best US Presidential campaign. Happy faces, verdant green pastures, bright blue skies, a scattering of students and young people as the septuagenarian leadership of India's politics would imagine them to be, carefree farm hands, free flowing jet streams of pure white water, and the general portrayal of life in India as bliss, carefully arranged in immaculate sequences with melodious beats among soft lights became the spearhead of the NDA's campaign. The inevitable outcome of this splurge was meant to induce a 'feel good factor' which began to be uttered mantra-like by political leaders who did not have and probably will never have any idea about what it meant. To be fair to the BJP, which has seldom misjudged the mood of its own core electorate, the publicity probably kept its supporters together, particularly its urban voters. A more thought provoking or cerebral campaign for the minds of that constituency would have created confusion in that particular unthinking upper-middle-class mindset. The previews had started early in the year and, to begin with, it was difficult to understand what the advertising was in aid of. Subsequently, it became a daily feature issued, as all such features inevitably are, in the public interest. Only much later was the political sponsorship fully confessed to. By then, it transpired that the cost of telling the Indian public how good it was feeling was paid for from the pockets of the same public.

There were ancillaries to the India Shining campign too, novel and curious methods such as cellular text messages and telephone calls asking voters to support the BJP and playing recordings of Vajpayee himself. The usual banter of rallies, public meetings, whistle stop tours and airborne media interviews accompanied the NDA leadership's resolve to win another term. It was during this election campaign that the role of pop-stars, sport icons, film personalities and other such glamorous accessories became greater than ever before, not merely as campaigners but as contestants too. The 2004 Lok Sabha election was the first state-organised circus that appealed to and exhorted voters to discharge their electoral duties so ceremoniously. That election, more than any preceding one, was on a technologically higher plain. It was the most technical, most carefully choreographed and most professionally arranged reporting of the world's largest democratic exercise.

As the obvious extravagance of the NDA's campaign became more pronounced, so did the falsehood of what it was portraying. Media, more than public perception, had already decreed a walk-over for the NDA and this did not change, not until the first round of polling in early May when the mood of Andhra Pradesh began to suggest that all was not well. That, however, was still far off in the prevailing mood of early April. After all, the NDA merely had to hold on to its seats and votes. With its objectives minimised, despite professions of senior BJP leaders aiming to get an absolute majority for the party on its own, and its campaign managed by the best paid and most professional events and publicity managers that money could buy, the senses of the media were lulled. It was not the media alone which became intoxicated by the NDA's radiance. Politicians from across party lines flocked to its banner. Secular fundamentalists, who less than two years ago had been among the most vociferous critics of the BJP over the Gujarat pogrom were among the first to join its ranks. Najma Hepatullah, too animated by a sense of her own significance, deemed the Congress an unworthy patron for her pursuit of politics and was tempted over by the BJP. From another field, Arif Mohammad Khan, a sometime doyen of secular politics and rabid anti-communalist as he believed himself to be, was not long in taking the plunge. Others professed a new found liking for Vajpayee in the hope that he would hear them now and recompense them later.

Thus, long established and supposedly shrewd political leaders became nothing more than victims of a belief they had themselves spun around their politics. They did not see that the biggest and perhaps only achievement in real terms of the Vajpayee government had been that it had lasted in power. There had been no significant unfolding of any new vision, no national consensus or political progression that could have made a change to the conduct of Indian politics. If anything, the offensive of the BJP in office was directed at a personality, its defences were in aid of bloodshed and violence. For a party claiming its roots in urban India it had initiated nothing for its cities. Politicking had reigned over a cumber some administrative apparatus which in turn stifled real governance. Redressal was minimal. Writing about the BJP rather early on in its tenure, Shiv Vishvanathan made some hard hitting but genuine complaints. His views published in the *Economic and Political Weekly* are incredible, not for their polished condemnations but for the precience with which he was able to articulate the problems of the BJP, he stated:

> The BJP has offered nothing new. Its success lies in affable advertising, its debating strength. Remember Arun Shourie, Jaitley, Vajpayee, Jaswant Singh, Govindacharya make a potent debating team, next to which other groups sound forgettable. In terms of governance, the BJP has offered nothing. It is just that liberalisation initially is more efficient than bureaucratic socialism. The BJP's real success is an appropriation of discourses. As an advertising creation, as a politically consumable entity, the Vajpayee regime is a success. But as a system of governance, as a democratic imagination, as a vision of India beyond tutorial college nationalism, the regime has failed. The BJP fits the World Bank's good boy theory of democracy. If anything domesticates the BJP, it is not democracy but the logic of power. The BJP has been too long in the wilderness and there is no doubt it is fond of the trappings of power. It will make adjustments to stay in power. In playing this politics of limits, it has been a success. But it is an impoverished success and a desiccated politics that India is celebrating.

In its refusal to accept, and to largely gloss over, balanced criticisms from non-partisan quarters, the NDA made its second mistake. Closer and closer to election day, the coalition was too deafened by its own pomp to allow free and adequate soundings. Its course would remain unaltered, its tactics unrepentant, its confidence absolute, even to the cost of its own interests. It was against this background and in this mood that India's first successful non-Congress government approached the hustings. Its opposition was nothing more than a lady it labelled a foreigner who traversed the country alone and appeared to be undaunted by the forces arrayed against her. She stood to lose the most, perhaps everything, but in her own mind the possibility of defeat exercised no influence. India had witnessed a similar figure doing the same thing before, but that had been a long, long time ago.

'Making Cosmos out of Chaos'

"They do not know the stuff I am made of."

Sonia Gandhi, 1999

Late in the afternoon of December 27, 2003, Sonia Gandhi strolled across to her neighbour Ram Vilas Paswan's house for a tete-a-tete over tea. The Dalit leader was expecting her, and as she sounded him out on the details of a coalition arrangement for the forthcoming Lok Sabha elections, Paswan already began calculating formulations. Paswan has been a factor in the unwieldy state of Bihar for almost two decades now. Like his co-regionalists, George Fernandes, Nitish Kumar, Sharad Yadav and Laloo Prasad Yadav, Paswan too was one of the bright stars of the socialist Third Front. Among all these leaders, only Laloo Prasad Yadav had consistently stayed away from the BJP extending unconditional support to Sonia Gandhi and forming a coalition government with the Congress in Bihar in 2000. Paswan had only recently walked out of the NDA, on the pretext of opposition to Narendra Modi. Sonia Gandhi now had the tough task of convincing him to come to an agreement with Laloo, with whom he has shared an intense rivalry. Contrary to expectations, she succeeded. A crucial state like Bihar, with 42 seats to Parliament, was patched up in a day, and a Congress Paswan and Laloo came into existence to give competition to the India Shining Campaign in the fractious state of Bihar. She pitched politics against publicity and came away from the meeting satisfied.

Meanwhile, the election campaign began to escalate as paraphernalia became visible, leaders got approachable and television time waxed and waned between family soaps and the India Shining campaign. The Congress was not visible. By mid-January most pundits began issuing 'victory certificates' to the NDA as election 2004 was described as the most one-sided electoral contest in living memory.

January 15th saw a rapprochement between Sharad Pawar and his former boss as Sonia Gandhi called on him personally at his residence. A decision was conveyed to the media, the choice of Prime Minister would be taken based upon a consensus. Sonia Gandhi did not present herself as a Prime Ministerial candidate. This meeting consolidated Maharashtra and western India for the Congress Party. A real coalition was slowly coming together. The BJP did not bat an eyelid; theirs was a tried and tested alliance, Sonia Gandhi's an attempt to create a hurried patchwork. That is what the NDA media-managers said. An unruffled L.K. Advani decided to fulfil his penchant for long drives and, amidst much fanfare, udertook another yatra, covering the length and breadth of India. The BJP's election machinery went into over-drive, its leaders panning out across the country, in chartered jets and modified caravans, speaking of how India had entered a new shining phase of progress and resolve. Congress was nowhere in the presentations.

Writing around this time, the irrepressible and outspoken chief of the *Seminar* Magazine, Malvika Singh wrote in a column:

> Talking about the Congress presence the only presence that you can feel and sense is that of Sonia Gandhi. She is constantly on the move combing districts in different states, meeting constituents. She comes across as energised, upbeat and in fighting form. Juxtaposed to her are the many others who appear more like wimps than political players. Are they just stumped that the reticent leader they thought she was is emerging as a fighter? Are they trying to 'sabotage' her potential, her future? What are they up to? What is their strategy?'March 11, 2004.

She saw something others perhaps didn't. If they did, they certainly didn't articulate it. Soon after the defeat of the party in the October Assembly elections, Sonia Gandhi had begun a series of mass contact programmes. These 'road-shows', as the media called them, had been highly successful. The first one, in western UP had drawn enthusiastic crowds. Sonia Gandhi knew all too well that enthusiasim did not automatically translate into electoral gain. Yet she persisted, alone, often unaccompanied by other leaders and always ready to launch herself into spontaneous roadside meetings. This 'jan-sampark abhiyaan' as the Congress called the mass-contact programme ran parallel to the one on one meetings she had with regional satraps and potential allies. The Congress Party's was a highly individualistic campaign conducted by its leader, in attendance was a waning enthusiasm displayed by other senior leaders. What sustained Sonia Gandhi on these long tours was the response of the public and the spontaneous energy of party workers who accosted her wherever she arrived.

Returning late from one such meeting on the night of February 5th and going immediately into a meeting overseeing election strategy, she was radiant and forthcoming at a lunch the following day. The gruelling schedule appeared to lift her. The luncheon meeting, hosted for prospective allies on February 6th saw the entire Left Front, individual forces of influence such as Chandra Shekhar and regional satraps such as the DMK, turning up at her door. Even the Samajwadi Party, in a state of perpetual hostility, was invited. Another luncheon was convened the following day for journalists covering the Congress Party, at which she remarked to a gathering that the NDA government, 'was putting pressure on some political parties not to align with us.' This round of pleasantries and public relations completed, she was back on the road. Exactly two days later, on February 9th, the issue of *India Today* titled 'Landslide for Atal' portrayed a beaming Prime Minister incumbent on the magazine cover with a halo of the BJP lotus rising like a resplendent sun in the background. It seemed as though the media was fighting Sonia Gandhi on behalf of the ruling NDA. Her own efforts received hardly any attention at all. By early May, she had travelled over 65,000 kilometres, addressed close to a hundred rallies and meetings and was seen by not less than 500 million people, either in the flesh or through some electronic medium. Yet a hostile media did not relent. Tavleen Singh wrote in *The Indian Express*:

> If Sonia had done more rural touring in the past five years, she might have discovered long ago that about the only issue that is meaningful about her political career is that she happens to be Italian by birth and not Indian.

Describing Sonia Gandhi's campaign as her 'cow-dust hour' she continued;

> The only political party that seems not to have understood the extent to which things have changed is Congress so, election after election, they offer us a member of the Nehru-Gandhi dynasty as their magic wand. It does not work any more. No matter how many days Sonia spends eating chutney roti with peasants, no matter how much of a super-hit the media thinks she is, it will make little difference unless she can convince people that the Congress Party has more to offer than her and Priyanka. So enjoy the cow dust hour Soniaji, but if you think a few tours of rural India can make you Prime Minister, please think again.

It was the launch of Rahul Gandhi, a stunning display that evoked a forgotten degree of emotional spontaneity, particularly within Uttar Pradesh, that finally persuaded the BJP to take notice. There is little fairness in political utterances during elections but the quality of the debate sunk further with Narendra Modi joining the fray and turning abusive. In turn the NDA mood as a whole turned its focus away from highlighting the details of India Shining and turning in a more calibrated attack on Sonia Gandhi and her family instead. So sharp was this line that *Outlook* magazine felt compelled to give it attention in its final issue for April. Saba Naqvi Bhaumik wondered:

> The BJP-NDA is seen to be streets ahead in the electoral game. So, if Sonia is being dismissed as a non-starter (at least as a Prime Ministerial candidate), why are BJP netas wasting so much time and energy abusing her, her foreign origins and her children? Why are the saffronwallahs so

obsessed with Sonia and her children?

She concluded:

> ...No one in the BJP can match Rahul and Priyanka for drawing huge spontaneous crowds.

The manifesto of the NDA, launched on April 8th, devoted a promise to debar people of foreign origin from occupying important offices of the Indian state.' This issue as basis for a national agenda was political hyperbolism of the kind consistently promoted against Sonia Gandhi by the BJP. Much of the subsequent vitriol voiceo by her opposition is too vulgar to merit a reference.

As D-day approached most of the Congress leadership continued to be moribund and comatose, the BJP-led NDA remained on a high, Sonia Gandhi pushed on her campaign relentlessly. Evidence of the intensity of her campaign can be seen in the last week of April. On the 22nd, she addressed the first poll meeting in her own constituency of Rae Bareli, Indira Gandhi's former seat. The very next day, she was deep in rural Andhra Pradesh, holding a 'road show' in Guntur, and rural Nellore in Andhra Pradesh. Twenty-four hours later she had reversed routes and was in Faizabad, criss-crossing the heart of Awadh, in Uttar Pradesh. April 27th found her addressing a rally in Dausa in rural Rajasthan and canvassing support for the late Rajesh Pilot's son, Sachin. The intervening days were spent in Haryana campaigning, making assessments in New Delhi, circulating with the press and approving further engagements.

Even *Outlook* magazine, less certain as it was than its competitors about the impending BJP victory, gave Atal Behari Vajpayee a whopping 61 per cent as the people's choice for Prime Minister. Sonia Gandhi followed with 29 per cent and L.K. Advani, Jyoti Basu and Manmohan Singh with a per cent each. This was two weeks before polling day.

On the May 11th the election process ended across the country. No amount of campaigning, interviews, hype or advertising could now change the results lying inside the voting machines. The following day found an atmosphere of India waiting.

The morning of May 13th was like any other morning, Indians woke up, early as they usually do, not many went to work, not even in rural India. Instead, they radioed in to transistors or television sets or crowded around such devices wherever they were available at a public place. It was counting day and results began to come in steadily after nine in the morning. The initial counting indicated what everyone had been saying all along, the NDA opened its account with a strong showing in Rajasthan and Madhya Pradesh but there the advance stopped as Congress candidates first equalled and then surpassed their NDA counterparts. Within minutes the NDA was lagging behind first marginally, then substantially. In Andhra Pradesh, the Congress landslide was gargantuan, in UP the BJP downslide unstoppable. It was Gujarat that held everyone's attention. In the BJP laboratory the experiment had gone all wrong; the Congress score stood alongside the BJP's. In Bihar and Tamil Nadu, Sonia Gandhi's efforts to forge cross-party unity had remarkable consequences for her alliance. Where Congress did not peak, the Left stood its ground and affected an expansion. There were disappointments for the party too, states like Kerala, Punjab and Karnataka halted the lead. What should have been a substantial surplus from the landslides in Delhi and Haryana had to become buffers that compensated for the deficit in these states. It was not just rural India that gave the NDA the boot. Bombay, Madras, Calcutta and Delhi all voted for anti-NDA parties.

The verdict, stunning as it was, overturned the studied opinion and prediction of the NDA, of psephologists and pollsters and editors and columnists. Most of all, it surprised the Congress Party.

In the end, the degree of difference between the Congress and the BJP was not all that large, a mere seven seats separated the party. Congress won 145 seats, the BJP 138, a gain of 30 seats for Congress, a loss of 45 for the BJP. It was the respective alliances that decided the winner. The Congress-led alliance won 217 seats, the NDA wilted at 185. A loss of almost 130 seats for the NDA. A far cry from what the managers of the

BJP had been maintaining all along, that the party would get 300 seats on its own. It did not even get half of that. It was Pramod Mahajan, wearing a ruffled look, on whom it fell to represent the defeated demeanour of his party bosses. His confession that he was 'half stunned and half heart-broken' very much reflected the BJP mood.

Sonia Gandhi did not appear surprised at all. The streets around her New Delhi home looked as if they had witnessed a coup detat. Hundreds of thousands of party supporters, and onlookers began celebrating the party's return to power. It was a spontaneous celebration for no one had expected the Congress to even come close to victory, leave alone achieving it. Not only had she covered her deficit, she had overtaken the BJP, its high falutin strategy now lay ravaged by her efforts, its leadership it seemed had simply evaporated. Confronting every challenge, against all odds, contrary to most expectations, Sonia Gandhi had humbled the unassailable Atal Behari Vajpayee. The lady they labelled a foreigner had been duly elected by the people of India to lead her country. She had swept Vajpayee back whence he had been carefully lifted and painstakingly crafted to appear the popular, awe-inspiring national icon and competitor to Jawaharlal Nehru which he never ever was.

'All election victories look inevitable in retrospect; none in prospect,' wrote Margaret Thatcher in her autobiography. This one, even in retrospect, was hard to believe. In a special column of his *Outlook* magazine, Vinod Mehta commented:

Not only has the country been stunned by the awesome verdict, the entire free world must learn from the courage of the poor, the illiterate, the voiceless and the underprivileged of the earth's largest democracy as they punish rulers who thought their realm consisted of 150 million for whom India was definitely 'shining'. That this resentment against a callous, corrupt, divisive government, with a seemingly benign leader, was not picked up by the news media or political parties should keep researchers engaged for a few years. Since the news media is made up of people comprising India Shining, it did not submit the dubious slogan to the scrutiny and skepticism it deserved.

Six years after she had stepped into politics Sonia Gandhi had already reached its peak. The struggle to get to the pinnacle of power was now behind her. The opportunity to exercise and harness this power lay in front of her. The present signified only a triumph of will.

Epilogue
The Second Renunciation or Nehru Found

On the evening of May 18th, the Central Hall of Parliament was packed to capacity. Newly elected MPs, defeated members of Parliament, leaders, workers and other members of the Congress Party lunged for space alongside ancient benches which could not accommodate any more people. Despite the air-conditioning the air was stuffy and the odour of flower petals sat heavily upon the over-crowded chamber, the atmosphere was hyper-charged. Press-men were everywhere. Within this enclosure was encapsulated the largest and substantially representative concentration of the Indian National Congress. There was scarcely a dry eye among them, no voice remained unemotive, a singular motivation ran through most of those present. The Congress Party could not have exhibited a more unified picture had it tried to engineer it. Facing this unruly, emotional mass of her party-men sat Sonia Gandhi. She had just rejected the office of the Prime Minister of India.

'Power in itself has never attracted me, nor has position been my goal.' Unbelievable words, insincere too, had they been uttered by any other politician in India. Sonia Gandhi had not only just spoken them, she had acted upon them. 'I was always certain that if I ever found myself in the position that I am in today, I would follow my own inner voice. Today, that voice tells me I must humbly decline this post.' And she did. Her three hundred word speech took over 30 minutes to read, due to emotional outbursts and interruptions throughout. The following speeches, very few of them contrived, took three hours as the speakers tried variously to influence a change of mind. They were futile speeches. Her decision had been final. Pitting her sentiment against their disappointment, the following day Sonia Gandhi issued a missive which finally and firmly read:

> To all of you who are disappointed, I have this to say: I am not going anywhere. I am still very much in politics. I will continue as Congress President and Chairperson, Congress Party in Parliament for as long as you want me to. I am one of you. And nothing will ever change that...I appeal to you to understand the depth of my sentiment, when I say that I cannot reverse my decision.

Within a span of a week, Sonia Gandhi had accomplished far more than what even her most die-hard supporters could have expected. These seven days must have formed the most challenging week of Sonia Gandhi's public life. On May 13th, she led her party to victory; upsetting myriad calculations, the Congress Party was once more in power after a hiatus of eight years. On the 15th she was unanimously elected leader of the Congress Parliamentary Party and was set to become the Prime Minister of India. Meetings with the President of India and alliance partners between the 16th and the 18th resulted in the formation of the United Progressive Alliance (UPA), their agenda for governance was drafted and ready for the following day. The evening of the 18th saw an unprecedented rejection of the Prime Minister's office. This act of renunciation evoked an outstanding variety of reactions; emotional upheavals among Congress workers ran parallel to a deep mental shock among most of the party's leaders. The Indian public, awash with cynicism for its politicians were doused in a new hope that bordered on disbelief. Among her opposition and critics there was acute bewilderment and gloom because in a single swoop she demolished what they had been saying all along. As one Samajwadi MP put it, 'she killed six hundred birds with one stone'. Within a week of the results being announced, the UPA government had been formed with Manmohan Singh as its Prime Minister.

Sonia Gandhi laid down the founding principles of the soon to be formed UPA government on May 15th. It was at the meeting of the CPP, which elected her leader, that she underlined, 'The commitment to provide a strong and stable government dedicated to promoting social harmony and peace unites all of us in the coalition. The commitment to provide a firm resolute government devoted to the welfare of the kisans and khet mazdoors, of youth and women, of weaker sections of society unites us all in the coalition.

Writing on the day that the UPA government took office, Mark Tully wrote in a London journal:

> Because Sonia is such a private person, we will probably never know what "the inner voice" she said she listened to when deciding to stand down, told her. But this is certainly not the end of the Nehru-Gandhi dynasty or Sonia Gandhi. With her enhanced charisma, she will be an invaluable asset when Congress turns, as it undoubtedly will, to one of her children. For the immediate future, her problem will be avoiding back-seat driving. She will still be the most powerful person in Congress and in that fractious party there will be many pressures on her to exercise her power.

Meanwhile, the UPA has completed a year in office. The events of the last year are too recent to recount in this book. Despite a strong, sometimes aggressive, left-wing influence, it will complete its full term. The only potential 'jacket' for trouble may develop in 2006, when the Congress Party must confront its own allies at the Centre in electoral contests at the state level. So far though there is no evidence of a national mood against the party or any development of an anti-incumbency factor. Certainly the party has come a long way from the time when assessments about its future were largely dismal. It was only in 1997, a year before Sonia Gandhi took over as Congress President that the scholar Achin Vanaik wrote:

> So serious has been the decline of the Congress that it is no longer out of place to wonder whether its crisis is terminal or whether India is entering a post-Congress future......The Congress may still survive as a significant force in the Indian polity. But if the Congress is to survive it must do so in a new form and shape. The old Congress is dying even if it is too early to write definite epitaphs. A new Congress is yet to emerge.

Whether the Congress under Sonia Gandhi is a 'new' Congress is uncertain. It is certainly a renewed political force that has grounded itself strongly within its original core political philosophy to a far larger and deeper extent than previous Congress regimes. For the foreseeable future the developments of any Congress Party 'ideology', the creation of its 'vision' as it were, must happen through critiques and arguments within the parameters of the Nehruvian Consensus. Above all, this means the consolidation of secularism as the sanctum sanctorum of India's political agenda. That, simply put, is at the core of Sonia Gandhi's politics.

Sonia Gandhi and her main national opposition, the BJP, have a differing vision on the method and process of political evolution.

This dynamic is bound to guide the exchange between government and opposition for the next few years. Conflict is the inherent principle in any such division and it will continue to operate itself until a consensus for governance is established. This consensus must be found on two issues above all others. First, a definition of secularism must evolve, a definition that is specific and relevant to the social and political realities of India. Second, there has to be an agreement on the direction of economic policy even though there will be difference of opinion on the details of particular policy initiatives and reform. Sonia Gandhi views the former point as a pre-condition while the latter is allowed to be subjected to expert opinions and arguments. Like Pandit Nehru, if there is any one theme which brings out her intellectual and political brilliance it is the theme of liberal politics and its ancillaries of social diversity, secularism, multiplicity, plurality and representative democracy. She outlined her creed in her first Presidential address to the 81st Plenary Session of the Indian National Congress in Bangalore in 2001 when she said:

> The Congress mirrors India in all its diversity. It represents, like no other party does, the plurality of India. It is the only pan-Indian party that draws its support and sustenance from each and every section of our society that appeals to and derives its encouragement from all Indians, irrespective of caste, community, religion, language or region. Other parties use our diversity to divide us. We are the only party that uses our diversity to keep us united, the only party that recognises that without social harmony, nothing else is possible. A fractured India cannot prosper.

A divided India cannot progress. Only the Congress can ensure a strong Centre, strong states and strong local bodies in villages, towns and cities. If we do not watch out, regionalisation of our polity could lead to parochialism and a weakening of the national will. This is so very essential for maintaining the political unity of India.

In the course of the same speech, she elaborated on the theme and formed the apothesis of her political will and outlook:

It is only the Congress Party whose very core is secular. We need no certificate for this. For us secularism is an article of faith. We are a party whose leaders have become martyrs at the altar of secularism. Secularism, for us, is freedom of religion, not freedom from religion. For us, secularism is not religion versus religion.

This revivalist (and radical) brand of secularism has been the ideological fulcrum that has propelled the Congress Party back into government. India's secularism was founded on an indigenous, self-derived synthesis and cultural coexistence. It was subverted by an imperialistic British autocracy and revived by a Westernised elite as a process of the Independence Movement. In its half understood form it was the focus of the right-wing's political critique, another subversion, until it became in the late 1990s a pun, a term little understood and much maligned. Sonia Gandhi's biggest contribution has been in re-converting secularism, reviving it as a guiding principle within politics, in a form which resembles, most closely, the original. This hubristic and radically deviant move has made her politics different to the traditional terms of engagement used by Indian political leaders. Hers is a more empirical, more rational response to the perceived challenges of the Indian polity. She has come close to achieving the status of her forbears despite the disadvantages of her provenance; the given primordials of a person such as her religion, birthplace, language and culture. The remarkable exchange is that the majority of Indians have dismissed these non-rational foundations of identity and elected her their leader. Her renunciation of prime-ministerial office, therefore, as an acknowledgement of this favour, is a personal act of faith and understanding. It is this understanding that has converted even larger numbers to her side.

The six distinct intellectual components in Sonia Gandhi's politics are: a revivalist secularism, a retrospective determinism, an intellectual continuity, sociological cohesion, a lack of authoritarian incorporation and economic empowerment based upon a sustainable subsidiarity. None of these is as esoteric as the phrases may suggest. They are based upon rational foundations and modernist interpretations of politics, in a deeply conservative and highly politicised society. In a very substantial degree, her political personality unites the principles of a Nehruvian ideal with the pragmatism of Indira Gandhi's brand of politics. The retrospective determinism spoken of here is a reading of past Congress history which for a large part is also her family history, and turning this reading into the culmination of a creed for the modern day Congress. This in turn necessitates an intellectual continuity, that is, a unity of ideological thought which forms an unbroken mental chain between Pandit Nehru and Sonia Gandhi. The result of this is sociological cohesion. This is something that Sonia Gandhi has been successful in creating; taking 'secularism' as an experiment and bridging elite perceptions with majoritarian or mass realities to create integration. The mobilisation of regional and small political parties around a Congress centre was in itself an unprecedented task, to successfully direct this mobilisation into a focused attack on communal politics, to effect an ideological engagement was an improbability made possible. So much so that the BJP's largest ally, the TDP, blamed the riots of Gujarat for its own defeat in Andhra Pradesh.

Certain social groups are inherently attached to party ideologies because no other party involves itself with these groups. Sonia Gandhi has attempted to integrate as many of these social fronts in as high a proportion as possible with the Congress Party. This means widening the party's outlook, looking ahead and providing a diversity of services to these various groups. This is not a new phenomenon. It is a reversal to the days of one party rule, of a dominant political formation. It is far from complete, in fact it has only just begun. The deconstruction of the right wing has happened far more rapidly than anyone would have thought. The project is still nascent but the BJP's 'cultural nationalism' thesis was an elitist and esoteric concept which promoted negative integration; against a particular community, it is no longer operable. Sonia Gandhi has been deliberately inclusive and responsive towards a coalition of interests.

The challenge that awaits a more concentrated and wilful effort from Sonia Gandhi is organisational reform, particularly in Uttar Pradesh. She has not been successful so far in tackling the perceived injustices of party workers in such crucial states because too much delegation and devolution to a combination of panels, individual leaders and dominating factions means that this bureaucratisation of the party reform programme is unable to operate outside rigid parameters. This feudalistic party bureaucracy which represents the interface between the party leadership and its workers is the single most threatening facet for the modern day Congress Party. Competing pressures of acoommodation in party posts and a demand for organisational empowerment which cannot be granted all contribute to an ever increasing culture of complaint within. A fragmentation of interests within the party requires a mechanism to negotiate these same interests. While it is possible to control this at the highest levels of the party organisation, through her persona and inter-active leadership, it is difficult to extend this 'healing touch' across the country to workers on a regular basis. For this she must rely on her representatives in their respective states. The natural dynamics of party politics are therefore subject to the level of influence and control exercised by these various leaders. Very few of them are able to manage the party in their charges as she would perhaps like them to, all the time.

There is therefore a dual integration required between the levels of the party hierarchy as well as between the various interest groups. Excessive autonomy will lead to further fragmentation, excessive authoritarianism may subvert inner party democracy. This balance between the two must be set by Sonia Gandhi herself.

The identity of the Indian National Congress and its 'cultural' sustenance was developed by a diverse political experience. The ideas of Mahatma Gandhi, the vicissitudes of the Independence Movement with its varying brands of nationalism, communalism within politics and its sectarian branches of thought and, most of all, the diversity of political thought among the Congress leadership all contributed to the development of Congress culture. These in turn were blended into the outlook of Pandit Jawaharlal Nehru who meditated upon and modified the messages he received, until, like a prophet of a newly proclaimed race, he was individually responsible for the creation of a definition of modern India. Mahatma Gandhi may have been the Father of India as an ideal, but it was Pandit Nehru who fathered India into modernity. The descendant of this creation became the Congress Party which began to shake off its identity soon after Nehru's death. It was both replenished and reduced by Indira Gandhi, in varying degrees. Rajiv Gandhi restored it, almost successfully but his project remained incomplete because of his premature death by assassination. The ideological destruction of the party under Rao left it vulnerable where it mattered most, in the Hindi heartlands. If any individual can at all be called the guide who returned Congress to its roots, in the closest degree possible, she has to be Sonia Gandhi. This tone of triumph cannot be sounded just because the party has returned to power, that power is shared with others. It does not signify anything as profound as a victory of secularism over its rival ideologies. Nor does it mean that the vision of Nehru is once again the lens through which the progress of India must be viewed. No. The triumph is real because Sonia Gandhi has altered, through sheer physical and intellectual endeavour, the course that the Congress was taking. She is the 'heroine' of the act because she has prepared the ground from which the project of a Congress revival, wedded to the larger objective of national progress may be achieved. Will she lead this 'revolution' herself, or will it be a successor, is too early to say. The future holds choices to be made, for Sonia Gandhi, the Indian National Congress and, most crucially, for the people of India. That is why this story is only the beginning.

APPENDICES

Appendix I

Narasimha Rao's Congress Government. June 10, 1991.

Prime Minister	P.V. Narasimha Rao
Human Resource Development	Arjun Singh
External Affairs	Madhavsinh Solanki
Finance	Manmohan Singh
Defence	Sharad Pawar
Home	S.B. Chavan
Agriculture	Balram Jhakar
Railways	Jaffer Sharief
Civil Aviation and Tourism	Madhavrao Scindia
Petroleum and Natural Gas	B. Shankaranand
Parliamentary Affairs	Ghulam Nabi Azad
Law Justice Company Affairs	Vijaya Bhaskar Reddy
Health and Family Welfare	M.L. Fotedar
Urban Development	Sheila Kaul
Welfare	Sitaram Kesri
Water Resources	V.C. Shukla

Appendix II

'We, who had no voice..." – A paper written by Salman Khurshid, 1997

Unprecedented events within the Congress Party in the last few months were expected to usher in a rapid process of revitalisation. Events in the country moved a little faster and before we were really prepared, Punjab and sundry by-elections were upon us. The results of these elections are both interesting and distressing. We will go through the usual protests and protestations. One group will scream for "long knives," while the other will resort to sophistry to shame restoration rakes. But the fact remains that there is something rotting in the Congress. And rot in the Congress is rot in this land of ours – in the 58th year of our independence.

The problem is the problem itself. We have no way to sincerely talk about our sudden atrophy. We, therefore, have no way of countering it. There was, for a while, great hype about a Narora-type camp at Mt. Abu. But the cool dry climate of the resort didn't permit any nuclear activity. We wanted our top leadership (intellectual, if you please) to do a brainstorming to prevent scenarios such as the Punjab results. Instead the Punjab results prevented the brainstorming. And now, we are told, we shall try again – this time closer to God at Vrindavan. Soon the yatras and rallies will begin and political parrots will fly in all directions, with messages for which there are no takers any more. The Congress Party symbol is "no longer a passport to power", we are told by the wise. How to acquire a fresh and valid travel document no one bothers to tell us. We have lost in 1996 because we were splintered and fragmented. We have lost in 1997 because we are together. Our colleagues who served the last Congress Party President maintain we lost because "chargesheeted" leaders were denied tickets to run. Our colleagues who serve the President now have said: "Chargesheeted leaders have lost, so we will not give them tickets." Perhaps we are all overlooking the view that leaders ought not to be chargesheeted, in the first place. At least not on flimsy grounds which might titillate an adversary's political palate but would not convince a serious common lawyer.

So where should we begin – we, who had no voice...?

Although Congress is a thoroughly democratic party, and needs no lessons from the likes of six-day wonders like Mr. T.N. Seshan, the fact is that our leader is first "chosen" and then accepted and appreciated. Mr. Kesri is the leader of our party but "popularly" elected by less than 250 legislators and a handful of members of the Congress Working Committee. Undoubtedly a few months from now over a thousand AICC members will endorse his elevation. But, as in the case of his predeccessor, Mr. Kesri was not thought of as a possible aspirant or contender a few months ago. Very rapidly he has moved to take charge and establish his control over the party. He means well, even if his dramatic break with the recent past has embittered those unable to adjust quickly to the changes. The President wants to revive the Congress and to pass its eternal torch to a new generation. The process of his elevation inevitably did not provide for a "warming up" or preparation. Since many active and thinking Congress leaders were coincidentally outside Parliament, we did not have a say. We may have wished him to take the reins but nobody was asking us. Since we were not voting we could not demand attention to certain priorities. Those who voted did not necessarily have the same priorities. There is very sound reason for such disparities – those who won are largely from constituencies not mauled by caste and communalism. We, who lost were massacred by just that twin menace.

Many of our colleagues underrate the contribution and capability of Mr. Narasimha Rao due to the seemingly inexplicable failure over Ayodhya and the unacceptable failure in the polls. However, he had worked to a plan that not only kept a minority government going for five years but also gave the most imaginative and economically pathbreaking administration in many years. Unless we are clear about the reasons that wrecked his Camelot, and are honest enough to accept them, we will not get our little world in order.

To begin with there was never a serious enough case made out for "one man one post". It was essentially a euphemism for saying: "We want greater share in power." The oft repeated criticism of certain decisions, too, may not have had much to do with their merits. For if it did, we would have applied ourselves with expedition to rectifying them. Most of us, in any case, know that a bipolar Congress leadership is an invitation to disaster. Democratic parties ought to be able to function with bipolar or even collective leadership. But historically they have become accustomed – nay it is time to admit – they have been consciously designed to function under one undisputed leader. If some of us consider that to be an unwholesome principle, we will have to change the way we think in the party. Forcing a bipolar leadership will not resolve any problem. Our present President need hardly worry about this. There are many other more important issues to worry about.

Congress may be tired and defeated. But no other party has discovered the talisman to rule India. The Janata Party and the federal parties have all peaked and discovered that politics of opposition is a song compared to the stress of ruling. But the issues on which they all ran a spurious campaign to oust the Congress still need a response from the Congress – corruption, casteism, communalism and, finally, the very panacea for all these ills, economic reform and liberalisation. Unfortunately our positions on the first three have tied themselves into knots over the last decade and on the last it has been a "step forward, two steps back". Let us examine each one of these and prepare an agenda of substance to replace the empty slogans.

Corruption is what corruption does. It aberrates society, making it inefficient and self-deprecating. Transitions often lead to corruption, as post-Soviet Union Russia has discovered to its distress. Economic systems are supported by moral systems and vice versa. When one breaks down the other inevitably feels the shocks or after shocks. Unnatural economic systems do not get moral support and create moral "air pockets" as well as opportunities for corruption – large governmental monopoly over opportunities, widespread lack of transparency, a small commercial elite class, total absence of laws providing for financing political activity, need for large sums of money for politics due to the vastness of the political terrain, and finally a woefully faceless prolix and slumberous legal system. Fortunately a vigilant – nay inquisitive press – has in recent years exposed the entrails of corruption repeatedly. Although in truth much of the credit should go to faceless "Deep Throat" characters who feed the press. Add to all this our natural penchant for hypocrisy and you have a haven for the corrupt.

Liberalisation was supposed to arrest corruption or at least reduce it to tolerable levels. But unfortunately, we did not go far enough in the name of "sovereignty" on the inevitable concern for the "poor man". Pre-liberalisation meant certain services and goods would not be available at the Indian market except by courtesy of smugglers. Post-liberalisation (a la 1991) meant they would be available at the pleasure of the Minister, the Secretary or the Prime Minister's Office. "How much, of what, for whom," without reference to an acceptable principle of freedom, was a recipe for disaster that cooked our goose. On the chopping block were our colleagues like Kalpanath Rai, Sukh Ram, Sheila Kaul, Satish Sharma, et al. They were condemned and convicted before trial. Many other colleagues who had benefited from their generosity (for such was the system) kept a conspicuous silence. The political form of sati was never in fashion in our party. How many of them were collecting partially, if not wholly, for the party will never be known. Are they to be punished for bad accounting?

The party received its egg on the face in the hawala proceedings. Understandably the Supreme Court was indignant about the loose morals of politicians. The best and the worst were bunched together; foot soldiers and holders of Constitutional office were mixed in a frightening cocktail. Some blamed their discomfiture on Mr. Rao and sought vindication through victory in an election – Mr. Madhavrao Scindia and Kalpanath Rai. Others tried but failed – Messrs. Buta Singh and Kamal Nath. But the story is not over. We continue to hear talk of tainted leaders. The extent of confusion is reflected in the incomprehensible decision of an outstanding Mr. Motilal Vohra resigning his office on grounds of being "chargesheeted" and yet formally heading the Congress Party election campaign in the UP Assembly elections of 1996. One man's meat is another's poison.

Corruption has become a recurring theme song of political campaigns in the last decade. Inevitably those who ousted a predecessor government on grounds of corruption quickly proceeded to feather their own nest. Not once was a genuine effort made to provide a system to obliterate the canker of corruption.

Of the many reasons for developing a socialist state, some were lofty and noble but at least one was simply pragmatic. The political elite (public persons and public servants (how the two are different, in a minute) structured power for itself through state control and monopoly. The State controlled goods and services through the public sector. Civil servants ran the public sector and politicians used it – jobs for the boys, contracts for supportive businessmen, transportation and accommodation on quite a lavish scale for the boss (the Indian dachas!). As a Minister I was told I could not take an air-conditioned official car on long and tedious journeys across UP So MMTC and STC obliged. In big cities I could not stay at comfortable hotels on government account. So the State Tourism Boards obliged. All this will have to go with liberalisation. But so should the myopic rules. If you want the best minds in the country to rule, you will have to give them compatible working conditions. After all it is not easier to run India than it is to run Tata Sons. Congress will have to take a stand. We do not live in ashrams any more and the highest we aspire for the Motherland is not the eight feet drop from the gallows (as our forefathers did in the Independence movement). So let us stop pretending and start living.

Putting liberalisation on the right track will contain corruption – and only that will. We have heard some Jurassic roars in the party about repudiation of "Manmohaneconomics". Here please pay heed to our lesser voice. We did not lose because of Dr. Manmohan Singh. We lost despite him. And if his critics say that his economics is deaf and blind I can only say: "There are none so blind, as those who will not see." History tells us that nations move when they have (or create) a common enemy or else when they have shared dreams. Hitler followed the first path; the tigers of Asia have taken the latter. Let us choose with care.

So why did we lose despite Dr. Manmohan Singh? In the streets of Uttar Pradesh they will tell you to rest your researches. The answer is all too evident – "Mandal and Kamandal". We had no position on the first except to let the courts decide. We have no position on the second except to say that the courts will decide. Is it surprising that people think we do not want to rule any more?

Why have people turned to parties which take extreme and exclusive postures on these issues? To begin with, not because the voter prefers an absolute position to an accommadative position; or an extremist position to a liberal one. The real problem is that they had to choose between an aggressive position and an absence of one. Take Ayodhya. We could not prevent the demolition of the Babri Masjid. So we should apologise. If that does not work we should put our former leaders on trial. If that does not work we should say that Muslims have more urgent needs like education and jobs. If that does not work let us appoint more Muslim office bearers. And if that does not work......? The BJP are gloating that they are finally writing the national agenda. They scribe the word "Ayodhya" on the wall and freeze our faculties and our fortunes alike. On the other side of the wall the Janata Dal and the Samajwadi Party trace the same lethal graffiti. We exhaust ourselves in sadhbhavana yatras and end up supporting those very bandicoots who ran off with our golden goose. Is it not time that we scale the wall or even bring it down? If the Berlin Wall can come down so can the artificial barriers built by Advani and Mulayam Singh Yadav.

Let us state our position on the minorities clearly. We repudiate the charge of appeasement. Welfare of the minorities is a solemn constitutional guarantee. We will uphold it in substance and form. In education and opportunity creation we will do the utmost to undo the disadvantages of the past. If reservation policies continue let the minorities have their share. Unimaginable damage has been caused to minority electoral expectations by the management of the Panchayat system of reservations. Let it be known that whenever reservations will be claimed on the ground of educational and economic backwardness, Muslims will get their share.

We, who had no voice, would like the Congress to do some creative thinking to break the stranglehold of mediocrity imposed by reservations and yet deliver far greater benefits to Muslims and backwards than their self-appointed benefactors. "We are not in power, how do we do it?" some sceptics will say. Well, let us go out and sell this idea to the people and we will be in power again.

Ayodhya scares us even more. We do not like talking about it. And when we are forced to, we end up apologising – only to deny that we apologised. The mosque cannot be rebuilt, some tell us with pedagogic authority. Why don't we taunt Mulayam Singh Yadav with this then? He is the Defence Minister. Though UP State is no longer under Central Rule, Singh continues to have a strong rapport with an understanding and secular-minded Governor. Mulayam Singh is the darling of the Muslim masses. Why does he not rebuild the mosque? Status quo ordered by the Supreme Court ought not to stand in the way. The Court will be more than pleased to meet a government which will relieve it of the onerous responsibility. But, of course, we do not live in Alice's world which gets "curiouser and curiouser". So let us take the bull (if I might be permitted to say) by the horns. Let us take a position on Ayodhya. BJP claims Hindus support them and Mulayam Singh claims Muslims support him. Let us find out who and what has India's support. Let us ask for a referendum between Hindus and Muslims; not a referendum between the Gita and the Quran. We want a referendum on what should happen at Ayodhya.

A temple
A mosque
Nothing
Both a temple and a mosque – but built 100 feet apart

Let everybody stand and be counted. There will be no CMs, MPs and PM in the running. No political musclemen and booth capturing. Just an opinion. Secularism will prevail in a natural condition. We will also learn how disputes can ultimately be settled in a democracy. We, who had no voice, would like the Congress to demand a referendum.

A successful political movement is made up of ideas and persons. We have tried to give voice to the ideas which gave the Congress some punch again. But ideas need to live in the able bodies and minds of people. The Congress Party needs transfusions of fresh blood which has been thoroughly checked and tested for political disease. The last mass entry into the Congress Party was way back in 1975. Since then no significant political induction has taken place. We are an ageing party with a generous touch of black hair dye. A combination of experience and youth is, of course, ideal. But a few fifty-year-olds do not make a youthful party. If we are planning a serious future we will need many more young people.

One major problem all political parties face today is that the kind of people who wish to join politics today are not the kind parties need or necessarily want. In our reaffirmation of the Gandhi-Nehru traditions if only we could acquire the skill and charm of drawing flowers of society to us we might just reduce the sting of political culture. Picking up a test cricketer and a film star now and then is not what I have in mind. Galaxies of brilliant minds, professionals, social activists, human rights activists, etc. shold be manning the front line of the Party. Some of these will not be able to become Lok Sabha MPs. Indeed, they may well become ineffective and useless as Lok Sabha MPs. We can bring them to the Rajya Sabha. We can give them party posts. It is time for leaders to lead. Give people positions commensurate with their talents and their nuisance value. The party needs both depth and wide cover. Some people will be good as

MPs; others will be good as Ministers; yet others will be good as party administrators; and some will be good field workers and salesmen. We allow one person to reserve too many caps for himself. As a result, we lose too many good hands and shoulders. Let not too many people say: "We, who had no voice......"

There has been much talk about a brainstorming session – first at Mt. Abu, then at Vrindavan. Perhaps this venue, too, may change. Whenever this session takes place a few, a lucky few, will attempt to charter the future of the Congress Party. There will be concerned attempts to dissect the past, both the distant and the recent. There will be *ad hominem* arguments. There will be no further opportunity to take stock of reality for a while.

And we will have no voice. Unless someone is listening.

Appendix III

Executive Summary of the Sangma Task Force's Report. 1998.

In the 12th Lok Sabha formed after the 1998 General Elections, the Congress has a strength of 139 Members, two Members more than in the 11th Lok Sabha. The BJP has improved its position from 161 to 181 Members. The Congress is still centre stage in Indian politics with a vote share of 25.81 per cent against the BJP vote share of 25.34 per cent. Relative, however, to 1952 when the Congress vote share was 45 per cent, the party has indeed suffered. The Congress has also lost presence in major states, while the BJP is extending its presence in its non traditional areas.

The Congress ideology continues to be sound and valid. However, preservation of Parliamentary Democracy has to be emphasised; that Socialism is quite consistent with the Reform Process has to be clarified, bringing home that Reforms are necessary for the sustainable advancement of the poor; and further it should also be clarified that the secularism of Congress is without admixture of religion and politics and is quite distinct from the so-called "Cultural Nationalism" of the BJP, which is an open negation of the diversity of India and an implicit admixture of religion and politics.

The vision of the party for the future should be for the establishment of an equitable socio-economic order in which the people will be healthy (population growth being contained), educated, enlightened, skilled and productive and enjoy peace and high quality of life; the youth will grow into satisfied and responsible citizens; women will be at par with men in the household, work-place, society and governance; children will face no exploitation with full opportunities to grow into capable adults; environment will be protected; governance will be good and transparent; the economy will be one of the foremost in the world, commanding political respect by its own strength.

For the rejuvenation of the party and safeguarding its unity and integrity, the urgent requirements are: restructuring of field formations; structural and functional decentralisation; observance of inner party democratic processes; membership strength of the field formations being large enough to be comprehensively representative and lean enough for effective management and business transactions; and deliberative and communication processes being kept active and alive through systematised and programmed meetings of the field formations. An approach based on meeting these requirements is bound to instil a sense of participation in, and belonging to, the party which will contribute to its unity and integrity.

Restructuring of the PCCs should be carried out at the earliest, membership reflecting participation by all sections – SCs, STs, OBCs, Minorities, Women, etc; and the youth should be given special weightage and projection.

Decentralisation of the field formations of the party should give special attention to major states like UP and Bihar. The structure for UP and Bihar should specially provide respectively, for Uttarakhand Regional Congress Committee and Chota Nagpur Regional Congress Committee. In addition, there should also be Divisional Congress Committees for these states. The tenure of the committees should be four years instead of two years as at present.

Inner Party democracy should be strengthened by holding periodic elections without default and ad hocism should be strictly avoided.

Membership strength of the PCCs should be strengthened by holding of periodic elections without default and ad hocism should be strictly avoided.

Regular meetings of the PCCs and other committees at the various levels should be held according to a stipulated timetable.

The party and its functioning at all levels should be ideological and programme-oriented.

There should be regular and mandatory Party Conferences at all levels.

The party should establish and draw upon the expertise of resourceful think tanks at the National and Pradesh levels.

For the reinforcement of the stake and role of the grass-root level workers, grass-root teams should be established; each team shall consist of three workers at the minimum; 7.5 lakh teams (2.25 million workers) are required for covering the whole country; the basic strategy is to do service-oriented work with close and regular contacts with individual households; the grass-root teams should be instruments for delivery of services locally required and redressal of public grievances.

The party workers should do service within the framework of a permanent agenda, addressing the concerns of the youth, women, the working people in the organised and the unorganised sectors, the farmers, old people and children.

The organised programmes and activities of the party should be less in terms of one shot rallies and public meetings and more in terms of orderly and systematised mass contacts: the party cadres should be given special training on the provisions of important social legislations relating to land reforms, labour, women, children, etc. for the purpose, there should be decentralised training arrangements.

For broadening and strengthening the support base of the party, regular membership drives should be organised; if in the restructuring of the party formations, special categories of persons cannot secure positions through elections, they should be nominated with voting rights; Article XIV of the Constitution and the rules framed thereunder should be amended for the prupose.

There should be regular monitoring of the Special Component Plans, Tribal Sub-Plans and 15-Point Programme for Minorities; special attention should also be given for the vocational training of the Dalit and Minority Communities in their traditional skills.

For implementing "Minorities"-oriented programmes the party may concentrate on these communities as understood under the National Policy on education and as per the numerical minority status of the communities in individual states.

The party should continue to mobilise the youth in their rank and file targeting Universities, Colleges and even post-Secondary students; the NSUI should enhance its profile through membership drives every academic year, dissemination of Congress ideology, actively participating in elections and in the programmes of the Universities like the National Service Scheme; apart from organising cultural and sports activities and interacting with teachers organisations.

The Indian Youth Congress should be strengthened and be involved in social campaigns against female infanticide and drug abuse and campaigns for containment of population growth, AIDS awareness, eradication of illiteracy and protection of environment.

The Youth Congress should start their membership drive and hold elections within a year.

The intelligentsia should be mobilised through the membership drives of the party; professionals like lawyers, engineers, doctors, teachers, management specialists, etc, should be enrolled; they should also be given placements in the party structure apart from consultative status; further hopes should be held out for them for their participation in the government as and when the party comes to power.

Women should be a special target group in membership drives; they should be given one-third representation in positions of party hierarchy as done in the UK, Australia, Scandinavian countries, Latin American countries, etc.; women should be given special training on participation in political life and electoral processes. Women's electoral campaigns should be given special training on participation in political life and electoral processes. Women's electoral campaigns should also be funded without discrimination; publicly funded women's programmes should be closely monitored for ensuring efficient delivery of services.

Separate National Advisory Councils for the youth, women and special groups should be established, the model of the Liberal Party of Canada being adapted.

The Parliamentary Wing and Legislature Parties should be strengthened. The Legislative Affairs Committee recommended in the Interim Report should scrutinise all legislative proposals of the government from constitutional, legal, technical and substance points of view.

The financial position of the party should be improved by measures such as enhancement of primary membership fee from Re. 1/- to at least Rs. 3/- collection of contributions from 1 lakh Congress sympathisers at Rs. 1000/- per annum, collection of contributions from business houses transparently, adoption of Kerala method of fund collection, collection of contributions from active members at Rs. 150/- per annum, collection of annual contributions from MLAs, MPs and office bearers at Rs. 1200/- per annum, avoidance of wasteful expenditure at party functions, publication of annual souvenirs, and or professional periodicals.

Ethics committees should be established in the PCCs with bylaws stipulating modalities for ensuring ethical behaviour and standards of the Party workers, particularly to prevent corruption and criminalisation.

Accountability should be ensured up the party hierarchy; PCCs and other field formations should be allowed to function autonomously in their own well-laid out areas of competence without interference from above; there should be disciplinary action committees right down to block levels to discipline errant party functionaries.

A three-member North East Cell should be established. This should be headed by a member of the Congress Working Committee.

An Indian National Overseas Congress should be established to mobilise the support of Indians Overseas; and the Congress should be projected as an experienced and natural party of good governance with modern orientation. This organisation should function under the supervision of the Dept. of External Affairs of the AICC.

For making the party responsive to socio-economic concerns in the changing world scenario, issues involved in world developments including globalisation should be presented to the party cadres in a demystified manner, special learning materials in simple and local languages being produced and distributed, and information dissemination seminars being conducted with the help of think tanks; seminars should also be conducted to get feedback on grass-root level responses to programmes implemented with reference to global compulsions so that such feedback could be useful inputs for policy formulation and correction.

Appendix IV

Members of the Congress Working Committee, the Chief Minister, delegates, brothers and sisters.

First of all, I welcome you all to this Brainstorming camp. We have gathered here at a time when our country is passing through a severe crisis. We shall sit here together to discuss vital issues concerning our party. We will hold serious deliberations on them.

The Congress Party is a great national institution and we all take pride in being part of it. We have to lay stress on how we can bring an awakening into this great organisation. This is our commitment.

I would like camps of this kind to be organised regularly at the national and other levels. We have so much in our lives today, but little scope for looking back; do serious thinking and self-introspection. We need all those three things. We have an opportunity, in this beautiful place, to do some quiet thinking. We must make use of it.

Papers about the issues that will be discussed thoroughly in this camp have been supplied to you. The camp will discuss, specially, the political, agricultural, national, international matters and those concerning the organisation. In the next three days, besides the discussions, we shall review our activities and make plans for the future. We can tackle fast the crisis and hurdles in our way by inducting freshness in the party.

Our party has been serving the people since the days of Mahatma Gandhi. We should remember what Gandhiji said: political work can be done only by adhering to ideals and morality. We must remember that programmes, plans and preparations for election always go on in a political party. The party should remain alert about its doctrines, programmes and conduct.

I hope that we will gain a lot from this camp, which will be an achievement for our party. You will recall that five months ago, at a programme in Delhi, I had spoken about inducting a new force and strengthening the party. For this purpose, I had constituted a task force.

I am happy to tell you, here today, that the task force has done commendable work. Several of its recommendations have been implemented after their approval in the Congress Working Committee meeting held in Delhi last June.

Some of us often see only the dark side. I have neither the 'all is well' and so 'sit back hand in hand' attitude nor do I see despair and defeat all around. We must harbour neither of these in our minds. Neither complacence nor pessimism will behove us. We have to look forward to the future. We have to learn from the past, not remain stuck with it.

I can now see a new discipline and goal in our method of working. A beginning has been made to induct a new work-culture in the AICC and the Pradesh Congress Committees. This will go on. No organ of the Congress Party will remain inactive.

New programmes are being given to the frontal organisations. These include both political and social campaigns.

A committee has been constituted for amendments in the party constitution. It has to pay special attention as to how tribals, minorities, backward classes and women can be given a larger role in the organisation. The committee will soon be submitting its report.

Programmes have been launched to impart training at several levels and giving a boost to the party. This way workers will get new knowledge and also political education.

The conduct and discipline committees have begun their work. I keep myself informed about it.

We have launched a monthly journal called *Congress Sandesh* from August 15. It will be sent to all members of the PCCs and the AICC. The next issue is devoted to the Pachmarhi's brainstorming session.

Our immediate challenge is the forthcoming Assembly Elections in Madhya Pradesh, Mizoram, Rajasthan and Delhi. Preparations have already begun. The Task Force's programme implementation committee has already interacted at considerable length with the Presidents of these four states. The Committee has also had discussions with the Chiefs of Frontal Organisations and CLP leaders.

The salient points which emerged through these interactions included updating of electoral roll, selection of candidates on merit, preparation of state manifestos at an early date, a comprehensive strategy to be adopted for fighting these elections, appointment of Central observers, publicity, etc.

It is becoming clearer every day that the graph of the Congress Party is going up and that of the BJP-led coalition government is going down. We are winning the battle of ideas and eventually if we act unitedly and vigorously we will win the full support of our people.

In less than two hundred days, the BJP-led coalition has proved its inability to govern India. There is no evidence of firm and decisive direction in any branch of its activities. The economy is stagnant, inflation is on the rise. Investors and business confidence is at an all time low. Foreign policy is in a shambles. The coalition in Delhi is at war with itself. Internal contradictions are being exposed every day. The BJP and its allies are speaking with different voices on vital national and international issues. The expansion of the Central Cabinet has been postponed indefinitely, it seems. Our stand of not rushing into bringing this government down has been appreciated all round.

I once again wish to make it clear that as and when the need arises our party will fulfil its constitutional obligations without hesitation and provide stability and purpose. We have never opposed for the sake of opposition. We have highlighted the failures and follies of the government. We will continue to do so.

We have always rejected the fascistic notion of one nation, one culture, one people. We believe that India is one nation, with plural cultures, diverse peoples. Diversity has defined us for centuries. Let us not allow political parties to divide us, to inflame religious passions, to ignite caste tensions and to fan regional sentiments. A divided India cannot survive. A fractured India cannot prosper. An India in which Indian is set against Indian cannot keep its 'tryst with destiny' The respect for plurality and the celebration of diversity constitute the very essence of Indian civilisation. That essence is under threat. It is only the Congress that can meet this threat effectively.

The people of India have rejected our opponent's vision of India because that vision is both narrow and flawed.

It is the Congress Party which under the leadership of Jawaharlal Nehru, Indira Gandhi and Rajiv Gandhi has brought and woven together sections of society harmoniously. We are the only political party that has not, does not and will not practise the policies of exclusion and the polities of spreading animosities. The Congress has had a place of dignity and respect for all communities, for all religions, for all languages, for all regions that make up the kaleidoscopic mosaic of India. The Congress Party is being once again called upon to fulfil this role.

Let us now remind ourselves of other important tasks that I would like to discuss here freely, frankly and responsibly.

First, we must take up the ideological crusade against the communal virus from whatever source it arises and spreads. Religious fundamentalism is alien to our culture but let us not be smug about this. Forces of religious fundamentalism of all kinds are out to destroy this tradition of tolerance and mutual accommodation. Many of us thought that economic development and progress would roll back the spread of communal ideologies and put an end to the politics of hate. This has clearly not happened. The question we must ask ourselves is whether we have, in any way diluted our commitment to the fight against communal forces. It would perhaps be tempting to say we have not. However, there is a general perception that we have at times compromised with our basic commitment to the secular ideal that forms the bedrock of our society.

During our deliberations we must all apply our minds to this vitally important question.

Second, we must acknowledge that we have not successfully accommodated the aspirations of a whole new generation of Dalits, Adivasis and backward people particularly in the northern parts of the country. Could this be one of the reasons for our decline in states like Uttar Pradesh and Bihar? Regrettably, we have not paid enough attention to the growth of such sentiments and feelings and consequently have had to pay a heavy price. It is not enough to make promises. The Congress Party must ensure to this section of our people full and equal representation. Great damage has been done to national-level politics itself on account of our decline in north India particularly. Electoral reverses are inevitable and are, in themselves, not cause for worry. What is disturbing is the loss of our social base, of the social coalition that supports us and looks up to us. What is also worrying is that Intra-Party discord seems to take up so much of our time and energy when it ought to be canalised for working together to regain popular support and public credibility.

Third, we have a special responsibility for attracting and retaining good people into our fold. Our party must dedicate itself to cleansing public life, we must be a more responsive political force. An effective instrument of social justice. We are committed to electoral reforms to reduce the role of money and muscle power. We must demand and ensure that an Electoral Reforms Bill be introduced in the winter session of Parliament.

Similarly, a systematic campaign is called for to enhance the image and the standing of the Congress among special groups in society-among the youth, for example, and among the educated sections of society. Already, 60 per cent of India is under the age of 24. We must not alienate ourselves from this vast, growing and dynamic segment of our society. Our programmes and policies must be such that they engage and draw the youth to our party. Their concerns must be addressed. It has now become clear that college degrees are not going to solve the problem of educated youth. What we need is education that is job-oriented and we intend to put this into effect when in office. The Indian freedom movement was dedicated to a purpose and not to a doctrine and the purpose was to eliminate as far as possible, in a pluralistic society, inequalities and caste bias. The fragmentation of society that we see today in the name of caste is both alarming and distressing. We must categorically reject casteism and we must resist its growth with all our might. Politics in the last few years has certainly given new identities to disadvantaged groups and has empowered oppressed communities. But we must take the social justice movement into its next phase, into a phase that stresses basic issues of health, education, food, security, nutrition and family planning. Let us be very clear it is the parliamentary system that is leading to social empowerment and that is giving representation to groups and communities who have been subjugated for centuries. This is as it should be. At the same time, we must also take serious note of the growing sense of frustration with the parliamentary form of government among the thinking and educated sections for our society. While seeking to understand the roots of this frustration, we must be in the forefront of a campaign that will ensure that the parliamentary form of government is not tampered with in the name of stability. There is nothing permanent about uncertain mandates and coalitions. Society itself is in a state of great transition and flux. To a large extent, shifting alliances in society reflect themselves in changing electoral mandates. We must not jettison these processes in the name of stability. We must also take the lead in championing the cause of electoral reforms, reforms that put the parliamentary form of government on a sounder foundation.

Fourth, we must constantly reinterpret our economic philosophy in the light of changing circumstance emerging challenges and the experience we gain while implementing policies. Our economic policy will have to be multi-dimensional to meet the needs of our people at various levels. No one dogma, no one formula will cater to the diverse needs of the economy and of our society. The abolition of poverty within the next 10-15 years must remain our fundamental objective. The assurance of a better quality of life and an improved standard of living to all citizens must remain our primary preoccupation. Sustaining a higher level of growth in agriculture, industry and other sectors is absolutely essential for abolishing poverty and expanding employment opportunities, it is imperative to control inflation, since inflation hits the poor the hardest. Expenditure on anti-poverty, rural development and wage employment programmes must increase, as also investments in primary education and public health. But we must also concern ourselves with making these expenditures more effective. The nation today spends close to Rs. 15,000 core every year on anti-poverty programmes. This is not an insubstantial amount and we must as a political party be in the forefront of a campaign and a movement to ensure that existing programmes, schemes and Yojanas reach those they are intended for. The Congress Party must also spearhead socio-economic campaigns and movements. We must press for land reforms, put pressure on governments to strengthen Panchayats and Nagarpalikas, and ensure that the public distribution system works to the benefit of the poor. It is not necessary to be in government to make sure that development programmes and schemes are implemented effectively. I am glad to note that our host State of Madhya Pradesh has been the first to conduct elections to panchayats after the passage of the 73rd Amendment to the Constitution and that administrative and financial powers have been given to almost 30,000 panchayats in the State. The role of the government at every level has to be redefined in the light of changing circumstances to make it a vehicle of economic change and social transformation. This is the essence of economic reforms. Government expenditure must add to the country's productive investment capacity and must be focused on improving the nation's physical and social infrastructure. We cannot spend our way to prosperity. Efficiency and productivity in all economic activities is a prerequisite for meeting social goals. The pattern of public expenditure must undergo a fundamental reorientation at both the Centre and in the states to enable us to invest more in poverty alleviation and social development programmes.

Fifth, we have to understand that foreign policy is not something of concern only to diplomats. It affects each and every one of us. It is fundamental to our security, to our standing in the world, to our very sovereignty. It impacts on the economy, on our exports, on our ability to mobilise foreign investment for development. The very financial position of the government is affected by foreign policy. The world has changed beyond recognition in the last ten years. It continues to change every day. India itself faces a whole new world scenario following the recent nuclear tests conducted by it and by Pakistan. We must now consolidate our technological capacities for defence and deterrence avoiding confrontationist or needlessly provocative postures. Simultaneously, we must endeavour to become part of the international mainstream on disarmament without in any way jeopardising our society's options. India must acquire a leadership role in the international community on the basis of its strengths and its achievements. Peace with our neighbours is an essential prerequisite. In the matter of a few weeks, the present coalition government destroyed what the Congress had painstakingly achieved over a ten-year period to normalise our relations with China. Our policy towards Pakistan is also confused and unclear. We have made no special efforts to repair our relationship with traditional friends and allies who opposed our nuclear tests.

The Congress Party's greatest asset has been the ability to reinvigorate, modify and adapt itself to suit changing times.

India is passing through a difficult time as it prepares to enter the sixth millennium of its existence as a civilisation. But as I said earlier there is no need for gloom or despair. The Congress Party and the Indian nation have in the past overcome stupendous challenges. We should therefore look to the 21st century with hope and high expectation.

I am confident that India will play a major role in shaping the political, economic, social technological, environmental contours of the coming century.

Let us at Pachmarhi resolve to restore the Congress to its original values of service and sacrifice.

Let us at Pachmarhi resolve to restore to the Congress its ethical and moral foundation.

Let us at Pachmarhi resolve to continue relentlessly in building a new Congress, a Congress that once again represents the hopes and aspirations of a growing number of our people, a Congress that embodies an India marching confidently forward providing prosperity, dignity and pride to all its citizens.

Letter from Sonia Gandhi, Chairman, National Advisory Board to Dr. Manmohan Singh, Prime Minister of India.

Sonia Gandhi., Chairperson
National Advisory Council
September 16, 2004

Dear Prime Minister,

I have been informed that the government is considering the reconstitution of the Divestment Commission and setting up, in its place, a new Board for Reconstruction of Public Sector Enterprises.

In this regard, I would like to draw your attention to the following commitment made in the National Common Minimum Programme:

"The UPA is pledged to devolve full managerial and commercial autonomy to successful, profit-making companies operating in a competitive environment."

In this regard, I would like to suggest that the first item in the terms of reference of the new board should be such as to enable it to look into ways and means for strengthening public sector enterprises, in general, and making them more autonomous and professional.

The functioning of the board should not be limited only to restructuring or advising on the closure or sale of public sector enterprises that are referred to it by the government.

I hope this matter will be considered on priority and a clear decision taken before the constitution of the Board for Reconstruction of Public Sector Enterprises.

With regards,
Yours sincerely,

Sonia Gandhi

Acknowledgements

Malvika Singh – A Godmother in every sense of the term. For her rebukes and her praises, for keeping an open house and dragging me out of the mess I keep getting into, for always being there. **Romi Chopra** – For all his words of encouragement and all his deeds of kindness. **Salman Khurshid** – for allowing me to make DEPCO my 'intellectual home' while he remained its Chairman, and for helping me preserve my sanity when I came close to losing it in the Genesis of my political career. **Shamim Akhtar** – The 'Chief Whip' at DEPCO office, companion (and antagonist) who was always understanding in the end. **Shivraj Patil** – For his courteous and helpful insights into the politics of the Congress Party early on. **Nandini Mehta** – who offered all help and her time with the manuscript. **Sandip Sharma** – For being an ever-present Guru and never losing patience with a most erring disciple, and more than that for being a very true friend. **William Stanton** – For urging me on in his own inimitable way to keep at it and finish the work I had started. **Willem van Lynden** – 'Top mate' and a swashbuckler of a friend in deed. **Sophiya Khan** – For urging me, every time I returned to Delhi to 'finish the book' and for remaining 'on my case' until I had done so. **Rashi Bhargava** – For being a constant friend and for reading my material when all others thought it 'boring political stuff'. **Tony Price and Angela Lambert** – For encouraging me very early on with my work and going to great lengths to find me a publisher even while this book was in its preliminary stages. **Sauvik' Bob' Barua** - For his timely intervention and help with the images. **Bhai Tripura** – A great companion, a rare friend and comrade in arms. **PR Kyndiah** – A father figure to many a young Congressman for his kindness and insights into the politics of the North-East.

Phillip Cottam – My own 'Friend, Philosopher and Guide' when I was a very difficult teenager at Stowe and was likely to hurt myself. He taught me early on in life that "there are no re-runs". I know I would have been a much lesser man without him. To my *Mamunjaan*, **Raja Saheb Mahmudabad**. How many kindnesses can I possibly thank him for? **Jaisal Singh** - The most hospitable man of my generation and a constant friend. To **Ham** and **Ha** for being themselves. **Amma and Abba** - What can I write, I owe them everything.

Index

Advani, L. K.
  Congress victory in
  Gandhinagar city seat, 248
  Godhra massacre, 240
  Hawala Scandal, 88
  Hindutva politics, 12
  Laloo Yadav's arrest during the
  Rath yatra in Samastipur, 13, 56
  on AIDMK withdrawal of support
  from NDA, 150
  on Congress stand on Kargil war,
  177
  Outlook magazine report of people's
  choice for prime minister, 271
  Rath yatra, 13, 67, 268
  reappointment as BJP president, 166
  reply to the motion moved by
  Narasimha Rao, 34-35
  Sonia's citizenship issue, 166
Agha, Zafar, 120
AIADMK, 18, 93, 97, 148, 150, 178
All India Congress Committee (AICC),
  60, 157, 158, 190, 213, 214, 221
  Avadi session, 130
  Bombay session, 127
  Calcutta session, 117
  Congress presidential election, 115
  demand for convening a session, 111
  Indira Gandhi as Congress
  President, 65
  Jitendra Prasad as Vice-President,
  222
  Kesri dismisses Congress General
  Secretaries, 116
  members, 287

  resolution to install Sonia
  Gandhi as head of both AICC and
  CPP, 126
  resolution at Simla Conclave, 253,
  254
  Surajkund session, 63
  West Bengal Assembly elections,
  204
Aiyar, Mani Shankar, 215
Allahabad, 26, 82, 180
Ambedkar, Dr. B. R., 72
Amethi, 18, 67, 75, 76, 77, 78, 79, 80,
  180, 181, 182, 183
Andhra Pradesh, 20, 26, 27, 29, 37, 49,
  50, 59 - 62, 95, 97, 191, 222, 265,
  271 - 272, 280
Antony Committee Report, 189-190
Antony, A. K., 114, 189
Antulay, A. R., 154, 156
Anwar, Tariq, 158, 164
Asghar Ali Engineer, 52
Assam, 95, 253
Assembly Elections
  of 1993, 97
  BJP victory in Gujarat, 247, 248,
  261, 252
  BJP victory in Jharkhand, 260
  Congress defeat, 195, 268
  Congress defeat in Chhattisgarh, 260
  Congress defeat in Rajasthan, 260
  Congress victory in Jammu &
  Kashmir, 125, 248-251
  in Karnataka, 59, 60, 61
  Madhya Pradesh, 140
  Maharashtra, 154

TDP victory in
Andhra Pradesh, 59, 60
in Sikkim, 59
UP (1996), 81, 82, 290
West Bengal (1997), 207-209
Ayodhya Movement, 12-13, 45-58, 63,
71, 74, 76, 100, 101, 211, 240, 247,
287, 291, 292
Azad, Ghulam Nabi, 111, 180, 248-250,
285
Azad, Maulana, 54

Babri Masjid, 71
and Nehru, 47
BJP leaders' arrest, 58
Congress position, 75
Debate in Parliament, 58
demolition, 123, 218
Mulayam Singh and 55
Muslim disenchantment with, 211
Narasimha Rao and, 55-58, 100-101
S.B. Chavan's statement, 56
Sangh volunteers' role in the
demolition, 55-56
Karsevaks, 55
Bahuguna, H. N., 73
Balasubramaniam, S. R., 93
Banerjee, Mamata 117
Bangalore Plenary, Session
Bangladesh, 49, 163, 173
Bano, Begum Noor 220
Bano, Shah, 54
Basu, Jyoti, 109, 121, 146, 149, 150,
151, 207, 208, 271
Bellary, 95, 180, 181, 182
Bhattacharya, Budhadev, 208
Bhaumik, Saba Naqvi, 270

Bihar, 13, 55, 68, 69, 88, 93, 96, 114,
147, 148, 189, 201, 202, 203, 267,
272, 296, 305
Bharatiya Janta Party (BJP)
Advani's reappointment as
president, 166
advocate of Hindu revivalism, 93
and Muslims, 74
Ayodhya issue, 12, 251-252
coalition government at the Centre,
142-143
CPI (M) and, 146
confrontation with the Congress, 266
cultural nationalism thesis, 281, 295
defeat in Delhi Assembly elections,
260
dismissal of MP government in
1993, 137
Economic policy, 130-131
election campaign style, 96, 266,
268
fall of Vajpayee government, 178
Communal tensions, 95
Gujarat riots, 241-242
Gujarat Order, 199
Hindutva politics, 47
identification with religion and
religious symbols, 72-73
India Shining Campaign, 264
Janta Dal's alignment with, 50
Laloo and, 58, 201
National Executive Committee
meeting in Goa, 246
Muslims and, 49-51
Ram Mandir Movement, 69
single largest party in 1996 election,
110

Sonia Gandhi and, 80, 209, 210, 231-232

Trimamool Party understanding, 209

Sushma Swaraj as BJP candidate against Sonia Gandhi, 180, 183

Bangaru Lakshman as Party President, 232, 233

Uma Bharati as MP Chief Minister candidate, 259

victory in Gujarat Assembly election, 247,247

victory in Rajasthan and Jharkhand assembly election, 207

Vote share in 1998 election, 295

website, 179

West Bengal Assembly election, 201-208

withdrawal of support from the V.P. Singh government, 13

Bofors Scandal, 11, 93

Brar, Harcharan Singh, 92

Brass, Paul, 48, 49

Bahujan Samaj Party (BSP), 72, 75, 81, 82, 83, 134, 212, 218

Bundela, Sujan Singh, 220

Caste Politics, 7, 12

CBI, 23, 86, 87, 88, 89, 112

Central Vigilance Commission (CVC), 257

Chatterjee, Pulok, 76

Chaturvedi, Bhuvnesh, 61, 77, 92

Chavan, S. B., 56, 57, 62, 92, 154, 285

Chidambaram, P., 40, 42, 93, 149

Chowdhary, A.B.A. Ghani Khan, 208

Chowdhary, Saifuddin, 146

CPI, 150, 207

Congress Party / Indian National Congress

alliance with AIADMK

Assembly elections, 82-83

Babri Masjid Issue, 55-59

Bangalore Plenary session, 278

Bengal Mahajot, 207-211

Calcutta session, 115-116

Assembly election 1998, 177

Dalits and, 72

defeat in MP Assembly election, 260

defeat in 1996 general elections, 8

defeat in 1999 general elections, 195

dissatisfaction and resentment within, 14, 62-64

dissidents' role, 80

economic policy, 101

economic reform, 187

11th general elections, 91-97

factions on the Rajya Sabha nominations, 204-207

fall of percentage of votes in 1996 general election, 67

fall of voting percentage in the Assembly elections, 97

Gujarat Assembly elections and defeat, 243-244, 248

India Today report, 119

Introspection Committee Report - 1999 general elections, 189-192

issues before the Panchmari Camp, 305-309

landslide victory in Punjab and J & K elections, 251-252

largest Party in the Parliament 1989, 29

launching agitation on Gujarat
Order, 199-200
leadership crisis, 217-227
Mahatma Gandhi's advice to, 85
Mandal and communalisation
politics, 7
middle class creation, 183-184
minority government at the
Centre, 36
myth of Muslim
appeasement, 45-54
Narasimha Rao as President, 27
New Economic Policy, 42, 189
number of seats in the 1991
general elections, 34
number of MPs' election, 295
outside support to the United Front,
110
Panchmari Conclave, 127-133,
140-142
Parivartan Yatra, 236
Paswan and Laloo alliance in
Bihar, 267
Percentage of votes secured, Lok
Sabha elections, 187, 295
Position in 1996 elections, Lok
Sabha, 110
post- Independence period, 16-17
Prime Ministerial candidate issue,
165-166, 168-169
Rao resigns as president, 112-113
regional parties support, 75
rejection of Rao's politics, 103
relations between the United Front
and, 113
resolution on J & K government
formation, 250

Sangma Task Force Report of
1998, 295-300
Simla Conclave, 252-255
Sitaram Kesri's appointment as
President, 107 113-114
Sonia's efforts at organisational,
reforms, 281
Sonia Gandhi as President, 107, 126,
133, 142, 170, 217-220
split in 1969, 162
splits in state party units, 81
support to Chandra Shekhar
government, 15
Tirupati session, 100
UP affairs, 28, 134-136, 211-213
victory in the Delhi Assembly
elections, 260
victory in 2004 general elections,
272-273
Constitution Amendment Bill, 229
Congress Parliamentary Party (CPP)
fertiliser price, 43-44
Rao continues as the Chairperson,
113
Congress split, 78, 212
Congress Working Committee (CWC)
Assembly election, 61
Composition after Jitendra Prasad's
death, 227
economic resolution, 129-130
meeting, 62-64, 151
meeting after the fall of the Vajpayee
government, 156-161
resolution on the Kargil war, 176-
177
resolution on Mandal, 68-69
Sonia's resignation at meeting , 160

Desai, Morarji, 29
Deshmukh, Vilasrao, 200
Devaluation (of the rupee) 40, 41
Devi, Rabri, 147, 201, 202
Dhawan, R. K., 23, 111
Dixit, Sheila, 179, 259, 260
Dravida Munnetra Khazagham (DMK),
    93, 118, 148, 149, 269
Dwivedi, Devendra, 92, 112

Election Commission of India, 95
Elections (General Elections)
    Congress, seat from UP, 134
    By-elections in Rajasthan, Congress
    defeat, 252
    of 1984, 69
    of 1991, 29
    of 1992, 262
    of 1996, 94, 95, 98, 157, 187
    Congress position, 166
    fractured mandate, 110
    of 1998, 108, 120, 122, 123, 125,
    137, 147, 146, 157, 187
    Congress defeat, 124, 187
    of 1999, 203, 204
    Congress defeat, 108, 195, 229
    New Economic Policy rejection,
    188, 189
    NDA's performance and
    number of seats, 2004, 272, 273

Fernandes, George, 12, 161
    Bihar politics, 267
    resignation from Defence Ministry
    on Tehelka issue, 233
    sacking naval Chief Vishnu
    Bhagwat, 145
    on Sonia Gandhi, 183

Tehelka expose, 232, 233
Fotedar, M. L., 41, 42, 150, 285
French, Patrick, 48

Gandhi, Feroze, 24, 76
Gandhi, Indira
    assassination, 24
    charisma, 102
    As Congress President, 32
    Congress defeat in the south in 1977
    election, 62
    Congress Party under, 156
    estrangement with Chandra
    Shekhar, 14
    Gharibi Hatao slogan, 17
    leadership, 26, 32, 304
    Sanjay Gandhi's death, 23, 24
    socialist programmes in, 1971
    and Sonia Gandhi, 25, 166, 249
    Syndicate's role in elevation as the
    Congress President, 65
Gandhi, Mahatma, 48, 54, 85, 199, 282,
    301
Gandhi, Priyanka, 18, 20, 25, 76, 77,
    79, 118, 181, 270, 271
Gandhi, Rahul, 270
Gandhi, Rajiv
    and V.P. Singh, 11
    assassination, 3-4, 7-8, 18-21, 30, 37
    61, 74, 80, 166, 170, 236, 282
    Bofors allegations, 11
    Congress Party under, 156
    economic policy, 129-130
    economic reforms under, 187
    election tours, 18
    entry into politics, 23-24
    fall from power, 14

government surveillance and
spying, outside his residence, 16
Jain Commission's Interim Report,
118
leadership, 304
Leader of the Opposition, 17
meeting with Sonia in Cambridge,
166
Moscow and Tehran Visits 1991, 17
security arrangements, 18
statement on the fall of the Chandra
Shekhar government, 16
revival of Congress culture, 282
support to Chandra Shekhar
government, 15
Gandhi, Sanjay
death, 23, 24
leadership, 26
Gandhi, Sonia
address to *Hindustan Times*
conference, 261
address to leaders of PCCs and
CLPs, 152
birth, 1, 166
Calcutta rally, 146
citizenship issue, 160-161, 167
Congress Organisational reform
efforts, 281
Congress plenary address in
Bangalore, 232, 278-279
Congress President, 107, 126, 133,
142, 213, 277
on Dalit massacre in Jehanabad
district, 147
declines the office of the Prime
Minister, 1, 275-276
education, 1, 166

election campaign 1998, 123-124
Emergency, 23
entry into electoral
politics, 179
favours Sitaram Kesri's
candidature for the Congress
President, 115
foreigner issue, 166, 179
Godhra massacre, 242-243
Gujarat Assembly elections and
defeat of the Congress Party, 243-
244, 248
and Indira Gandhi, 24-25, 166
and Jitendra Prasad, 217-227
lead campaigner in 1998 general
elections, 120
leader of the Congress Party, 1-2,
141-142, 156-157
elected leader of the Congress
Parliamentary Party, 126, 161, 167,
276
liberal politics, 278
letter to Manmohan Singh, 310- 311
Mark Tully on, 277
mass contact programmes, 268, 269
media coverage of her election
campaign, 271-272
Member of Parliament and
leader of the Opposition, 195
method of leadership , 252
movement towards installing a
Congress government, 143
And Murli Manohar Joshi, 232- 233
No-confidence motion against
the NDA government, 257-259
nomination from Bellary
and Amethi constituencies for Lok

Sabha poll and victory, 189-183
on saffronisation of education, 229-232
ORG - MARG survey regarding Prime Minister, 142
own vision of politics, 254-255
organisational reforms under, 281- 282
Panchmari Camp, 127-137, 140
Presides over the Congress Chief Minister's Conference Guwahati (2002), 244-246
programmes in Amethi, 78
primary member of the Congress party in 1997, 121
Public appearance in Amethi, 75-81
Rajesh Pilot's death, 216
Rajiv Gandhi's assassination, 3-4
rapprochement between Mamata Banerjee and, 117
President of India, 166
resignation letter from CWC, 161-163
role in Jammu & Kashmir government formation, 280-281
role in the Panchmari Conclave, 127-137, 140
role in the UPA formation, 270
Simla Conclave, 252-253
speech on POTO legislation, 246- 247
Talkatora speech, 168-171
threat to her leadership, 237
UN General Assembly address, 234
US tour, 234-235
victory in 2004 general election, 271-274
George, Vincent, 76

Godhra, 240, 241, 242
Gomang, Giridhar, 201
Gowda, H.D. Deve, 107, 109, 110
Gujarat, 13, 74, 195, 197, 198, 199, 220, 229, 239, 240, 241, 242, 243, 244, 245, 246, 247, 248, 251, 252, 255, 261, 265, 272, 280
Gujarat Order, 199, 200
Gujarat Riots, 280
Gujral, I. K., 42, 107, 118, 120, 124, 141, 150, 177
Gupta, Indrajit, 35, 124
Guwahati Conference, 244, 246

Hasan, Zoya (Notes), 54, 70
Hawala Scandal/Scam, 81, 87
Hepatullah, Najma, 265
Himachal Pradesh, 58, 92, 251
Hindutva, 3, 12, 47, 53, 57, 69, 70, 243, 247, 251
Hyderabad, 30, 123, 180

IMF, 39
India Shining Campaign, 263, 264, 267, 268
India Today, 18, 119, 125, 139, 142, 143, 145, 150, 216, 269
Indian Union Muslim League, 158
IPKF, 19, 173

Jain Brothers, 187
Jain Commission, 81, 118
Jaiswal, Sri Prakash, 215, 236
Jaitley, Arun, 241
Jaitley, Jaya, 232
Jammu & Kashmir, 34, 125, 248, 249, 250, 251, 252, 253
Janata Dal, 61

Jayalalitha, 18, 93, 148, 149, 150, 161, 177, 178
Jhakkar, Balram, 43
Jharkhand Bribery Case, 112
JMM, 87, 101
Jogi, Ajit, 259
Joshi, Murli Manohar, 231, 232

Kamaraj, 32, 65, 208
Karnataka, 29, 37, 50, 59, 60, 61, 62, 95, 97, 109, 110, 180, 181, 182, 203, 249, 272
Kargil war, 173, 174, 175, 176, 177, 178, 179
Karunakaran, K., 111, 119, 222
Karunanidhi, Dr., 109, 148
Kerala, 29, 37, 49, 97, 189, 222, 272, 299
Kesri, Sitaram
    Congress President, 114
    decision to resign from office of Congress President, 125
    dismisses Congress General Secretaries, 116
    General Elections of 1998, 120
    leader of the Congress Parliamentary Party (CPP), 126
    losing control over the Congress, party, 164
    replacement as Congress President, 213
    treasurer of the Congress Party, 114
    victory in Congress Presidential election, 115, 216, 225
Khan, Arif Mohammad, 265
Khurana, Madan Lal, 88, 260

Khurshid, Salman, 63, 78, 135, 136, 164, 187, 213, 214, 215, 221, 223, 224, 251, 286, 313
Kidwai, Mohsina, 76, 79
Kidwai, Rashid, 246
Kumaramangalam, R., 40

Lakhubhai Pathak Cheating Case, 87
Lal, Bhajan, 201
Lal, Devi, 14, 15, 50
Laxman, Bangaru, 232, 233
Left Parties, 36, 50, 54, 146, 200
Lok Sabha, 31, 34, 36, 38, 40, 50, 52, 69, 70, 83, 88, 89, 94, 119, 126, 137, 146, 147, 150, 151, 154, 156, 157, 163, 174, 178, 179, 183, 200, 208, 209, 217, 229, 261, 262, 264, 267, 293, 295
Loktantrik Congress, 212
LTTE, 19, 173
Lucknow, 75, 76, 77, 78, 133, 136, 197, 211, 215

Madhya Pradesh, 27, 58, 62, 74, 76, 92, 94, 97, 127, 136, 137, 139, 140, 142, 145, 236, 239, 259, 262, 272, 303, 307
Mahajan, Pramod, 183, 273
Mahajot, 197, 207, 208, 209, 210, 211
Maharashtra, 49, 97, 126, 153, 154, 155, 156, 157, 158, 178, 191, 200, 204, 205, 216, 221, 268
Mahato, Shailendra, 87
Mandal Commission, 7, 11, 67
Manipur, 201, 202
Mayawati, 72, 133
MDMK, 149
Mehta, Harshad, 87

Mehta, Vinod, 273
Mizoram, 145, 253, 303
Modi, Narendra, 240, 241, 243, 267, 270
Moopanar, G. K., 81, 93, 96
Mukherjee, Pranab, 28, 30, 39, 115, 207
Munshi, Priyaranjan Das, 209

Naidu, Venkaiah, 262
Naik, Sudhakar Rao, 155
Nath, Kamal, 139, 209, 290
National Common Minimum Programme (CMP), 310
National Council of Applied Economic Research (NCAER), 51
National Front Government, 10, 11, 14
NCERT, 231
NDA Government
    AIADMK support and withdrawal of support, 14-150
    attack on Sonia and her family, 270
    Bihar issue, 201-202
    election campaign, 268
    election manifesto, 261, 262, 271
    extravagance on election campaign, 265
    fall, 107
    failure, 303
    flop show of, 145
    graph going down, 303
    Gujarat Order, 197, 199
    India Shining Campaign launch, 263-264
    Mamata Banerjee and, 208
    New Economic Policy, 189
    No-confidence debate against, 195
    nuclear tests, 145
    number of seats in 2004 elections, 272, 273
    President's Rule in Bihar ratification issue, 147
    Ram Vilas Paswan leaves, 267
    Sonia's attack, 269
    Sonia Gandhi and, 229-231, 257-259, 269
    Tehelka episode, 232-233
    Vote of Confidence 1999, 150
Nehru, Arun, 15, 50
Nehru, Pandit Jawaharlal,
    On Babri Masjid in Ayodhya, 47
    Congress Party under, 26, 83, 156
    Economic Outlook, 43
    first Prime Minister of India, 1, 7, 9, 33, 44, 47, 79, 304
New Economic Policy (NEP), 3, 8, 9, 38, 44, 60, 123, 128, 189, 200
Nuclear Tests, 142, 145, 184, 308

Orissa, 20, 201, 202, 203, 222
Owaisi, Salauddin, 49

Pachauri, Suresh, 62, 79
Pakistan, 26, 30, 32, 46, 48, 53, 100, 146, 148, 167, 173, 174, 176, 308
Panchmari Conclave/Resolution, 107, 109, 127, 142
Pant, Govind Ballabh, 47
Parivartan Yatras, 236, 238
Paswan, Ram Vilas, 68, 267
Patel, Ahmad, 111, 138
Patnaik, J. B., 92, 222
Pawar, Sharad
    Congress leader in the Lok Sabha, 156, 157, 126

Congress Presidential election, 115, 156

as Defence Minister, 135, 156, 285

General election of 1996, 157

General election of 1998, 125, 157

Gujarat election role in, 248

letter to Sonia Gandhi, 158, 159

number of MPs from his own state, 126

Maharashtra politics, 155

Pilot, Rajesh, 43, 61-62, 64, 78, 111, 135-138, 153, 155-156 195, 216, 220, 225, 239

Pilot, Sachin, 271

PDP, 250

Prabhakaran, 19

Prasad, Jitendra, 76, 81, 83, 119, 136, 217-220, 222, 227,

Prasad, Mahavir, 72, 134

Press Club of India, 91

Punjab, 34, 48, 92, 98, 173, 251, 253, 272, 282, 286

Rae Bareli, 77, 271

Rajasthan, 58, 88, 139, 142, 145, 216, 217, 252, 259, 260, 262, 271, 272, 303

Rajiv Gandhi Foundation (RGF), 76, 78

Rajya Sabha, 28, 62, 89, 179, 203, 204, 205, 220, 293

Ram Janamabhoomi Movement, 3, 12, 45, 47, 67, 75

Ram, Babu Jagjivan, 72

Ram, Kanshi, 72

Ramesh, Jairam, 40, 205

Rangarajan, C., 41

Rao, K. Vijaya Rama, 87

Rao, N. T. Rama, 60, 109

Rao, P. V. Narasimha

accepts dissidents' resignations, 66, 112, 113

achievements, 287, 288

address to US Congress, 99

analysis of his performance, 102-103

Andhra Assembly election debacle, 59-60

as External Affairs Minister, 101

break from the Nehruvian consensus, 33, 103

Arjun Singh and, 36, 65-66

Babri Masjid demolition, 55-58

birth, 27

challenge to his leadership, 59, 78, 155

as chief minister of Andhra Pradesh, 30

confidence motion, 33-36

completes five years as Prime Minister, 81

As Congress President, 27, 30

Congress under, 92-93, 113, 123

consensus builder, 37

continues as chairperson of the Congress Parliamentary Party, 113

dissidents demand his dismissal, 80

dismisses Madhavrao Scindia on Hawala issue, 236

economic reforms, 100

election campaign in 1996 election, 93, 94, 95, 96, 98

elevation to the office of the Prime Minister, 32

failure of Ayodhya issue, 100, 287

first address to Lok Sabha as PM, 31, first Prime Minister from the South, 29, 59
Hawala Scandal, 87
Home Minister under Rajiv Gandhi, 30
in active politics before 1991 General election, 29
JMM bribery case, 87
Lakhubhai Pathak cheating case, 87, 112
member of the AICC, 30
Minister of Defence and External Affairs, 30
Minister Planning, Minister of Human Resource Development, 30
minority government, 36
Muslims' alienation during his regime, 73
New Economic Policy, 38-45
no-confidence motion, 35-36
pressure group against, 44
reaction to the state assembly results, 61
resignation from the office of Congress President, 112-113
return to parliament in a by-election, 31
rise and fall of, 8
selection of his cabinet, 33
St. Kitts case, 112
Sworn in as Prime Minister, 27, 30, 38, 163
Telangana movement, 30, 77
Vir Sanghvi on, 102
Rao, P.V. Ranga, 60

Rashtrapati Bhavan, 15, 161
RBI, 41
Reddy, Vijaya Bhaskar, 222, 285
Rashtriya Janta Dal (RJD), 147, 150, 201, 202
RSS, 47, 159, 167, 181, 197, 198, 199, 242

Saikia, Hiteshwar, 95
Samajwadi Party (SP), 50, 55, 71, 75, 134, 151, 152, 212, 214, 248, 269, 291
Sangh Parivar, 52, 242
Sanghvi, Vir, 100, 103, 121
Sangma, P. A.
    adviser to the Congress President, 163
    letter to Sonia Gandhi, 158
    senior position in Parliament, 164
Sangma Report, 163
Speaker of the Lok Sabha, 163
Sangma Task Force, 128, 134, 142, 295
Sanjay Gandhi Memorial Trust, 78, 79
Sathe, Vasant, 205
Sayeed, Mufti Mohamed, 250
Scindia, Madhavrao, 155
    death, 163, 229, 239
    deputy leader in the parliament, 236, 238
    dismissal from Rao cabinet, 236 Jain Hawala issue, 236
    leadership issue, 237, 238
    and Sonia Gandhi, 237
    Parivartam Yatra, 236, 238
Scindia, Vasundhara Raje, 259
Shankaranand, B., 41, 285
Sharief, Jaffer, 203, 205
Sharma, Satish, 79, 289

Shastri, Lal Bahadur, 26, 32

Shekhar, Chandra, 7-10, 14-17, 35, 39, 247, 269

Shimla Conclave, 195, 253

Shinde, Sushil Kumar, 147

Shiv Sena, 56, 155, 209, 262

Shukla, V.C., 61, 87, 88, 137, 285

Sibal, Kapil, 205

Singh, Amar, 151

Singh, Arjun
Chairman of Cabinet
Committee, 63
challenge to Narasimha Rao, 59, 93-94, 155
defeat in the election of 1998, 137
differences with Congress High Command, 82
dissidents group around, 61-62
inner party democracy, 65
leaves Congress Party, 78
retaining minority goodwill, 74
resigns, from the CWC, 101
resignation from the Council of Ministers, 64-65
resignation letter, 66
support to Narasimha Rao, 36-36
and Tiwari Congress, 82

Singh, Beant, 98

Singh, Digvijay, 74, 79, 92, 109, 127, 136, 137, 138, 139, 140, 153, 206, 259, 260

Singh, Dr. Manmohan, 9, 38, 39, 40, 41, 42, 43, 44, 187, 188, 205, 271, 276, 285, 291, 310

Singh, Kunwar Uday, 255

Singh, Malvika, 268

Singh, V.P., 7,11-13,15,35,68,73,93,109

Singh, Vir Bahadur, 73

Singh, Virbhadra, 92, 253

Sinha, Jaswant, 266

Subramanyam Committee Report, 200

Sukhram, 89

Supreme Court, 89, 136, 260, 289, 292

Surajkund, 63

Surjeet, Harkishen Singh, 149, 150

Swamy, Subramaniam, 148, 149

Swaraj, Sushma, 173, 179, 180-182

Tamil Maanila Congress, 81

Tamil Nadu, 20, 29, 37, 81, 93, 94, 97, 109, 148, 149, 170, 272

Tandon, Purshottam Das, 47

TDP, 60, 95, 131, 262, 280

Teen Murti Bhavan, 21

Tehelka, 232

Thakur, Rameshwar, 79

Third Front, 15, 126, 151, 152, 157, 267

Tirupati Session, 100

Tiwari, Pramod, 79, 212

Tiwari, N.D.
and Jitendra Prasad, 221
Challenge to Narasimha Rao, 155
Chief Minister of UP, 28
damage to Rao Election Campaign, 93, 94
a new patron, 80
leaves Congress Party, 78, 82
recognised leader of his community,

Tiwari Congress Formation, 76, 82
UP Congress leadership , 134

Tiwari Congress, 76, 82, 88, 97, 212

Tripathi, Kamlapati, 73

Tully, Mark, 277

United Front Government (UF), 107,
110, 112, 113, 124, 237
UPA Government, 276, 277
Uttar Pradesh, 8, 13, 28, 47, 54, 67,
68, 69, 70, 74, 75, 76, 77, 79, 81,
82, 83, 93, 96, 109, 133, 135, 137,
150, 170, 180, 181, 182, 211, 217,
218, 221, 227, 236, 249, 270, 271,
281, 291, 305
UPCC, 76, 83, 133, 134, 135, 136, 164,
212, 213, 215, 218, 220, 221
Uttaranchal, 28, 73

Vaghela, Shankersinh, 244
Vaiko, 149
Vajpayee, Atal Behari
achievements, 265
AIADMK support and
withdrawal, 148, 149, 150, 178
assumes power as the leader of
the BJP-led-coalition, 142
efforts to bring down his
government, 161
election campaign led by, 263
election campaign of 1996, 96
election 2004 results, 273
fall of his government, 157, 158,
178
Goa National Executive speech,
246
India Today Report on, 269
no-confidence debate, 195
nuclear test, 142
ORG-MARG survey, 142
Outlook report of his victory 271
13-day rule, 110
Vote of Confidence 1999,150
Venkataraman, R., 16
Venkataramanan, S., 41
Venkatswamy, G., 92
Vishnu Bhagwat (Admiral), 145

West Bengal, 92, 109, 117, 146, 200,
204, 207, 208, 209, 210
World Bank, 39, 266

Yadav, Balram Singh, 79
Yadav, Laloo Prasad, 13, 55, 68, 147,
201, 202, 267
Yadav, Mulayam Singh, 50, 55, 68, 71,
73, 75, 134, 150-152, 191, 214, 218,
248, 259, 291, 292
Yadav, Sharad, 68, 88, 267